YEARBOOK
OF THE
INTERNATIONAL
LAW COMMISSION

2007

**Volume II
Part Two**

*Report of the Commission
to the General Assembly
on the work
of its fifty-ninth session*

UNITED NATIONS
New York and Geneva, 2014

NOTE

Symbols of United Nations documents are composed of capital letters combined with figures. Mention of such a symbol indicates a reference to a United Nations document.

References to the *Yearbook of the International Law Commission* are abbreviated to *Yearbook ...,* followed by the year (for example, *Yearbook ... 2007*).

The *Yearbook* for each session of the International Law Commission comprises two volumes:

Volume I: summary records of the meetings of the session;

Volume II (Part One): reports of special rapporteurs and other documents considered during the session;

Volume II (Part Two): report of the Commission to the General Assembly.

All references to these works and quotations from them relate to the final printed texts of the volumes of the *Yearbook* issued as United Nations publications.

*

* *

A/CN.4/SER.A/2007/Add.1 (Part 2)

UNITED NATIONS PUBLICATION
Sales No.: E.12.V.14 (Part 2) ISBN: 978-92-1-133799-0 e-ISBN: 978-92-1-055659-0
ISSN: 0082-8289

CONTENTS

DOCUMENT A/62/10*

Report of the International Law Commission on the work of its fifty-ninth session (7 May–5 June and 9 July–10 August 2007)

CONTENTS

---

* Initially distributed as *Official Records of the General Assembly, Sixty-second Session, Supplement No. 10.*

ABBREVIATIONS

ICJ	International Court of Justice
NATO	North Atlantic Treaty Organization
OHCHR	Office of the High Commissioner for Human Rights
PCIJ	Permanent Court of International Justice
UNESCO	United Nations Educational, Scientific and Cultural Organization
WTO	World Trade Organization

*

*   *

AJIL	American Journal of International Law (Washington, D.C.)
BYBIL	The British Year Book of International Law
I.C.J. Reports	ICJ, Reports of Judgments, Advisory Opinions and Orders
ILM	International Legal Materials (Washington, D.C.)
P.C.I.J., Series A	PCIJ, Collection of Judgments (Nos. 1–24: up to and including 1930)
P.C.I.J., Series B	PCIJ, Collection of Advisory Opinions (Nos. 1–18: up to and including 1930)
P.C.I.J., Series A/B	PCIJ, Judgments, Orders and Advisory Opinions (Nos. 40–80: beginning in 1931)
UNRIAA	United Nations, Reports of International Arbitral Awards

*

*   *

In the present volume, the "International Tribunal for the Former Yugoslavia" refers to the International Tribunal for the Prosecution of Persons Responsible for Serious Violations of International Humanitarian Law Committed in the Territory of the Former Yugoslavia since 1991.

*

*   *

NOTE CONCERNING QUOTATIONS

In quotations, words or passages in italics followed by an asterisk were not italicized in the original text.

Unless otherwise indicated, quotations from works in languages other than English have been translated by the Secretariat.

*

*   *

The Internet address of the International Law Commission is **www.un.org/law/ilc/**.

MULTILATERAL INSTRUMENTS CITED IN THE PRESENT VOLUME

Source

Pacific Settlement of International Disputes

Treaty of Paris of 1856 (Paris, 30 March 1856)	F. L. Israel (ed.), *Major Peace Treaties of Modern History, 1648–1967*, vol. II, New York, Chelsea House, 1967, p. 947.

Privileges and Immunities, Diplomatic and Consular Relations, etc.

Convention on the Privileges and Immunities of the United Nations (New York, 13 February 1946)	United Nations, *Treaty Series*, vol. 1, No. 4, p. 15, and vol. 90, p. 327.
Vienna Convention on Diplomatic Relations (Vienna, 18 April 1961)	*Ibid.*, vol. 500, No. 7310, p. 95.

Human Rights

1919 Convention concerning Employment of Women during the Night (Washington, D.C., 28 November 1919)	See www.ilo.org.
Convention on the Prevention and Punishment of the Crime of Genocide (New York, 9 December 1948)	United Nations, *Treaty Series*, vol. 78, No. 1021, p. 277.
Convention for the Protection of Human Rights and Fundamental Freedoms (European Convention on Human Rights) (Rome, 4 November 1950)	*Ibid.*, vol. 213, No. 2889, p. 221.
Protocol No. 4 to the Convention of 4 November 1950 for the Protection of Human Rights and Fundamental Freedoms, securing certain rights and freedoms other than those already included in the Convention and in the first Protocol thereto (Strasbourg, 16 September 1963)	*Ibid.*, vol. 1496, No. 2889, p. 263.
Protocol No. 6 to the Convention of 4 November 1950 for the Protection of Human Rights and Fundamental Freedoms, concerning the abolition of the death penalty (Strasbourg, 28 April 1983)	*Ibid.*, p. 281.
Protocol No. 7 to the Convention for the Protection of Human Rights and Fundamental Freedoms (Strasbourg, 22 November 1984)	*Ibid.*, vol. 1525, No. 2889, p. 195.
Protocol No. 13 to the Convention for the Protection of Human Rights and Fundamental Freedoms, concerning the abolition of the death penalty in all circumstances (Vilnius, 3 May 2002)	*Ibid.*, vol. 2246, No. 2889, p. 110.
Convention on the Political Rights of Women (New York, 31 March 1953)	*Ibid.*, vol. 193, No. 2613, p. 135.
International Convention on the Elimination of All Forms of Racial Discrimination (New York, 21 December 1965)	*Ibid.*, vol. 660, No. 9464, p. 195.
International Covenant on Civil and Political Rights (New York, 16 December 1966)	*Ibid.*, vol. 999, No. 14668, p. 171.
Optional Protocol to the International Covenant on Civil and Political Rights (New York, 16 December 1966)	*Ibid.*
International Covenant on Economic, Social and Cultural Rights (New York, 16 December 1966)	*Ibid.*, vol. 993, No. 14531, p. 3.
American Convention on Human Rights: "Pact of San José, Costa Rica" (San José, 22 November 1969)	*Ibid.*, vol. 1144, No. 17955, p. 123.
International Convention on the Elimination of All Forms of Discrimination against Women (New York, 18 December 1979)	*Ibid.*, vol. 1249, No. 20378, p. 13.
African Charter on Human and Peoples' Rights (Nairobi, 27 June 1981)	*Ibid.*, vol. 1520, No. 26363, p. 217.
Convention against Torture and Other Cruel, Inhuman or Degrading Treatment or Punishment (New York, 10 December 1984)	*Ibid.*, vol. 1465, No. 24841, p. 85.

Convention on the rights of the child (New York, 20 November 1989)	*Ibid.*, vol. 1577, No. 27531, p. 3.
International Convention on the Protection of the Rights of All Migrant Workers and Members of their Families (New York, 18 December 1990)	*Ibid.*, vol. 2220, No. 39481, p. 3.
Arab Charter on Human Rights (Tunis, 23 May 2004)	*Boston University International Law Journal*, vol. 24, No. 1 (2006), p. 147.

Narcotic Drugs and Psychotropic Substances

United Nations Convention against Illicit Traffic in Narcotic Drugs and Psychotropic Substances (Vienna, 20 December 1988)	United Nations, *Treaty Series*, vol. 1582, No. 27627, p. 95.

Refugees and Stateless Persons

Convention relating to the Status of Refugees (Geneva, 28 July 1951)	United Nations, *Treaty Series*, vol. 189, No. 2545, p. 137.
Convention relating to the Status of Stateless Persons (New York, 28 September 1954)	*Ibid.*, vol. 360, No. 5158, p. 117.
Convention on the reduction of statelessness (New York, 30 August 1961)	*Ibid.*, vol. 989, No. 14458, p. 175.

International Trade and Development

Convention relating to a uniform law on the formation of contracts for the international sale of goods (The Hague, 1 July 1964)	United Nations, *Treaty Series*, vol. 834, No. 11930, p. 169.
European Convention providing a Uniform Law on Arbitration (Strasbourg, 20 January 1966)	Council of Europe, *European Treaty Series*, No. 56.
North American Free Trade Agreement Between the Government of Canada, the Government of the United Mexican States, and the Government of the United States of America (Mexico City, Ottawa and Washington, D.C., 17 December 1992)	Washington, D.C., United States Government Printing Office, 1993.

Penal matters

Convention on Consent to Marriage, Minimum Age for Marriage and Registration of Marriages (New York, 10 December 1962)	United Nations, *Treaty Series* , vol. 521, No. 7525, p. 231.

Law of the Sea

Geneva Conventions on the Law of the Sea (Geneva, 29 April 1958)	
Convention on the Continental Shelf	United Nations, *Treaty Series*, vol. 499, No. 7302, p. 311.
Convention on the High Seas	*Ibid.*, vol. 450, No. 6465, p. 11.
United Nations Convention on the Law of the Sea (Montego Bay, 10 December 1982)	*Ibid.*, vol. 1833, No. 31363, p. 3.

Law applicable in armed conflict

Treaty of Peace between the Allied and Associated Powers and Germany (Treaty of Versailles) (Versailles, 28 June 1919)	British and Foreign State Papers, 1919, vol. CXII, London, HM Stationery Office, 1922, p. 1.
Geneva Conventions for the protection of war victims (Geneva, 12 August 1949)	United Nations, *Treaty Series*, vol. 75, Nos. 970–973, pp. 31 *et seq.*
Convention for the Protection of Cultural Property in the Event of Armed Conflict (The Hague, 14 May 1954)	*Ibid.*, vol. 249, No. 3511, p. 215.

Law of Treaties

Vienna Convention on the Law of Treaties (Vienna, 23 May 1969)	United Nations, *Treaty Series*, vol. 1155, No. 18232, p. 331.
Vienna Convention on succession of States in respect of treaties (Vienna, 23 August 1978)	*Ibid.*, vol. 1946, No. 33356, p. 3.
Vienna Convention on the Law of Treaties between States and International Organizations or between International Organizations (Vienna, 21 March 1986)	A/CONF.129/15.

Environment

Basel Convention on the control of transboundary movements of hazardous wastes and their disposal (Basel, 22 March 1989)	United Nations, *Treaty Series*, vol. 1673, No. 28911, p. 57.
Convention on Environmental Impact Assessment in a Transboundary Context (Espoo, 25 February 1991)	*Ibid.*, vol. 1989, No. 34028, p. 309.

Terrorism

International Convention against the taking of hostages (New York, 17 December 1979)	United Nations, *Treaty Series*, vol. 1316, No. 21931, p. 205.
International Convention for the Suppression of Terrorist Bombings (New York, 15 December 1997)	*Ibid.*, vol. 2149, No. 37517, p. 256.
International Convention for the Suppression of the Financing of Terrorism (New York, 9 December 1999)	*Ibid.*, vol. 2178, No. 38349, p. 197.

Chapter I

ORGANIZATION OF THE SESSION

1.   The International Law Commission held the first part of its fifty-ninth session from 7 May to 5 June 2007[1] and the second part from 9 July to 10 August 2007 at its seat at the United Nations Office at Geneva. The session was opened by Mr. Giorgio Gaja, First Vice-Chairperson of the fifty-eighth session of the Commission.

A.   Membership

2.   The Commission consists of the following members:

Mr. Ali Mohsen Fetais AL-MARRI (Qatar)

Mr. Ian BROWNLIE (United Kingdom of Great Britain and Northern Ireland)

Mr. Lucius CAFLISCH (Switzerland)

Mr. Enrique CANDIOTI (Argentina)

Mr. Pedro COMISSÁRIO AFONSO (Mozambique)

Mr. Christopher John Robert DUGARD (South Africa)

Ms. Paula ESCARAMEIA (Portugal)

Mr. Salifou FOMBA (Mali)

Mr. Giorgio GAJA (Italy)

Mr. Zdzislaw GALICKI (Poland)

Mr. Hussein A. HASSOUNA (Egypt)

Mr. Mahmoud D. HMOUD (Jordan)

Ms. Marie G. JACOBSSON (Sweden)

Mr. Maurice KAMTO (Cameroon)

Mr. Fathi KEMICHA (Tunisia)

Mr. Roman KOLODKIN (Russian Federation)

Mr. Donald M. MCRAE (Canada)

Mr. Teodor Viorel MELESCANU (Romania)

Mr. Bernd H. NIEHAUS (Costa Rica)

Mr. Georg NOLTE (Germany)

Mr. Bayo OJO (Nigeria)

Mr. Alain PELLET (France)

Mr. A. Rohan PERERA (Sri Lanka)

Mr. Ernest PETRIČ (Slovenia)

Mr. Gilberto Vergne SABOIA (Brazil)

Mr. Narinder SINGH (India)

Mr. Eduardo VALENCIA-OSPINA (Colombia)

Mr. Edmundo VARGAS CARREÑO (Chile)

Mr. Stephen C. VASCIANNIE (Jamaica)

Mr. Marcelo VÁZQUEZ-BERMÚDEZ (Ecuador)

Mr. Amos S. WAKO (Kenya)

Mr. Nugroho WISNUMURTI (Indonesia)

Ms. Hanqin XUE (China)

Mr. Chusei YAMADA (Japan)

B.   Officers and Enlarged Bureau

3.   At its 2914th meeting, on 7 May 2007, the Commission elected the following officers:

Chairperson: Mr. Ian Brownlie

First Vice-Chairperson: Mr. Edmundo Vargas Carreño

Second Vice-Chairperson: Mr. Pedro Comissário Afonso

Chairperson of the Drafting Committee: Mr. Chusei Yamada

Rapporteur: Mr. Ernest Petrič

4.   The Enlarged Bureau of the Commission was composed of the officers of the present session, the previous Chairpersons of the Commission[2] and the Special Rapporteurs.[3]

5.   On the recommendation of the Enlarged Bureau, the Commission set up a Planning Group composed of the following members: Mr. Edmundo Vargas Carreño (Chairperson), Mr. Ali Mohsen Fetais Al-Marri, Mr. Lucius Caflisch, Mr. Enrique Candioti, Mr. Pedro Comissário Afonso, Ms. Paula Escarameia, Mr. Salifou Fomba, Mr. Giorgio Gaja, Mr. Zdzislaw Galicki, Mr. Hussein Hassouna, Mr. Mahmoud Hmoud, Ms. Marie Jacobsson, Mr. Bernd Niehaus, Mr. Georg Nolte, Mr. Alain Pellet, Mr. Rohan Perera, Mr. Gilberto Vergne Saboia, Mr. Narinder Singh, Mr. Eduardo Valencia-Ospina, Mr. Marcelo Vázquez-Bermúdez, Mr. Nugroho Wisnumurti, Ms. Hanqin Xue, Mr. Chusei Yamada and Mr. Ernest Petrič (*ex officio*).

C.   Drafting Committee

6.   At its 2915th, 2938th and 2943rd meetings, on 8 May, 18 July and 26 July 2007, respectively, the Commission established a Drafting Committee, composed of the following members for the topics indicated:

---

[1] See paragraph 373 of the present report.

[2] Mr. Enrique Candioti, Mr. Zdzislaw Galicki, Mr. Alain Pellet and Mr. Chusei Yamada.

[3] Mr. Ian Brownlie, Mr. Giorgio Gaja, Mr. Zdzislaw Galicki, Mr. Maurice Kamto, Mr. Alain Pellet and Mr. Chusei Yamada.

(*a*) *Reservations to treaties*: Mr. Chusei Yamada (Chairperson), Mr. Alain Pellet (Special Rapporteur), Mr. Enrique Candioti, Ms. Paula Escarameia, Mr. Salifou Fomba, Mr. Giorgio Gaja, Mr. Mahmoud Hmoud, Mr. Roman Kolodkin, Mr. Donald McRae, Mr. Bernd Niehaus, Mr. Georg Nolte, Mr. Rohan Perera, Mr. Narinder Singh, Mr. M. Vázquez-Bermúdez, Mr. Nugroho Wisnumurti, Ms. Hanqin Xue and Mr. Ernest Petrič (*ex officio*).

(*b*) *Responsibility of international organizations*: Mr. Chusei Yamada (Chairperson), Mr. Giorgio Gaja (Special Rapporteur), Ms. Paula Escarameia, Mr. Salifou Fomba, Mr. Zdzislaw Galicki, Mr. Mahmoud Hmoud, Ms. Marie Jacobsson, Mr. Roman Kolodkin, Mr. Donald McRae, Mr. Alain Pellet, Mr. Rohan Perera, Mr. Gilberto Vergne Saboia, Mr. Narinder Singh, Mr. Eduardo Valencia-Ospina, Mr. Stephen Vasciannie, Mr. Marcelo Vázquez-Bermúdez, Mr. Nugroho Wisnumurti, Ms. Hanqin Xue and Mr. Ernest Petrič (*ex officio*).

(*c*) *Expulsion of aliens*: Mr. Chusei Yamada (Chairperson), Mr. Maurice Kamto (Special Rapporteur), Mr. Enrique Candioti, Ms. Paula Escarameia, Mr. Salifou Fomba, Mr. Giorgio Gaja, Mr. Roman Kolodkin, Mr. Donald McRae, Mr. Bernd Niehaus, Mr. Rohan Perera, Mr. Gilberto Vergne Saboia, Mr. Narinder Singh, Mr. Edmundo Vargas Carreño, Mr. Stephen Vasciannie, Mr. Marcelo Vázquez-Bermúdez, Mr. Nugroho Wisnumurti, Ms. Hanqin Xue, Mr. Ernest Petrič (*ex officio*).

7. The Drafting Committee held a total of 16 meetings on the three topics indicated above.

D. Working Groups

8. At its 2920th, 2928th and 2929th meetings, on 16 May, 31 May and 1 June 2007, respectively, the Commission also established the following Working Groups:

(*a*) *Working Group on shared natural resources*:[4] Mr. Enrique Candioti (Chairperson), Mr. Chusei Yamada (Special Rapporteur), Mr. Ian Brownlie, Mr. Pedro Comissário Afonso, Ms. Paula Escarameia, Mr. Giorgio Gaja, Mr. Zdzislaw Galicki, Mr. Hussein Hassouna, Mr. Mahmoud Hmoud, Ms. Marie Jacobsson, Mr. Donald McRae, Mr. Georg Nolte, Mr. Rohan Perera, Mr. Gilberto Vergne Saboia, Mr. Narinder Singh, Mr. Marcelo Vázquez-Bermúdez, Mr. Nugroho Wisnumurti, Ms. Hanqin Xue and Mr. Ernest Petrič (*ex officio*).

(*b*) *Working Group on effects of armed conflict on treaties*:[5] Mr. Lucius Caflisch (Chairperson), Mr. Ian Brownlie (Special Rapporteur), Mr. Pedro Comissário Afonso, Ms. Paula Escarameia, Mr. Salifou Fomba, Mr. Giorgio Gaja, Mr. Mahmoud Hmoud, Ms. Marie Jacobsson, Mr. Roman Kolodkin, Mr. Donald McRae, Mr. Bernd Niehaus, Mr. Georg Nolte, Mr. Bayo Ojo, Mr. Alain Pellet, Mr. Rohan Perera, Mr. Edmundo Vargas Carreño, Mr. Marcelo Vázquez-Bermúdez, Mr. Nugroho Wisnumurti, Ms. Hanqin Xue, Mr. Chusei Yamada and Mr. Ernest Petrič (*ex officio*).

---

[4] Membership was announced at the 2921st meeting, on 18 May 2007.

[5] Membership was announced at the 2933rd meeting, on 10 July 2007.

(*c*) *Open-ended Working Group on the most-favoured-nation clause*: Mr. Donald McRae (Chairperson).

9. The *Working Group on the long-term programme of work* for the quinquennium was established by the Planning Group and was composed of the following members: Mr. Enrique Candioti (Chairperson), Mr. Ian Brownlie, Mr. Pedro Comissário Afonso, Ms. Paula Escarameia, Mr. Salifou Fomba, Mr. Giorgio Gaja, Mr. Zdzislaw Galicki, Mr. Hussein Hassouna, Mr. Mahmoud Hmoud, Ms. Marie Jacobsson, Mr. Roman Kolodkin, Mr. Donald McRae, Mr. Georg Nolte, Mr. Alain Pellet, Mr. Rohan Perera, Mr. Gilberto Vergne Saboia, Mr. Narinder Singh, Mr. Eduardo Valencia-Ospina, Mr. Marcelo Vázquez-Bermúdez, Mr. Amos Wako, Ms. Hanqin Xue and Mr. Ernest Petrič (*ex officio*).

10. The *Working Group on external publication of Commission documents* was established by the Planning Group and was composed of the following members: Mr. Giorgio Gaja (Chairperson), Mr. Enrique Candioti, Ms. Paula Escarameia, Mr. Hussein Hassouna, Mr. Mahmoud Hmoud, Mr. Maurice Kamto, Mr. Roman Kolodkin, Mr. Donald McRae, Mr. Georg Nolte, Ms. Hanqin Xue, Mr. Chusei Yamada and Mr. Ernest Petrič (*ex officio*).

E. Secretariat

11. Mr. Nicolas Michel, Under-Secretary-General, United Nations Legal Counsel, represented the Secretary General. Ms. Mahnoush H. Arsanjani, Director of the Codification Division of the Office of Legal Affairs, acted as Secretary to the Commission and, in the absence of the United Nations Legal Counsel, represented the Secretary-General. Mr. George Korontzis, Principal Legal Officer, served as Principal Assistant Secretary, Mr. Trevor Chimimba, Senior Legal Officer, served as Senior Assistant Secretary. Mr. Arnold Pronto, Legal Officer; Mr. Pierre Bodeau-Livinec, Legal Officer; Mr. Santiago Villalpando, Legal Officer; and Mr. Gionata Buzzini, Associate Legal Officer, served as Assistant Secretaries to the Commission.

F. Agenda

12. At its 2914th meeting, the Commission adopted an agenda for its fifty-ninth session consisting of the following items:

1. Organization of the work of the session.

2. Shared natural resources.

3. Responsibility of international organizations.

4. Reservations to treaties.

5. Effects of armed conflicts on treaties.

6. The obligation to extradite or prosecute (*aut dedere aut judicare*).

7. Expulsion of aliens.

8. Programme, procedures and working methods of the Commission and its documentation.

9. Date and place of the sixtieth session.

10. Cooperation with other bodies.

11. Other business.

Chapter II

SUMMARY OF THE WORK OF THE COMMISSION AT ITS FIFTY-NINTH SESSION

13. Concerning the topic "Reservations to treaties", the Commission considered the eleventh[6] and twelfth (A/CN.4/584) reports of the Special Rapporteur and on the formulation and withdrawal of acceptances and objections and on the procedure for acceptances of reservations, respectively, and referred to the Drafting Committee 35 draft guidelines on the above issues. The Commission also adopted nine draft guidelines dealing with the determination of the object and purpose of the treaty as well as the question of incompatibility of a reservation with the object and purpose of the treaty, together with commentaries (see chapter IV).

14. Concerning the topic "Shared natural resources", the Commission considered the fourth report by the Special Rapporteur (A/CN.4/580), which focused on the relationship between the work on transboundary aquifers and any future work on oil and gas, and recommended that the Commission proceed with the second reading of the draft articles on the law of transboundary aquifers independently of any future consideration of oil and gas. The Commission also established a Working Group on shared natural resources which addressed (*a*) the substance of the draft articles on the law of transboundary aquifers adopted on first reading; (*b*) the final form that the draft articles should take; and (*c*) issues involved in the consideration of oil and gas, and in particular prepared a questionnaire on State practice concerning oil and gas for circulation to Governments (see chapter V).

15. In connection with the topic "Expulsion of aliens", the Commission considered the second[7] and third (A/CN.4/581) reports of the Special Rapporteur, dealing, respectively, with the scope of the topic and definitions (two draft articles), and with certain general provisions limiting the right of a State to expel an alien (five draft articles). Following its debate on the two reports, the Commission decided to refer the seven draft articles to the Drafting Committee (see chapter VI).

16. As regards the topic "Effects of armed conflicts on treaties", the Commission considered the third report of the Special Rapporteur (A/CN.4/578) and decided to establish a Working Group under the chairpersonship of Mr. Lucius Caflisch. The Commission subsequently adopted the report of the Working Group and decided to refer draft articles 1 to 3, 5, 5 *bis*, 7, 10 and 11, as proposed by the Special Rapporteur, and draft article 4, as proposed by the Working Group, to the Drafting Committee, together with the recommendations and suggestions of the Working Group (see chapter VII).

17. Concerning the topic "Responsibility of international organizations", the Commission considered the fifth report of the Special Rapporteur (A/CN.4/583), which focused on content of the international responsibility of an international organization. Following its debate on the report, the Commission referred 15 draft articles to the Drafting Committee and it subsequently adopted 15 draft articles, together with commentaries, dealing with the content of the international responsibility of an international organization (see chapter VIII).

18. Concerning the topic "The obligation to extradite or prosecute (*aut dedere aut judicare*)", the Commission considered the second report of the Special Rapporteur (A/CN.4/585), containing one draft article on the scope of application, as well as a proposed plan for further development. The Commission also had before it comments and information received from Governments (A/CN.4/579 and Add.1–4) (see chapter IX).

19. The Commission set up the Planning Group to consider its programme, procedures and working methods (see chapter X, section A). A Working Group on the long-term programme of work was established, under the chairpersonship of Mr. Enrique Candioti, which will submit its final report to the Commission at the end of the current quinquennium topic (see chapter X, section A.3). The Commission decided to include in its current programme of work two new topics, namely "Protection of persons in the event of disasters" and "Immunity of State officials from foreign criminal jurisdiction". In this regard, it decided to appoint Mr. Eduardo Valencia-Ospina as Special Rapporteur for the former topic, and Mr. Roman Kolodkin as Special Rapporteur for the latter topic (see chapter X, section A.4). The Commission also established a Working Group on the most-favoured-nation clause under the chairpersonship of Mr. Donald McRae to examine the possibility of considering the topic "Most-favoured-nation clause" (*ibid.*).

20. The Commission continued its traditional exchanges of information with the International Court of Justice, the Inter-American Juridical Committee, the Asian–African Legal Consultative Organization and the European Committee on Legal Cooperation and the Committee of Legal Advisers on Public International Law of the Council of Europe (see chapter X, section C). The Commission organized a meeting with United Nations and other experts in the field of human rights, which was devoted to discussions on reservations to human rights treaties (see chapter X, section A.9). The Commission also held an informal meeting with the International Committee of the Red Cross on matters of mutual interest (see chapter X, section C).

---

[6] *Yearbook ... 2006*, vol. II (Part One), document A/CN.4/574.

[7] *Ibid.*, document A/CN.4/573.

21.   An international law seminar was held with 25 participants of different nationalities. Members of the Commission gave lectures and were involved in other activities concerning the seminar (see chapter X, section E).

22.   The Commission decided that its next session be held at the United Nations Office at Geneva in two parts, from 5 May to 6 June and from 7 July to 8 August 2008 (see chapter X, section B).

Chapter III

SPECIFIC ISSUES ON WHICH COMMENTS WOULD BE OF PARTICULAR INTEREST TO THE COMMISSION

A. Reservations to treaties

23. The Special Rapporteur on reservations to treaties proposed to complete his presentation of problems posed by the invalidity of reservations in 2008. With this in view, the Commission welcomed replies from States to the following questions:

(*a*) What conclusions do States draw if a reservation is found to be invalid for any of the reasons listed in article 19 of the Vienna Convention on the Law of Treaties (hereinafter "1969 Vienna Convention") and the Vienna Convention on the Law of Treaties between States and International Organizations or between International Organizations (hereinafter "1986 Vienna Convention")? Do they consider that the State formulating the reservation is still bound by the treaty without being able to enjoy the benefit of the reservation? Or, conversely, do they believe that the acceptance of the reserving State is flawed and that the State cannot be considered to be bound by the treaty? Or do they favour a compromise solution and, if so, what is it?

(*b*) Are the replies to the preceding questions based on a position of principle or are they based on practical considerations? Do they (or should they) vary according to whether the State has or has not formulated an objection to the reservation in question?

(*c*) Do the replies to the above two sets of questions vary (or should they vary) according to the type of treaty concerned (bilateral or normative, human rights, environmental protection, codification, etc.)?

(*d*) More specifically, State practice offers examples of objections that are intended to produce effects different from those provided for in article 21, paragraph 3 (objection with minimum effect), or article 20, paragraph 4 (*b*) (maximum effect), of the 1969 and 1986 Vienna Conventions, either because the objecting State wishes to exclude from its treaty relations with the reserving State provisions that are not related to the reservation (intermediate effect), or because it wishes to render the reservation ineffective and considers the reserving State to be bound by the treaty as a whole and that the reservation thus has no effect ("super-maximum" effect). The Commission would welcome the views of States regarding these practices (irrespective of their own practice).

24. The Commission noted that it is aware of the relative complexity of the above questions, which are related to problems that are themselves highly complex and take into account a wide range of practice. The Commission suggested that the replies to these questions be addressed to the Special Rapporteur in writing through the Secretariat. It would be particularly useful if the authors could include with their replies as precise a description as possible of the practice they themselves follow.

25. The Commission had noted that, in the main, the formulation of objections to reservations is practised by a relatively small number of States. It would thus be particularly useful if States that do not engage in this practice could transmit their views on these matters, which are fundamental to the topic of "Reservations to treaties".

B. Shared natural resources

26. The Commission intended to study issues concerning oil and gas under the topic "Shared natural resources". It would be useful for the Commission in the consideration of these issues to be provided with relevant State practice, in particular treaties or other arrangements existing on the subject.[8]

C. Expulsion of aliens

27. The Commission would welcome any information concerning the practice of States under this topic, including examples of domestic legislation. It would welcome in particular information and comments on the following points:

(*a*) State practice with regard to the expulsion of nationals. Is it allowed under domestic legislation? Is it permissible under international law?

(*b*) The manner in which persons having two or more nationalities are dealt with under expulsion legislation. Can such persons be considered aliens in the context of expulsion?

(*c*) The question of deprivation of nationality as a possible precondition for a person's expulsion. Is such a measure allowed under domestic legislation? Is it permissible under international law?

(*d*) The question of the collective expulsion of aliens who are nationals of a State involved in an armed conflict with the host State. In such a situation, should a distinction be drawn between aliens living peacefully in the host State and those involved in activities hostile to it?

(*e*) The question of whether an alien who has had to leave the territory of a State under an expulsion order subsequently found by a competent authority to be unlawful has the right of return.

---

[8] A questionnaire on this issue was circulated to Governments.

(*f*)   Criteria that could be used to distinguish between the expulsion of an alien and the question of non-admission; more specifically, determining the point at which the removal of an illegal immigrant is governed by the expulsion procedure and not by the non-admission procedure.

(*g*)   The legal status of illegal immigrants located in the territorial sea or in internal waters, or in the frontier zone excluding port and airport areas. Specifically, apart from port and airport areas, is there an international zone within which an alien would be considered as not having yet entered the territory of the State? If so, how is the extent and breadth of such a zone determined?

(*h*)   State practice in relation to grounds for expulsion, and the question of whether and, where appropriate, the extent to which such grounds are restricted by international law.

28.   The Commission also approved the Special Rapporteur's recommendation that the Secretariat should contact the relevant international organizations in order to obtain information and their views on particular aspects of the topic.

D.   Responsibility of international organizations

29.   The Commission would welcome comments and observations from Governments and international organizations on draft articles 31 to 45, in particular on draft article 43, relating to an obligation of members of a responsible international organization to take, in accordance with the rules of the organization, all appropriate measures in order to provide the organization with the means for effectively fulfilling its obligation to make reparation.

30.   The Commission would also welcome views from Governments and international organizations on the two following questions, due to be examined in the next report:

(*a*)   Article 48 on responsibility of States for internationally wrongful acts provides that, in case of a breach by a State of an obligation owed to the international community as whole, States are entitled to claim from the responsible State cessation of the internationally wrongful act and performance of the obligation of reparation in the interest of the injured State or of the beneficiaries of the obligation breached.[9] Should a breach of an obligation owed to the international community as a whole be committed by an international organization, would the other organizations or some of them be entitled to make a similar claim?

(*b*)   If an injured international organization intends to resort to countermeasures, would it encounter further restrictions than those that are listed in articles 49 to 53 of the articles on responsibility of States for internationally wrongful acts?[10]

E.   The obligation to extradite or prosecute (*aut dedere aut judicare*)

31.   The Commission would welcome any information that Governments may wish to provide concerning their legislation and practice with regard to this topic, particularly more contemporary ones. If possible, such information should concern:

(*a*)   International treaties by which a State is bound, containing the principle of universal jurisdiction in criminal matters; is it connected with the obligation *aut dedere aut judicare*?

(*b*)   Domestic legal regulations adopted and applied by a State, including constitutional provisions and penal codes or codes of criminal procedures, concerning the principle of universal jurisdiction in criminal matters; is it connected with the obligation *aut dedere aut judicare*?

(*c*)   Judicial practice of a State reflecting the application of the principle of universal jurisdiction in criminal matters; is it connected with the obligation *aut dedere aut judicare*?

(*d*)   Crimes or offences to which the principle of universal jurisdiction in criminal matters is applied in the legislation and practice of a State; is it connected with the obligation *aut dedere aut judicare*?

32.   The Commission would also appreciate information on the following:

(*a*)   Whether the State has authority under its domestic law to extradite persons in cases not covered by a treaty or to extradite persons of its own nationality?

(*b*)   Whether the State has authority to assert jurisdiction over crimes occurring in other States that do not involve one of its nationals?

(*c*)   Whether the State considers the obligation to extradite or prosecute as an obligation under customary international law and, if so, to what extent?

33.   The Commission would also welcome any further information and views that Governments may consider relevant to the topic.

---

[9] *Yearbook ... 2001*, vol. II (Part Two) and corrigendum, pp. 126–128.

[10] *Ibid.*, pp. 129–137.

Chapter IV

RESERVATIONS TO TREATIES

A. Introduction

34. The General Assembly, in its resolution 48/31 of 9 December 1993, endorsed the decision of the International Law Commission to include in its agenda the topic "The law and practice relating to reservations to treaties".

35. At its forty-sixth session, held in 1994, the Commission appointed Mr. Alain Pellet Special Rapporteur for the topic.[11]

36. At its forty-seventh session, in 1995, the Commission received and considered the first report of the Special Rapporteur.[12]

37. Following that discussion, the Special Rapporteur summarized the conclusions he had drawn from the Commission's consideration of the topic: they related to the title of the topic, which should now read "Reservations to treaties"; the form of the results of the study, which should be a guide to practice in respect of reservations; the flexible way in which the Commission's work on the topic should be carried out; and the consensus in the Commission that there should be no change in the relevant provisions of the 1969 Vienna Convention, the Vienna Convention on succession of States in respect of treaties (hereinafter "1978 Vienna Convention") and the 1986 Vienna Convention.[13] In the view of the Commission, those conclusions constituted the results of the preliminary study requested by the General Assembly in resolutions 48/31 of 9 December 1993 and 49/51 of 9 December 1994. As far as the Guide to Practice was concerned, it would take the form of draft guidelines with commentaries, which would be of assistance for the practice of States and international organizations; these guidelines would, if necessary, be accompanied by model clauses.

38. Also at its forty-seventh session, the Commission, in accordance with its earlier practice,[14] authorized the Special Rapporteur to prepare a detailed questionnaire on reservations to treaties, to ascertain the practice of, and problems encountered by, States and international organizations, particularly those which were depositaries of multilateral conventions.[15] The questionnaire was sent to the addressees by the Secretariat. In its resolution 50/45 of 11 December 1995, the General Assembly took note of

the Commission's conclusions, inviting it to continue its work along the lines indicated in its report and also inviting States to answer the questionnaire.[16]

39. At its forty-eighth session, in 1996, the Commission had before it the Special Rapporteur's second report on the topic.[17] The Special Rapporteur had annexed to his report a draft resolution of the Commission on reservations to multilateral normative treaties, including human rights treaties, which was addressed to the General Assembly for the purpose of drawing attention to and clarifying the legal aspects of the matter.[18]

40. At its forty-ninth session, in 1997, the Commission adopted preliminary conclusions on reservations to normative multilateral treaties, including human rights treaties.[19]

41. In its resolution 52/156 of 15 December 1997, the General Assembly took note of the Commission's preliminary conclusions and of its invitation to all treaty bodies set up by normative multilateral treaties that might wish to do so to provide, in writing, their comments and observations on the conclusions, while drawing the attention of Governments to the importance for the Commission of having their views on the preliminary conclusions.

42. From its fiftieth session, in 1998, to its fifty-eighth session, in 2006, the Commission considered eight more reports[20] by the Special Rapporteur and provisionally adopted 76 draft guidelines and the commentaries thereto.

B. Consideration of the topic at the present session

43. At the present session the Committee had before it the eleventh[21] and twelfth (A/CN.4/584) reports of the

---

[11] See *Yearbook ... 1994*, vol. II (Part Two), p. 179, para. 381.

[12] *Yearbook ... 1995*, vol. II (Part One), document A/CN.4/470.

[13] *Ibid.*, vol. II (Part Two), p. 108, para. 487.

[14] See *Yearbook ... 1983*, vol. II (Part Two), p. 83, para. 286.

[15] See *Yearbook ... 1995*, vol. II (Part Two), p. 108, para. 489. The questionnaires sent to Member States and international organizations are reproduced in *Yearbook ... 1996*, vol. II (Part One), document A/CN.4/477 and Add.1, Annexes II and III.

[16] As of 31 July 2007, 33 States and 26 international organizations had answered the questionnaire.

[17] *Yearbook ... 1996*, vol. II (Part One), documents A/CN.4/477 and Add.1 and A/CN.4/478.

[18] *Ibid.*, vol. II (Part Two), p. 83, para. 136 and footnote 238.

[19] *Yearbook ... 1997*, vol. II (Part Two), pp. 56–57, para. 157.

[20] Third report: *Yearbook ... 1998*, vol. II (Part One), document A/CN.4/491 and Add.1–6; fourth report: *Yearbook ... 1999*, vol. II (Part One), documents A/CN.4/499 and A/CN.4/478/Rev.1; fifth report: *Yearbook ... 2000*, vol. II (Part One), document A/CN.4/508 and Add.1–4; sixth report: *Yearbook ... 2001*, vol. II (Part One), document A/CN.4/518 and Add.1–3; seventh report: *Yearbook ... 2002*, vol. II (Part One), document A/CN.4/526 and Add.1–3; eighth report: *Yearbook ... 2003*, vol. II (Part One), document A/CN.4/535 and Add.1; ninth report: *Yearbook ... 2004*, vol. II (Part One), document A/CN.4/544); and tenth report: *Yearbook ... 2005*, vol. II (Part One), document A/CN.4/558 and Add.1–2. See a detailed historical presentation of the third to ninth reports in *Yearbook ... 2004*, vol. II (Part Two), paras. 257–269.

[21] *Yearbook ... 2006*, vol. II (Part One), document A/CN.4/574 (see footnote 6 above).

Special Rapporteur, on the formulation and withdrawal of acceptances and objections and on the procedure for acceptances of reservations, respectively. The eleventh report had been submitted at the fifty-eighth session, but the Commission had decided to consider it at the fifty-ninth session, owing to a lack of time.[22]

44.   The Commission considered the eleventh report of the Special Rapporteur at its 2914th to 2920th meetings, on 7 to 11, 15 and 16 May 2007, and the twelfth report at its 2936th to 2940th meetings, on 13, 17 to 20 July 2007.

45.   At its 2917th, 2919th and 2020th meetings, on 10, 15 and 16 May 2007, the Committee decided to refer draft guidelines 2.6.3 to 2.6.6, 2.6.7 to 2.6.15 and 2.7.1 to 2.7.9 to the Drafting Committee, and to review the wording of draft guideline 2.1.6 in the light of the discussion. At its 2940th meeting on 20 July 2007, the Commission decided to refer draft guidelines 2.8, 2.8.1 to 2.8.12 to the Drafting Committee.

46.   The Drafting Committee was instructed to take into account the interpretation of draft guideline 2.8.12 resulting from an indicative vote[23] and an analysis of the provisions of article 20, paragraph 5, of the 1969 Vienna Convention as creating a presumption of tacit acceptance without such acceptance being considered acquired.[24]

47.   At its 2930th meeting, on 4 June 2007, the Commission considered and provisionally adopted draft guidelines 3.1.5 (Incompatibility of a reservation with the object and purpose of the treaty), 3.1.6 (Determination of the object and purpose of the treaty), 3.1.7 (Vague or general reservations), 3.1.8 (Reservations to a provision reflecting a customary norm), 3.1.9 (Reservations contrary to a rule of *jus cogens*), 3.1.10 (Reservations to provisions relating to non-derogable rights), 3.1.11 (Reservations relating to internal law), 3.1.12 (Reservations to general human rights treaties) and 3.1.13 (Reservations to treaty provisions concerning dispute settlement or the monitoring of the implementation of the treaty).

48.   At its 2950th and 2951st meetings, on 7 August 2007, the Commission adopted the commentaries relating to the aforementioned draft guidelines.

49.   The text of the draft guidelines and the commentaries thereto are reproduced in section C.2 below.

1.   INTRODUCTION BY THE SPECIAL RAPPORTEUR OF HIS ELEVENTH REPORT

50.   The Special Rapporteur briefly reviewed the history of the topic "Reservations to treaties", recalling the flexible regime established by the 1969 and 1986 Vienna Conventions, the uncertainties that the regime entailed and the Commission's fundamental decision not to call into question the work of the Vienna Conventions but to draw up a Guide to Practice consisting of guidelines which, while not binding in themselves, might guide the practice of States and international organizations with regard to reservations and interpretative declarations.

51.   The first group of draft guidelines included in the eleventh report (2.6.3 to 2.6.6) concerned the freedom to make objections to reservations. The Special Rapporteur recalled that it was merely a freedom, given that the Commission had not made it conditional on the incompatibility of a reservation with the object and purpose of the treaty, and that the United Nations Conference on the Law of Treaties had followed the Commission in that regard, despite the doubts of some delegations. That approach was in keeping with the spirit of consensus pervading all of treaty law, in the sense that a State could not unilaterally impose on other contracting parties the modification of a treaty binding them by means of a reservation. Limiting the freedom to make objections exclusively to reservations that were incompatible with the object and purpose of the treaty would render the procedure for acceptance of and objections to reservations under article 20 of the 1969 Vienna Convention ineffective.

52.   Yet the freedom to make objections was not arbitrary, but subject to conditions relating to both form and procedure, which were covered by draft guidelines 2.6.3 to 2.6.7. Grounds for objections could range from the (alleged) incompatibility of the reservation with the object and purpose of the treaty to political grounds. While the State was not obliged to mention incompatibility with the object and purpose of the treaty as the ground for its objection, surprisingly States very frequently invoked that very ground.

53.   Draft guideline 2.6.3[25] conveyed the idea that any State or international organization enjoyed the freedom to make objections.

54.   Turning to the relationship of the objection to entry into force of the treaty between the author of the reservation and the author of the objection, the Special Rapporteur recalled that although the Commission's special rapporteurs had in the past considered that the objection automatically precluded the entry into force of the treaty between those two parties, Sir Humphrey Waldock had subsequently supported the advisory opinion of the ICJ of 1951,[26] which held that the State that was the author of the objection was free to draw its own conclusions concerning the effects of its objection on its relations with the reserving State. In the event that the objecting State remained silent on the matter, the presumption made by the Commission in 1966 was that the treaty would not enter into force between the two parties.[27]

---

[22] The Commission held a meeting with United Nations and other human rights experts on 15 and 16 May 2007. See chapter X, section A.9, at p. 103 below.

[23] The Special Rapporteur having hoped that the Commission would take a clear position on this problem of principle in plenary meeting, the Commission did, following an indicative vote, express its support for retaining the principle set out in draft guideline 2.8.12.

[24] This interpretation was obtained by consensus.

[25] Draft guideline 2.6.3 reads as follows:

"2.6.3   *Freedom to make objections*

"A State or an international organization may formulate an objection to a reservation for any reason whatsoever, in accordance with the provisions of the present Guide to Practice."

[26] See *Yearbook ... 1962*, vol. I, 654th meeting, paras. 17 and 20. For the position of the ICJ, see *Reservations to the Convention on the Prevention and Punishment of the Crime of Genocide, Advisory Opinion of 28 May 1951, I.C.J. Reports 1951*, p. 15, at p. 26.

[27] See *Yearbook ... 1966*, vol. II, pp. 202–208.

That presumption, albeit logical, had nevertheless been reversed during the United Nations Conference on the Law of Treaties. As a result, the treaty was considered as being in force between the two parties concerned, with the exception of the provision covered by the reservation. Article 20, paragraph 4 (*b*), and article 21, paragraph 3, of the 1969 Vienna Convention reflected that presumption. While the Special Rapporteur was tempted to "revise" that wording, which was neither very logical nor satisfactory, he had ultimately decided not to change it, as it reflected current practice. It was therefore reproduced in draft guideline 2.6.4.[28]

55. Draft guideline 2.6.5[29] sought to answer a question that had been left pending by draft guideline 2.6.1, on the definition of objections, namely who had the freedom to make objections. Article 20, paragraph 4 (*b*), of the 1986 Vienna Convention provided guidance by referring to an objection by a contracting State or a contracting international organization. Any State or any international organization that was entitled to become a party to the treaty and that had been notified of the reservations could also formulate objections that would produce effects only when the State or organization became a party to the treaty.

56. With regard to draft guideline 2.6.6,[30] the Special Rapporteur said that in the absence of any relevant practice, the draft guidelines constituted an exercise in progressive development. It was the counterpart of draft guidelines 1.1.7 and 1.2.2 in the area of objections.

57. Introducing draft guidelines 2.6.7 to 2.6.15, on the form of and procedure for the formulation of objections, the Special Rapporteur recalled that, as far as form was concerned, article 23, paragraph 1, of the Vienna Conventions provided that objections must be formulated in writing; those were the terms used in draft guideline 2.6.7.[31]

58. Moreover, when a State or international organization intended that its objection should prevent the treaty from entering into force between it and the author of the

reservation, such an intention must be clearly expressed, in accordance with article 20, paragraph 4 (*b*), of the Vienna Conventions. Although practice in that area was not conclusive, draft guideline 2.6.8[32] followed the wording of the Vienna Conventions. In the interests of legal security, the intention should be expressed at the latest when the objection will produce its full effects. For that reason, the Special Rapporteur thought that a phrase along the following lines should be added at the end of draft guideline 2.6.8: "in accordance with draft guideline 2.6.13", since the latter concerned the time period for formulating an objection.

59. The Special Rapporteur then noted that the procedure for objections was no different from that for reservations. Thus it might be possible to consider reproducing all the draft guidelines that the Commission had already adopted on the procedure for formulating reservations, or else simply to refer to them, which was what draft guideline 2.6.9[33] did.

60. The question of the reasons for the objection, which was not covered in the Vienna Conventions, was taken up in draft guideline 2.6.10.[34] While the freedom to make objections was discretionary, it was nevertheless true that it would be useful to make the reasons for the objection known, both for the reserving State and for third parties called upon to assess the validity of the reservation, at least when the objection was based on incompatibility with the object and purpose of the treaty. The Special Rapporteur even wondered whether the Commission should not include a similar recommendation concerning the reasons for reservations in the Guide to Practice.

61. On the question of the confirmation of objections, the Special Rapporteur recalled that article 23, paragraph 3, of the 1986 Vienna Convention provided that objections did not require confirmation if they were made previously to confirmation of a reservation. That principle was also contained in draft guideline 2.6.11.[35] In his view, the same principle might also apply to the case in which a State or an international organization had formulated an

---

[28] Draft guideline 2.6.4 reads as follows:

"2.6.4   *Freedom to oppose the entry into force of the treaty vis-à-vis the author of the reservation*

"A State or international organization that formulates an objection to a reservation may oppose the entry into force of the treaty as between itself and the reserving State or international organization for any reason whatsoever, in accordance with the provisions of the present Guide to Practice."

[29] Draft guideline 2.6.5 reads as follows:

"2.6.5   *Author of an objection*

An objection to a reservation may be formulated by:

(*a*) any contracting State and any contracting international organization; and

(*b*) any State and any international organization that is entitled to become a party to the treaty.

[30] Draft guideline 2.6.6 reads as follows:

"2.6.6   *Joint formulation of an objection*

The joint formulation of an objection by a number of States or international organizations does not affect the unilateral nature of that objection."

[31] Draft guideline 2.6.7 reads as follows:

"2.6.7   *Written form*

"An objection must be formulated in writing."

[32] Draft guideline 2.6.8 reads as follows:

"2.6.8   *Expression of intention to oppose the entry into force of the treaty*

"When a State or international organization making an objection to a reservation intends to oppose the entry into force of the treaty as between itself and the reserving State or international organization, it must clearly express its intention when it formulates the objection."

[33] Draft guideline 2.6.9 reads as follows:

"2.6.9   *Procedure for the formulation of objections*

"Draft guidelines 2.1.3, 2.1.4, 2.1.5, 2.1.6 and 2.1.7 are applicable *mutatis mutandis* to objections."

[34] Draft guideline 2.6.10 reads as follows:

"2.6.10   *Statement of reasons*

"Whenever possible, an objection should indicate the reasons why it is being made."

[35] Draft guideline 2.6.11 reads as follows:

"2.6.11   *Non-requirement of confirmation of an objection made prior to formal confirmation of a reservation*

"An objection to a reservation made by a State or an international organization prior to confirmation of the reservation in accordance with draft guideline 2.2.1 does not itself require confirmation."

objection before becoming party to a treaty, and that was reflected in draft guideline 2.6.12.[36]

62. Draft guideline 2.6.13[37] concerned the time when the objection should be formulated and was based on article 20, paragraph 5, of the 1986 Vienna Convention. However, the Special Rapporteur noted that the third paragraph of draft guideline 2.1.6 (already adopted and entitled "Procedure for communication of reservations") dealt with the question of the period during which an objection could be raised, which might give rise to confusion. He therefore proposed that, in order to avoid any duplication with draft guideline 2.6.13, either the question should be reviewed on second reading or else the draft guideline 2.1.6 should be "revised" forthwith.

63. The Special Rapporteur then recalled a practice that had developed whereby States declared in advance that they would oppose certain types of reservations before they had even been formulated. Such pre-emptive objections seemed to fulfil one of the most important functions of objections, namely to give notice to the author of the reservation. Draft guideline 2.6.14[38] reflected that fairly widespread practice.

64. In contrast to pre-emptive objections, there were also late objections, formulated after the end of the time period specified in the Vienna Conventions. Such "objections" could not have the same effects as objections formulated on time or remove the implicit acceptance of the reservation. However, the Special Rapporteur thought that such "objections" were governed *mutatis mutandis* by the regime for interpretative declarations rather than by the regime for reservations and could still perform the function of giving notice. As practice reflecting that view did in fact exist, draft guideline 2.6.15[39] dealt with such late "objections".

65. With regard to draft guidelines 2.7.1 to 2.7.9, the Special Rapporteur said that the Guide to Practice should contain guidelines on the withdrawal and modification of objections, even though practice in that area was virtually non-existent. He also thought that the guidelines should be modelled on those relating to the withdrawal and modification of reservations. Draft guidelines 2.7.1[40] and 2.7.2[41] merely reproduced article 22, paragraph 2, and article 23, paragraph 4, respectively, of the Vienna Conventions. Draft guideline 2.7.3[42] also referred to the relevant guidelines on reservations, transposing them to the formulation and communication of the withdrawal of objections.

66. On the other hand, the effect of the withdrawal of an objection could not be compared with the effect of the withdrawal of a reservation. That question could give rise to highly complex issues, but it would be better to consider that the withdrawal of an objection was tantamount to an acceptance of reservations, and that was the principle that was established in draft guideline 2.7.4.[43] The date on which the withdrawal of an objection took effect was dealt with in draft guidelines 2.7.5[44] and 2.7.6[45], of which the former reflected the wording of article 22, paragraph 3 (*b*), of the 1986 Vienna Convention.

67. The Special Rapporteur also noted that, even in the absence of practice, it might be possible to contemplate the partial withdrawal of an objection, a situation which was covered by draft guideline 2.7.7.[46] As for

---

[36] Draft guideline 2.6.12 reads as follows:

"2.6.12 *Non-requirement of confirmation of an objection made prior to the expression of consent to be bound by a treaty*

"If an objection is made prior to the expression of consent to be bound by the treaty, it does not need to be formally confirmed by the objecting State or international organization at the time it expresses its consent to be bound."

[37] Draft guideline 2.6.13 reads as follows:

"2.6.13 *Time period for formulating an objection*

"Unless the treaty otherwise provides, a State or an international organization may formulate an objection to a reservation by the end of a period of 12 months after it is notified of the reservation or by the date on which such State or international organization expresses its consent to be bound by the treaty, whichever is later."

[38] Draft guideline 2.6.14 reads as follows:

"2.6.14 *Pre-emptive objections*

"A State or international organization may formulate an objection to a specific potential or future reservation, or to a specific category of such reservations, or exclude the application of the treaty as a whole in its relations with the author of such a potential or future reservation. Such a pre-emptive objection shall not produce the legal effects of an objection until the reservation has actually been formulated and notified."

[39] Draft guideline 2.6.15 reads as follows:

"2.6.15 *Late objections*

"An objection to a reservation formulated after the end of the time period specified in guideline 2.6.13 does not produce all the legal effects of an objection that has been made within that time period."

[40] Draft guideline 2.7.1 reads as follows:

"2.7.1 *Withdrawal of objections to reservations*

"Unless the treaty otherwise provides, an objection to a reservation may be withdrawn at any time."

[41] Draft guideline 2.7.2 reads as follows:

"2.7.2 *Form of withdrawal of objections to reservations*

"The withdrawal of an objection to a reservation must be formulated in writing."

[42] Draft guideline 2.7.3 reads as follows:

"2.7.3 *Formulation and communication of the withdrawal of objections to reservations*

"Guidelines 2.5.4, 2.5.5 and 2.5.6 are applicable *mutatis mutandis* to the withdrawal of objections to reservations."

[43] Draft guideline 2.7.4 reads as follows:

"2.7.4 *Effect of withdrawal of an objection*

"A State that withdraws an objection formulated earlier against a reservation is considered to have accepted that reservation."

[44] Draft guideline 2.7.5 reads as follows:

"2.7.5 *Effective date of withdrawal of an objection*

"Unless the treaty otherwise provides, or it is otherwise agreed, the withdrawal of an objection to a reservation becomes operative only when notice of it has been received by the State or international organization which formulated the reservation."

[45] Draft guideline 2.7.6 reads as follows:

"2.7.6 *Cases in which an objecting State or international organization may unilaterally set the effective date of withdrawal of an objection to a reservation*

"The withdrawal of an objection takes effect on the date set by its author where that date is later than the date on which the reserving State received notification of it."

[46] Draft guideline 2.7.7 reads as follows:

"2.7.7 *Partial withdrawal of an objection*

"Unless the treaty provides otherwise, a State or an international organization may partially withdraw an objection to a reservation. The partial withdrawal limits the legal effects of the objection on the treaty relations between the author of the objection and the author of the reservation or on the treaty as a whole.

(*Continued on next page.*)

draft guideline 2.7.8,[47] it was modelled on draft guideline 2.5.11 (Effect of a partial withdrawal of a reservation). Draft guideline 2.7.9[48] dealt with a case in which a State or international organization that had made a simple objection wished to widen its scope. Considerations of good faith and the inability of the reserving State to state its views led him to believe that widening of the scope of the objection should be prohibited.

2. Summary of the debate

68. With regard to draft guidelines 2.6.3 and 2.6.4, it was observed that it was possible to deduce from the 1951 advisory opinion of the ICJ[49] that a distinction could be drawn between "minor" objections (not relating to the object and purpose of the treaty) and "major" objections based on that incompatibility. The effects would be different, and it could be maintained that although the 1969 Vienna Convention did not expressly make any distinction between those two types of objection, the regime of objections was not necessarily the same. One might well ask whether the presumption of article 20, paragraph 4 (*b*), of the Vienna Convention applied to all objections or to "minor" objections only. The difference in regimes might also explain the practice of some States whereby an objection to a reservation that was allegedly incompatible with the object and the purpose of the treaty did not preclude entry into force of the treaty between the reserving State and the objecting State. It was also pointed out that article 20, paragraph 4 (*b*), was consistent with article 19 only when it referred to "minor" objections. The Commission should not adopt texts that seemed to imply that a uniform regime did in fact exist.

69. The view was also expressed that it was not necessary to draw a distinction between "major" and "minor" objections, since a reservation that was incompatible with the object and purpose of the treaty was considered void and therefore produced no legal effects. Draft guideline 2.6.4 could be clearer and state directly that if the reserving State did not withdraw its reservation and the objecting State did not withdraw its objection, the treaty did not enter into force.

70. It was noted that the distinction between "major" and "minor" objections would have consequences for the time period for formulating an objection. From that standpoint, the time period of 12 months specified in article 20, paragraph 5, of the Vienna Convention would not be applicable to objections relating to the validity of reservations (major objections), given that articles 20 and 21 of the Vienna Convention did not concern objections to the reservations mentioned in article 19.

71. Even if one considered that articles 20 and 21 applied to all types of reservations, the distinction between the two types of objections should not be systematically disregarded. It would be useful to have an additional guideline which would state that, in the absence of an express or implicit indication, an objection was presumed not to relate to the validity of the reservation.

72. Regarding the distinction between "making" and "formulating" [objections], the question arose as to whether it would not be simpler to use the term "formulate" throughout the Guide to Practice.

73. The view was also expressed that there was a discrepancy between the title and the content of draft guideline 2.6.3, given that the expression "to make" appeared in the title, whereas the term "to formulate" was used in the text of the guideline. It was also asked whether there were any limitations on the freedom to make objections, particularly with regard to treaties that expressly permitted certain derogations but called them "reservations", such as the North American Free Trade Agreement (NAFTA). It was further asked whether the original presumption, namely that the treaty did not enter into force between the objecting State or international organization and the author of the reservation, was not preferable to the current presumption reflected in article 20, paragraph 4 (*b*).

74. Concerning draft guidelines 2.6.3 and 2.6.4, it was further observed that the term "freedom" was not entirely appropriate, since what was involved was actually a right. The expression "for any reason whatsoever" also needed to be qualified at least by a reference to the Vienna Conventions or to general international law, since the Guide to Practice should not include objections contrary to the principle of good faith or *jus cogens*.

75. The view was also expressed that if reservations were allowed, and the reservation formulated by a State or an international organization was clear, other States did not have the freedom to formulate an objection. The Guide to Practice should also contain a clearer description of the possible forms of acceptance of reservations (express or implicit) that might limit the freedom to make objections, with a view to making treaty relations more secure. It was also observed that the discretionary right to formulate an objection was independent of the question of whether a reservation was or was not compatible with the object and purpose of the treaty, and that might be included in draft guideline 2.6.3.

76. With regard to draft guideline 2.6.5, it was asked whether one could speak of an "objection" by a potential party. It would be better to speak of a conditional objection. It was also asked whether there was a difference between an objection formulated jointly by several States and parallel or overlapping objections formulated in identical terms.

"The partial withdrawal of an objection is subject to the same formal and procedural rules as a total withdrawal and takes effect on the same conditions."

[47] Draft guideline 2.7.8 reads as follows:

"2.7.8   *Effect of a partial withdrawal of an objection*

"The partial withdrawal of an objection modifies the legal effect of the objection to the extent of the new formulation of the objection."

[48] Draft guideline 2.7.9 reads as follows:

"2.7.9   *Prohibition against the widening of the scope of an objection to a reservation*

"A State or international organization which has made an objection to a reservation cannot subsequently widen the scope of that objection."

[49] *Reservations to the Convention on the Prevention and Punishment of the Crime of Genocide* (see footnote 26 above), p. 27.

77.   It was further asked whether it was justified that States that had no intention of becoming party to the treaty should have the same right as the contracting parties to formulate objections. In that connection, the practice of States and regional organizations, and not only the practice of the Secretary-General of the United Nations, should be taken into consideration.

78.   It was also observed that the reference in draft guideline 2.6.5 to States or international organizations that were entitled to become party to the treaty was preferable to the criterion of "intention" to become a party, in that it was not easy to determine intention, which was closely linked to the internal procedures of States or international organizations. It was pointed out, however, that the problem stemmed from the inappropriate English translation of the original French text of the draft guideline. It was also noted that practice with regard to the formulation of objections by States or international organizations that were entitled to become party to the treaty was inconclusive.

79.   It was also noted that at the time that the effects of objections were considered, it should be made clear that an objection formulated by a State or international organization entitled to become a party to the treaty would not produce legal effects until such time as the State or international organization in question had actually become party to the treaty.

80.   As for guideline 2.6.6, the point was made that it did not seem useful as currently drafted, since it laid emphasis on the unilateral nature of joint objections.

81.   The basic thrust of draft guideline 2.6.10 met with general approval; however, one point of view held that there would be no need to extend that recommendation to reservations: a reservation, provided that it was clear, did not have to include the reasons, which were often of an internal nature, why it had been made, unlike objections, whose reasons might facilitate determination of the reservation's compatibility with the object and purpose of the treaty. According to another, more widely held point of view, such an extension to reservations would be desirable, since what was involved was only a recommendation.

82.   Regarding draft guideline 2.6.12, it was asked whether it might not be going too far to exempt States or international organizations that had formulated an objection prior to the expression of their consent to be bound by the treaty (or even prior to signature) to confirm the objection at the time of expressing their consent. The guideline should be reconsidered, bearing in mind the often lengthy period of time that elapsed between the formulation of such an objection and the author's expression of consent to be bound by the treaty.

83.   The view was also expressed that the phrase "prior to the expression of consent to be bound by the treaty" was vague. If an objection was formulated prior to the signature of the treaty by a State, and if signature was subject to ratification, acceptance or approval, the objection would need to be confirmed when the instrument of ratification, acceptance or approval was deposited if the State had not confirmed it at the time of signature. The question was also raised as to whether such "objections" made prior to the expression of consent to be bound by the treaty could be considered to be real objections. It was also maintained that only contracting parties should be able to make objections.

84.   With regard to draft guideline 2.6.13, it was pointed out that the 12-month period ran from the date on which a State or international organization received notification of the reservation; it was therefore necessary to draw a clear distinction between that date and the date on which the reservation was communicated to the depositary. The same distinction was drawn in draft guideline 2.1.6, which had already been adopted. According to another point of view, in the light of draft guideline 2.1.6, the third paragraph of draft guideline 2.1.6 could be deleted. The view was expressed that the meaning of the term "notification" should be clarified further.

85.   Concerning draft guideline 2.6.14, the view was expressed that "pre-emptive objections" could not have legal effects. States or international organizations should react to real reservations and not to hypothetical ones, and they had ample time to do so following notification of the reservation.

86.   Moreover, it was considered that such objections were real objections, which produced all their effects but did not become operational until all conditions—namely the formulation and notification of the reservation—were met. It might therefore be more appropriate to speak of "conditional objections". It was also noted that draft guideline 2.6.14 could give rise to confusion between political declarations and declarations intended to produce legal effects. According to one point of view, it was more a question of "preventive communications", which, in order to be termed objections, should be confirmed once the reservation had been formulated. The possibility of excluding part of the treaty was also mentioned.

87.   It was also observed that the expression "all the legal effects" in draft guideline 2.6.15 was not sufficiently clear; according to that view, late objections did not produce any legal effects. Rather, they could be likened to interpretative declarations, since they were an indication of the manner in which the objecting State interpreted the treaty. In any event, it had to be ascertained whether such objections were permissible and what kinds of effects they produced. That was why they were notified by the Secretary-General as "communications". It might be appropriate to include in the Guide to Practice reactions or "objecting communications" which were not objections; that was done with declarations that did not constitute reservations, and would reflect current practice.

88.   With respect to draft guideline 2.7.1, it was observed that the title ought in fact to read: "Time of withdrawal of objections to reservations".

89.   Several members expressed support for draft guidelines 2.7.2 and 2.7.3. It was asked whether the withdrawal and modification of objections also included pre-emptive and late objections.

90. With regard to draft guideline 2.7.4, the view was expressed that its title was too general, since the withdrawal of objections could have several effects. It would be better if the title was amended to read "Acceptance of a reservation by the withdrawal of an objection".

91. Draft guideline 2.7.7 sought to address the extremely complex issue of the partial withdrawal of objections, but should perhaps be amplified in the light of future deliberations on the effects of reservations and objections. The second sentence of draft guideline 2.7.7 could be moved to draft guideline 2.7.8. The same held true for the title of draft guideline 2.7.8. It was pointed out in connection with that guideline that there was no exact parallel between the partial withdrawal of an objection and that of a reservation, since the purpose of the objection was first and foremost to safeguard the integrity of the treaty.

92. With regard to draft guideline 2.7.9, several members wondered whether an absolute prohibition, even during the 12-month period, could be justified by the lack of practice. The principle of good faith, which had not been invoked for the widening of the scope of reservations, was of little avail. Since the Commission had accepted the widening of the scope of reservations under certain conditions, it would be logical to accept such a widening for objections, at least during the 12-month period, given that the Vienna Conventions were silent on the matter. An absolute prohibition seemed far too categorical to be justified. For other members, it was not possible to draw an exact parallel between widening of the scope of a reservation and widening of the scope of an objection. Moreover, if a signatory State had formulated an objection to a reservation before formally becoming a party to the treaty, it must be able to formulate an aggravated objection by becoming a party to the treaty within the 12-month period.

93. Other members pointed out that if an objection had been made without preventing the entry into force of the treaty between the reserving State and the objecting State, any further widening of the scope of the objection would be virtually without effect. On the other hand, if several reservations had been made, there was nothing to prevent a State or an international organization from raising successive objections to different reservations, still within the 12-month period. There was nothing to indicate that all objections had to be made at the same time. Similarly, if a reservation was withdrawn, an objection to that reservation would automatically cease to have any effect. The view was also expressed that draft guideline 2.7.9 was acceptable in that States should not have the impression that such widening of the scope was permissible, as that would make it possible for the author of an objection to circumvent all or some of its treaty obligations *vis-à-vis* the author of the reservation. It was also observed that there would be no problem in limiting draft guideline 2.7.9 to a situation in which a State that had formulated an initial objection which did not preclude the entry into force of the treaty between it and the reserving State subsequently widened the scope of its objection, precluding treaty relations.

94. One widely held point of view was that a draft guideline should be added recommending that States should explain the reasons for the withdrawal of their objection, which would help the treaty bodies understand why the reservation was being considered in another light; that might facilitate the "reservations dialogue".

3. Special Rapporteur's concluding remarks

95. Summing up the discussion, the Special Rapporteur said that he was pleased to note that a consensus seemed to be emerging to refer the draft guidelines to the Drafting Committee. He was rather attracted by the distinction between major and minor objections, but remained sceptical as to its appropriateness, given that it was based on a somewhat rare and unconvincing practice. Nothing in article 20, paragraph 4 (*b*), of the 1969 and 1986 Vienna Conventions, the *travaux préparatoires* or the Soviet proposal made during the United Nations Conference on the Law of Treaties made it possible to draw such a distinction, which had been mentioned in passing in the 1951 advisory opinion of the ICJ. The Conference had been particularly concerned with the idea of making the formulation of reservations as easy as possible, and consequently of limiting the effects of objections. The reversal of the presumption in article 20, paragraph 4 (*b*), posed problems of consistency. At best, the Vienna Conventions were silent on whether the rules they contained were applicable to all reservations or only to those that had passed the test of compatibility with the object and purpose of the treaty. In any case, that distinction—intellectually interesting as it might be—could have an impact only on the effects of reservations.

96. The Special Rapporteur endorsed the comments made concerning the discrepancy between the title and the text of draft guideline 2.6.3. The title should be aligned with the text, and "to make" should be replaced with "to formulate". He was sympathetic to the argument that the freedom to formulate objections was limited by rules of procedure and by the treaty itself, even if the treaty did permit certain reservations. He wondered, however, whether that last point ought to be mentioned in the text, given that the Guide to Practice only contained auxiliary rules, which States were free to follow or set aside by contrary treaty provisions.

97. The Special Rapporteur was also receptive to the argument that the phrase "for any reason whatsoever" should be understood in the context of the Vienna Conventions, general international law and the Guide to Practice itself. As for the freedom to formulate objections, he firmly believed that however discretionary that freedom might be, it was not arbitrary but circumscribed by law. He nevertheless found it difficult to imagine objections contrary to *jus cogens*, even if such objections were not totally inconceivable. The idea of stating that the freedom to formulate objections was independent of the validity of the reservation or of its compatibility with the object and purpose of the treaty seemed acceptable to him. Conversely, he was opposed to any reference in the Guide to Practice to the Vienna Conventions because the Guide to Practice should be self-contained.

98. The term "*faculté*" was perfectly appropriate in French, but in English a more satisfactory term than "freedom", which was used in the English translation of the report, could be found.

99.   The Special Rapporteur thought that all those observations could apply also to draft guideline 2.6.4, including with regard to the use of the term "freedom" in its title. The Drafting Committee might wish to give the matter careful consideration.

100.   Turning to draft guideline 2.6.5, he said he felt that several criticisms were the result of linguistic misunderstandings. The expression used in French—"*Tout État ... ayant qualité pour devenir partie au traité*"— made no mention of intention. The text itself was based on article 23, paragraph 1, of the Vienna Conventions. If regional organizations or States did not, in the exercise of their functions as depositary, communicate reservations to States entitled to become party to the treaty, they were not acting in accordance with article 23, paragraph 1, of the Vienna Conventions. As to the distinction between the two types of authors of objections, it could be explained in greater detail in the commentary without necessarily changing the wording of the draft guideline.

101.   With regard to draft guideline 2.6.6, the Special Rapporteur approved the observation that it was the possibility of the joint formulation of objections that should be stressed rather than their unilateral nature, which could simply be mentioned in the commentary. As for similar objections formulated by several States, he thought that they could not be considered as jointly formulated objections, but could be considered parallel, separate ones.

102.   The Special Rapporteur noted that draft guidelines 2.6.7, 2.6.8 and 2.6.9 had met with general approval and did not call for any specific commentary.

103.   Draft guideline 2.6.10 had elicited favourable comments; he found interesting the proposal that, in the event of silence on the part of an objecting State, a presumption could be established either along the lines that the objection was based on the incompatibility of the reservation with the object and purpose of the treaty or vice versa. However, he did not see the usefulness of such a presumption, since he doubted that the effects of the two types of objections were different.

104.   The Special Rapporteur also noted that the proposal for an additional guideline recommending that States should give the reasons for their reservations had met with considerable support notwithstanding some hesitation.

105.   He agreed with the comments made concerning draft guideline 2.6.12, namely that it would apply only to treaties that must be ratified or approved after signature and not to those which entered into force by signature alone, but he thought that this could be mentioned in the commentary. He was aware of the risk of too long a period elapsing between the time an objection was formulated and the time it took for the objection to produce the effects mentioned by some members, but he did not see how that risk could be avoided.

106.   With respect to draft guideline 2.6.13, the Special Rapporteur noted that most members were in favour of deleting the third paragraph of guideline 2.1.6, which duplicated it.

107.   Draft guidelines 2.6.14 and 2.6.15 had elicited the most criticism. The two draft guidelines concerned objections formulated outside the specified time period. Since he held a flexible view of the law, he had attributed to them effects that certain members had had difficulty in accepting. Pre-emptive objections produced their effects only when the reservation to which they referred was made. The question of pre-emptive objections with intermediate effect was complex and difficult, but it seemed to him that such objections could be compatible with the Vienna Conventions. The Special Rapporteur also thought that the terminology might be open to discussion; he was attracted by the English expression "objecting communications", but wondered how it ought to be translated into French.

108.   As far as draft guideline 2.6.15 was concerned, he thought that the question of validity was totally different from that of definition. A late objection, even if it was not valid, was always an objection. Yet from a positivist point of view it was correct to say that a late objection did not produce legal effects, and that could be reflected by rewording the draft guideline.

109.   The Special Rapporteur agreed with those members who thought that the time of withdrawal should be mentioned in draft guideline 2.7.1. He noted that draft guidelines 2.7.2, 2.7.3, 2.7.4, 2.7.5, 2.7.6, 2.7.7 and 2.7.8 had been supported by speakers, aside from a few comments of a drafting nature, which could be taken up in the Drafting Committee.

110.   Furthermore, he was not unsympathetic to criticisms of the way in which draft guideline 2.7.9 was worded. He thought that widening of the scope of an objection to a reservation could be permitted if it took place within the 12-month period, and provided that it did not have the effect of modifying treaty relations.

111.   The Special Rapporteur noted that the draft guidelines on the withdrawal and modification of objections covered pre-emptive objections, which were genuine potential objections, but not late objections that had no legal effect.

112.   In conclusion, the Special Rapporteur expressed the hope that all the draft guidelines would be referred to the Drafting Committee, which might wish to consider redrafting some of them.

4.   Introduction by the Special Rapporteur of his twelfth report

113.   In introducing his twelfth report, on the procedure for acceptances of reservations, the Special Rapporteur said that the report in fact constituted the second part of his eleventh report.[50] The starting point of that report was paragraph 5 of article 20 of the Vienna Conventions, which was not reproduced word for word in draft guideline 2.8;[51] rather, it was the main idea of that paragraph

---

[50] *Yearbook ... 2006*, vol. II (Part One), document A/CN.4/574 (see footnote 6 above).

[51] Draft guideline 2.8 reads as follows:

"2.8   *Formulation of acceptances of reservations*

"The acceptance of a reservation arises from the absence of objections to the reservation formulated by a State or international

that was reflected, as the draft guideline set out the principle of the tacit acceptance of reservations. The Special Rapporteur also set out the conditions under which the absence of an objection is acquired, either because the contracting State or international organization may have made an express declaration (express acceptance) to that end or because the State remains silent (tacit acceptance). The Special Rapporteur did not think that the distinction between tacit acceptances of reservations (resulting from the silence of a State that ratifies when the reservation has already been made) and implicit acceptances (resulting from silence maintained for 12 months after the formulation of a reservation) produced specific effects. In both cases the silence was equivalent to acceptance, and that distinction need not form the subject of a guideline in the Guide to Practice. Furthermore, there was no reason to consider treaty provisions that expressly authorize a reservation as advance acceptances. Such provisions precluding the need for an acceptance derogate from the ordinary law of reservations.

114. Draft guideline 2.8.1 *bis*[52] reproduced the substance of the provisions of draft guideline 2.6.13. As the Commission had referred the latter guideline to the Drafting Committee, draft guideline 2.8.1 *bis* seemed superfluous.

115. Draft guideline 2.8.1,[53] meanwhile, had the advantage of showing that acceptances and objections to reservations were two sides of the same coin. One could only question whether there was any need to retain the phrase "Unless the treaty otherwise provides", although it was also contained in article 20, paragraph 5, of the Vienna Convention. Maintaining it had the advantage of ensuring that the States negotiating the treaty could modify the 12-month time limit, a simple customary rule that was subject to derogation.

116. Draft guideline 2.8.2[54] illustrates the case of multilateral treaties with a limited number of participants

(referred to in article 20, paragraph 2, of the Vienna Conventions) or the requirement that unanimous acceptance should not be called into question by a new contracting State that opposed the reservation. The purpose of tacit acceptance—to ensure clarity and stability in treaty relations—would not be affected if each new accession threatened to call the participation of the author of the reservation to the treaty into question.

117. Draft guideline 2.8.3[55] provides that express acceptance of reservations can occur at any time before or after the 12-month time period.

118. Draft guidelines 2.8.4[56] and 2.8.5[57] deal with the form and the procedure for the formulation of express acceptances, respectively.

119. Draft guideline 2.8.6[58] reproduces in slightly modified form the provisions of article 23, paragraph 3, of the Vienna Conventions.

120. Draft guidelines 2.8.7 to 2.8.11 seek to solve problems specific to the acceptance of reservations to the constituent instrument of an international organization.

121. Draft guideline 2.8.7[59] reproduces the entire text of article 20, paragraph 3, of the Vienna Conventions, although the Special Rapporteur was aware that this principle was far from solving all the problems that arise, starting with the problem of the definition of the "constituent instrument of an international organization". The Special Rapporteur was not in favour of making a distinction between the rules applicable to reservations to institutional provisions and those applicable to reservations to substantive provisions of the same treaty because it was not easy to distinguish between the two

---

organization on the part of the contracting State or contracting international organization.

"The absence of objections to the reservation may arise from a unilateral statement in this respect [(express acceptance)] or silence kept by a contracting State or contracting international organization within the periods specified in guideline 2.6.13 [(tacit acceptance)]."

[52] Draft guideline 2.8.1 *bis* reads as follows:

"2.8.1 *bis* *Tacit acceptance of reservations*

"Unless the treaty otherwise provides [or, for some other reason, an express acceptance is required], a reservation is considered to have been accepted by a State or an international organization if it shall have raised no objection to the reservation by the end of a period of 12 months after it was notified of the reservation or by the date on which it expressed its consent to be bound by the treaty, whichever is later."

[53] Draft guideline 2.8.1 reads as follows:

"2.8.1 *Tacit acceptance of reservations*

"[Unless the treaty otherwise provides, a] [A] reservation is considered to have been accepted by a State or an international organization if it shall have raised no objection to the reservation in accordance with guidelines 2.6.1 to 2.6.14."

[54] Draft guideline 2.8.2 reads as follows:

"2.8.2 *Tacit acceptance of a reservation requiring unanimous acceptance by the other States and international organizations*

"A reservation requiring unanimous acceptance by the parties in order to produce its effects is considered to have been accepted by all the contracting States or international organizations or all the

States or international organizations that are entitled to become parties to the treaty if they shall have raised no objection to the reservation by the end of a period of 12 months after they were notified of the reservation."

[55] Draft guideline 2.8.3 reads as follows:

"2.8.3 *Express acceptance of a reservation*

"A State or an international organization may, at any time, expressly accept a reservation formulated by another State or international organization."

[56] Draft guideline 2.8.4 reads as follows:

"2.8.4 *Written form of express acceptances*

"The express acceptance of a reservation must be formulated in writing."

[57] Draft guideline 2.8.5 reads as follows:

"2.8.5 *Procedure for formulating express acceptances*

"Draft guidelines 2.1.3, 2.1.4, 2.1.5, 2.1.6 and 2.1.7 apply *mutatis mutandis* to express acceptances."

[58] Draft guideline 2.8.6 reads as follows:

"2.8.6 *Non-requirement of confirmation of an acceptance made prior to formal confirmation of a reservation*

"An express acceptance of a reservation made by a State or an international organization prior to confirmation of the reservation in accordance with draft guideline 2.2.1 does not itself require confirmation."

[59] Draft guideline 2.8.7 reads as follows:

"2.8.7 *Acceptance of reservations to the constituent instrument of an international organization*

"When a treaty is a constituent instrument of an international organization and unless it otherwise provides, a reservation requires the acceptance of the competent organ of that organization."

types of provisions, which occasionally coexisted within a single article. Moreover, article 20 did not draw such a distinction.

122.   On the other hand, the Special Rapporteur thought that attention should be devoted to another question that the Vienna Conventions had left unanswered, namely whether an acceptance required by the competent organ of the organization must be express or could be tacit. The Special Rapporteur was of the view that acceptance of the reservation by the competent organ of the organization could not be assumed because of the particular nature of constituent acts, and that was the principle that was reflected in draft guideline 2.8.8.[60]

123.   Draft guideline 2.8.9[61] sought to fill another gap in the Vienna Conventions, namely the very definition of the "organ competent" to accept a reservation. This provision, which systematized an uncommon practice, was nevertheless far from solving all problems that may arise in this connection, one of the most difficult being the case in which a reservation was formulated before the constituent instrument entered into force and thus before any organ existed with competence to determine whether the reservation was admissible. It was this problem that draft guideline 2.8.10[62] sought to address by stipulating that if a reservation were formulated prior to the entry into force of the constituent instrument, the reservation should be subject to the acceptance of all States and international organizations concerned, even if the wording should probably be reviewed.

124.   Draft guideline 2.8.11[63] took up another problem that was not resolved in the Vienna Conventions, namely that of whether the requirement of an express acceptance of reservations to the constituent act of an international organization precluded States from commenting individually on the reservation. While the opposite argument could be advanced, the Special Rapporteur thought that it would be useful to know what the positions of the contracting States and international organizations were, even if those positions were devoid of any legal effect. Those positions could help the competent organ take its own position and afford an opportunity for a reservations dialogue.

125.   Lastly, draft guideline 2.8.12[64] sought to establish the definitive and irreversible character of acceptances to reservations. Given the silence of the Vienna Conventions on the matter, the Special Rapporteur thought it would be contrary to the purpose and the object of article 20, paragraph 5, of the Conventions to state that, once an acceptance had been secured, the accepting State or international organization could reverse its acceptance, which would be counter to the general principle of good faith and might pose serious problems of legal security in terms of the reserving State's participation.

5.   SUMMARY OF THE DEBATE

126.   With regard to draft guideline 2.8, it was noted that the words in brackets should be retained for the sake of clarity. The wording of the draft guideline could also be simplified. It was further pointed out that the clear predominance of the tacit acceptance was more akin to standard practice than to a rule. The view was also expressed that it would be useful to establish a guideline on implicit acceptances, provided for in article 20, paragraph 5, of the Vienna Conventions, or at any rate to draw a distinction between implicit and tacit acceptances. According to another point of view, there was no need to draw a distinction between implicit and tacit acceptances; rather, a single term should be used to indicate the absence of an express objection.

127.   The view was also expressed that the Vienna Convention did not seem to preclude the possibility of formulating an acceptance of a reservation prior to the expression of consent to be bound by the treaty. In that case, such an acceptance would produce effects only when bilateral relations were established between the reserving State and the State accepting the reservation.

128.   It was further pointed out that the phrase "considered to have been accepted" in article 20, paragraph 5, of the Vienna Conventions referred more to a determination than to a "presumption". Another view was that, according to the Vienna Convention, the absence of an objection gave rise to the notion of presumption, and that the words "tacit acceptance" should be replaced with the words "presumption of acceptance" in draft guidelines 2.8, 2.8.1, 2.8.1 *bis* and 2.8.2. It was also suggested that such presumption applied only when reservations were valid in the sense of article 19 of the Vienna Convention.

---

[60] Draft guideline 2.8.8 reads as follows:

"2.8.8   *Lack of presumption of acceptance of a reservation to a constituent instrument*

"For the purposes of applying guideline 2.8.7, acceptance by the competent organ of the organization shall not be presumed. Guideline 2.8.1 is not applicable."

[61] Draft guideline 2.8.9 reads as follows:

"2.8.9   *Organ competent to accept a reservation to a constituent instrument*

"The organ competent to accept a reservation to a constituent instrument of an international organization is the one that is competent to decide whether the author of the reservation should be admitted to the organization, or failing that, to interpret the constituent instrument."

[62] Draft guideline 2.8.10 reads as follows:

"2.8.10   *Acceptance of a reservation to the constituent instrument of an international organization in cases where the competent organ has not yet been established*

"In the case set forth in guideline 2.8.7 and where the constituent instrument has not yet entered into force, a reservation requires the acceptance of all the States and international organizations concerned. Guideline 2.8.1 remains applicable."

[63] Draft guideline 2.8.11 reads as follows:

"2.8.11   *Right of members of an international organization to accept a reservation to a constituent instrument*

"Guideline 2.8.7 does not preclude the right of States or international organizations that are members of an international organization to take a position on the validity or appropriateness of a reservation to a constituent instrument of the organization. Such an opinion is in itself devoid of legal effects."

[64] Draft guideline 2.8.12 reads as follows:

"2.8.12   *Final and irreversible nature of acceptances of reservations*

"Acceptance of a reservation made expressly or tacitly is final and irreversible. It cannot be subsequently withdrawn or amended."

129. Some members expressed a preference for the "simplified" version of draft guideline 2.8.1, maintaining that there was no need to repeat draft guideline 2.6.13, as that guideline had already been referred to the Drafting Committee. Several other members, however, expressed their preference for the version appearing in draft guideline 2.1.8 *bis*, on the grounds that it was clearer and more practical. The words appearing in brackets should also be retained, given that they were more consistent with article 20, paragraph 5, of the Vienna Conventions. Reference was also made to the situation in which a State or an international organization became a party to a treaty without formulating an objection to a reservation before the 12-month time period had elapsed. It was pointed out that in such cases the State or international organization still had the option of formulating a reservation up until the expiry of the 12-month period, in keeping with the letter of article 20, paragraph 5, of the Vienna Convention.

130. With regard to draft guideline 2.8.2, some members expressed concern about the possibility that a reservation might be accepted by States or international organizations that were not yet parties to the treaty. A possible solution in the form of an additional draft guideline to clarify that point was even mentioned. It was also noted that the draft guideline seemed inconsistent with the Vienna Convention in that it restricted tacit acceptance of a reservation to the 12-month period following notification of the reservation, without taking into consideration the fact that a State could formulate an objection to the reservation when it expressed its consent to be bound by the treaty, even if such expression occurred subsequent to the 12-month period.

131. Several members endorsed draft guidelines 2.8.3, 2.8.4, 2.8.5 and 2.8.6, subject to some editorial modification. Some doubts were expressed as to the absolute character of draft guideline 2.8.4.

132. With regard to draft guideline 2.8.7, it was noted that replacement of the word "when" with the phrase "as far as" might solve the problem of distinguishing between substantive and constitutional provisions.

133. With regard to draft guideline 2.8.8, it was observed that it might be preferable to state explicitly that acceptance must be expressed in writing, if that was the intention of the draft guideline. According to one view, the notion of presumption should be replaced by the notion of tacit acceptance. If, on the other hand, the guideline referred to a decision by the international organization, it was questionable whether that procedure was consistent with practice. Moreover, the draft did not make it possible to clearly determine which provisions of draft guideline 2.8.1 did not apply.

134. Some members wondered whether draft guideline 2.8.9 was really necessary, given that the organ competent to accept a reservation to the constituent act of an organization was determined by the internal rules of the organization or by the organization's members. The view was also expressed that a distinction must be drawn between organs competent to decide on the admission of the author of the reservation to membership of the organization and organs competent to interpret the constituent act.

135. With regard to draft guideline 2.8.10, the question was raised as to whether the existence of two systems of acceptance of reservations to a constituent act of an international organization, depending on whether acceptance occurred before or after the entry into force of the act in question, did not undermine legal security. It should perhaps be stipulated that such a reservation would have to be accepted by all signatories to the treaty.

136. In addition, a preference was stated for replacing the word "concerned" with the phrase "which have expressed their consent to be bound by the treaty", for the sake of accuracy and clarity. It was asked what would happen if all the States that ratified the instrument did so making a reservation.

137. It was observed that the English word "right" did not correspond to the original French word "*faculté*" in draft guideline 2.8.11 and that the title of the guideline did not reflect its contents because the position taken on a reservation could be an objection. Other drafting improvements could also be made to the draft guideline. It was pointed out that the phrase "devoid of legal effects" was either too categorical or superfluous. An opinion could have the value of an interpretative declaration, contributing to the "reservations dialogue", or of a political declaration. The fact that the competent organ of the organization had accepted the reservation did not prevent States from formulating objections, and the question of legal effects of such objections should remain open.

138. With regard to draft guideline 2.8.12, some members considered that acceptances should not have, in all circumstances, a final and irreversible nature. It was also pointed out that an express acceptance should be considered final and irreversible only 12 months after the reservation was made, as was the case with tacit acceptances. During that period States should be able to withdraw their acceptance of a reservation, and such a regime should conform to the regime adopted for objections.

139. The view was also expressed that in certain cases, as, for example, when a State that had accepted a reservation discovered that the reservation had far wider repercussions than anticipated, or if a judicial interpretation was issued attributing to it significantly different content than had been supposed at the time it had been made, or if a fundamental change in circumstances occurred, the State that had accepted the reservation should be able to reconsider its position.

140. Another point of view held that in such cases the reaction of the State that had accepted the reservation should be a declaration explaining and interpreting the conditions of its acceptance.

6. Special Rapporteur's concluding remarks

141. The Special Rapporteur observed that despite the dry, technical nature of the topic, all statements had been in favour of referring draft guidelines 2.8 to 2.8.12 to the Drafting Committee. Several suggestions from Commission members had been of an editorial nature or concerned translation, and the Drafting Committee was competent to rule on them.

142. It seemed to him that the variant proposed in draft guideline 2.8.1 *bis* was the preferred one; that question, which raised no problems of principle, could again be settled in the Drafting Committee. He agreed with those who held that the phrase "whichever is later" in article 20, paragraph 5, of the Vienna Conventions necessarily implied that the contracting States and international organizations had at least one year in which to comment on a reservation. However, he questioned whether that argument should have any impact on the wording of draft guideline 2.8.1.

143. The same was not true, however, for the observations made regarding draft guideline 2.8.2, which led to the conclusion that a distinction must be drawn among four cases: (*a*) if a treaty made its own entry into force contingent upon the unanimous ratification of all signatories, the principle set out in article 20, paragraph 5, of the Vienna Convention clearly applied, since the treaty could not enter into force until all signatories had ratified it without opposing the reservation. The other cases were more subtle: (*b*) one involved the question of whether the reservations must be accepted by all the parties for another reason; (*c*) in another, which concerned the States or international organizations that were supposed to become parties, the Special Rapporteur felt that if the Commission wished to remain faithful to the spirit of article 20, it must accept that the parties had 12 months as from the date of notification in which to ratify, and at that time, or during that portion of the 12-month period that had yet to elapse, they could conceivably not accept the reservation; (*d*) in a case where the treaty had not entered into force, the parties could take a position on the reservation throughout the period running from notification to expiry of the 12-month period following notification, or until entry into force, whichever was later. In all cases, however, the Special Rapporteur maintained that it was still draft guideline 2.8.1 or draft guideline 2.8.2 that applied. The Drafting Committee could consider those questions further and decide to which case each of the draft guidelines should be attached, bearing in mind the need to safeguard treaty relations.

144. The Special Rapporteur did not, however, feel that the question of whether the phrase "presumption of tacit acceptance" ought to replace the expression "tacit acceptance" in draft guidelines 2.8, 2.8.1 and 2.8.2 was a mere editorial question. He had in fact been convinced that the maintenance of silence during 12 months or until ratification created a simple presumption of acceptance by virtue of the fact that the reservation could turn out to be impermissible for several reasons, for example by being incompatible with the object and purpose of the treaty. That position of principle was also compatible solely with article 20, paragraph 5, of the Vienna Convention, which stated that the reservation was "considered to have been accepted".

145. The Special Rapporteur believed that the insertion of the word "contracting" before the words "State or international organization" at the beginning of draft guideline 2.8.3 would be taken care of by the Drafting Committee.

146. The doubts expressed with regard to draft guideline 2.8.4 seemed to him unjustified; furthermore, they called into question one of the basic premises of the draft, which was respect for the text of the Vienna Convention,

article 23, paragraph 1, of which specifically stipulated that acceptance must be expressed in writing.

147. Nor was he any more favourably disposed to a proposal that a distinction should be drawn in draft guideline 2.8.6 between the institutional and substantive provisions of the constituent act of an international organization. That was not common practice, and one need not mention the theoretical and practical problems such a distinction would entail.

148. The Special Rapporteur did not think that a reference should be made to the rules of the international organization in draft guideline 2.8.8, for it was the transparency of the process and the certainty that must result therefrom that were important.

149. With regard to draft guideline 2.8.9, the Special Rapporteur believed that the principle of determination of the competent body by the rules of the organization did in fact need to be established, even if that in itself was not sufficient; the current wording remained valid in cases where the constituent act itself said nothing.

150. As to draft guideline 2.8.10, he believed that replacing the phrase "States and international organizations concerned" with the phrase "contracting States and international organizations" was likely to create problems; it might be preferable to refer to "signatory" States and international organizations.

151. He agreed that the title of draft guideline 2.8.11 did not correspond to the guideline's content; some thought would have to be given to new wording. He also recognized that what was said regarding legal effects would have to be reconsidered to avoid giving the impression that the members of the international organization could cast doubt on the position taken by the competent organ, which was binding on all, and also to avoid the current wording in favour of an approach that was not so heavily negative, such as the phrase "without prejudice to the effects that might be produced by its exercise".

152. Turning lastly to draft guideline 2.8.12, the Special Rapporteur saw no reason to align the legal regime of express acceptances with that of tacit acceptances. A State that had of its own accord taken the initiative of making a formal declaration of acceptance of a reservation could not take back that declaration, even if it had been made prior to the expiry of the 12-month period. That would be neither justified by the text of the Vienna Convention nor consistent with the principle of good faith. Moreover, an acceptance could produce fundamental effects on the situation of the reserving State insofar as the treaty was concerned, and the possibility of withdrawing an acceptance would be highly destabilizing from the standpoint of the security of legal relations. Nor did he agree with the suggestion that it ought to be possible to withdraw an express acceptance if it was made on the basis of a particular interpretation of the treaty that was subsequently refuted by a judicial interpretation. Such an interpretation would have the force of only relative *res judicata*, in which case the State that had accepted the reservation would have the possibility of formulating an interpretative declaration and could do so at any time, in accordance with draft guideline 2.4.3.

C. Text of the draft guidelines on reservations to treaties provisionally adopted so far by the Commission

1. TEXT OF THE DRAFT GUIDELINES

153. The text of the draft guidelines provisionally adopted so far by the Commission is reproduced below.[65]

RESERVATIONS TO TREATIES

GUIDE TO PRACTICE

Explanatory note

Some draft guidelines in the present Guide to Practice are accompanied by model clauses. The adoption of these model clauses may have advantages in specific circumstances. The user should refer to the commentaries for an assessment of the circumstances appropriate for the use of a particular model clause.

1. *Definitions*

1.1 *Definition of reservations*

"Reservation" means a unilateral statement, however phrased or named, made by a State or an international organization when signing, ratifying, formally confirming, accepting, approving or acceding to a treaty or by a State when making a notification of succession to a treaty, whereby the State or organization purports to exclude or to modify the legal effect of certain provisions of the treaty in their application to that State or to that international organization.

1.1.1 [1.1.4][66] *Object of reservations*

A reservation purports to exclude or modify the legal effect of certain provisions of a treaty or of the treaty as a whole with respect to certain specific aspects in their application to the State or to the international organization which formulates the reservation.

1.1.2 *Instances in which reservations may be formulated*

Instances in which a reservation may be formulated under guideline 1.1 include all the means of expressing consent to be bound by a treaty mentioned in article 11 of the Vienna Convention

on the Law of Treaties and the Vienna Convention on the Law of Treaties between States and International Organizations or between International Organizations.

1.1.3 [1.1.8] *Reservations having territorial scope*

A unilateral statement by which a State purports to exclude the application of a treaty or some of its provisions to a territory to which that treaty would be applicable in the absence of such a statement constitutes a reservation.

1.1.4 [1.1.3] *Reservations formulated when notifying territorial application*

A unilateral statement by which a State purports to exclude or to modify the legal effect of certain provisions of a treaty in relation to a territory in respect of which it makes a notification of the territorial application of the treaty constitutes a reservation.

1.1.5 [1.1.6] *Statements purporting to limit the obligations of their author*

A unilateral statement formulated by a State or an international organization at the time when that State or that organization expresses its consent to be bound by a treaty by which its author purports to limit the obligations imposed on it by the treaty constitutes a reservation.

1.1.6 *Statements purporting to discharge an obligation by equivalent means*

A unilateral statement formulated by a State or an international organization when that State or that organization expresses its consent to be bound by a treaty by which that State or that organization purports to discharge an obligation pursuant to the treaty in a manner different from but equivalent to that imposed by the treaty constitutes a reservation.

1.1.7 [1.1.1] *Reservations formulated jointly*

The joint formulation of a reservation by several States or international organizations does not affect the unilateral nature of that reservation.

1.1.8 *Reservations made under exclusionary clauses*

A unilateral statement made by a State or an international organization when that State or organization expresses its consent to be bound by a treaty, in accordance with a clause expressly authorizing the parties or some of them to exclude or to modify the legal effect of certain provisions of the treaty in their application to those parties, constitutes a reservation.

1.2 *Definition of interpretative declarations*

"Interpretative declaration" means a unilateral statement, however phrased or named, made by a State or by an international organization whereby that State or that organization purports to specify or clarify the meaning or scope attributed by the declarant to a treaty or to certain of its provisions.

1.2.1 [1.2.4] *Conditional interpretative declarations*

A unilateral statement formulated by a State or an international organization when signing, ratifying, formally confirming, accepting, approving or acceding to a treaty, or by a State when making a notification of succession to a treaty, whereby the State or international organization subjects its consent to be bound by the treaty to a specific interpretation of the treaty or of certain provisions thereof, shall constitute a conditional interpretative declaration.

1.2.2 [1.2.1] *Interpretative declarations formulated jointly*

The joint formulation of an interpretative declaration by several States or international organizations does not affect the unilateral nature of that interpretative declaration.

1.3 *Distinction between reservations and interpretative declarations*

The character of a unilateral statement as a reservation or an interpretative declaration is determined by the legal effect it purports to produce.

---

[65] See the commentary to guidelines 1.1, 1.1.2, 1.1.3 [1.1.8], 1.1.4 [1.1.3] and 1.1.7 [1.1.1] in *Yearbook ... 1998*, vol. II (Part Two), pp. 99–107; the commentary to guidelines 1.1.1 [1.1.4], 1.1.5 [1.1.6], 1.1.6, 1.2, 1.2.1 [1.2.4], 1.2.2 [1.2.1], 1.3, 1.3.1, 1.3.2 [1.2.2], 1.3.3 [1.2.3], 1.4, 1.4.1 [1.1.5], 1.4.2 [1.1.6], 1.4.3 [1.1.7], 1.4.4 [1.2.5], 1.4.5 [1.2.6], 1.5, 1.5.1 [1.1.9], 1.5.2 [1.2.7], 1.5.3 [1.2.8] and 1.6 in *Yearbook ... 1999*, vol. II (Part Two), pp. 93–126; the commentary to guidelines 1.1.8, 1.4.6 [1.4.6, 1.4.7], 1.4.7 [1.4.8], 1.7, 1.7.1 [1.7.1, 1.7.2, 1.7.3, 1.7.4] and 1.7.2 [1.7.5] in *Yearbook ... 2000*, vol. II (Part Two), pp. 108–123; the commentary to guidelines 2.2.1, 2.2.2 [2.2.3], 2.2.3 [2.2.4], 2.3.1, 2.3.2, 2.3.3, 2.3.4, 2.4.3, 2.4.4 [2.4.5], 2.4.5 [2.4.4], 2.4.6 [2.4.7] and 2.4.7 [2.4.8] in *Yearbook ... 2001*, vol. II (Part Two) and corrigendum, pp. 180–195; the commentary to guidelines 2.1.1, 2.1.2, 2.1.3, 2.1.4 [2.1.3 *bis*, 2.1.4], 2.1.5, 2.1.6 [2.1.6, 2.1.8], 2.1.7, 2.1.8 [2.1.7 *bis*], 2.4, 2.4.1, 2.4.2 [2.4.1 *bis*] and 2.4.7 [2.4.2, 2.4.9] in *Yearbook ... 2002*, vol. II (Part Two), pp. 28–48; the commentary to the explanatory note and to guidelines 2.5, 2.5.1, 2.5.2, 2.5.3, 2.5.4 [2.5.5], 2.5.5 [2.5.5 *bis*, 2.5.5 *ter*], 2.5.6, 2.5.7 [2.5.7, 2.5.8] and 2.5.8 [2.5.9], to model clauses A, B and C, and to guidelines 2.5.9 [2.5.10], 2.5.10 [2.5.11] and 2.5.11 [2.5.12] in *Yearbook ... 2003*, vol. II (Part Two), pp. 70–92; the commentary to guidelines 2.3.5, 2.4.9, 2.4.10, 2.5.12 and 2.5.13 in *Yearbook ... 2004*, vol. II (Part Two), pp. 106–110; the commentary to guidelines 2.6, 2.6.1 and 2.6.2 in *Yearbook ... 2005*, vol. II (Part Two), and the commentary to guidelines 3, 3.1, 3.1.1, 3.1.2, 3.1.3 and 3.1.4, as well as the commentary to guidelines 1.6 and 2.1.8 [2.1.7 *bis*] in its new version, in *Yearbook ... 2006*, vol. II (Part Two). The commentary to guidelines 3.1.5, 3.1.6, 3.1.7, 3.1.8, 3.1.9, 3.1.10, 3.1.11, 3.1.12 and 3.1.13 are reproduced in section 2 below.

[66] The number between square brackets indicates the number of this draft guideline in the report of the Special Rapporteur or, as the case may be, the original number of a draft guideline in the report of the Special Rapporteur which has been merged with the final draft guideline.

1.3.1   *Method of implementation of the distinction between reservations and interpretative declarations*

To determine whether a unilateral statement formulated by a State or an international organization in respect of a treaty is a reservation or an interpretative declaration, it is appropriate to interpret the statement in good faith in accordance with the ordinary meaning to be given to its terms, in light of the treaty to which it refers. Due regard shall be given to the intention of the State or the international organization concerned at the time the statement was formulated.

1.3.2 [1.2.2]   *Phrasing and name*

The phrasing or name given to a unilateral statement provides an indication of the purported legal effect. This is the case in particular when a State or an international organization formulates several unilateral statements in respect of a single treaty and designates some of them as reservations and others as interpretative declarations.

1.3.3 [1.2.3]   *Formulation of a unilateral statement when a reservation is prohibited*

When a treaty prohibits reservations to all or certain of its provisions, a unilateral statement formulated in respect thereof by a State or an international organization shall be presumed not to constitute a reservation except when it purports to exclude or modify the legal effect of certain provisions of the treaty or of the treaty as a whole with respect to certain specific aspects in their application to its author.

1.4   *Unilateral statements other than reservations and interpretative declarations*

Unilateral statements formulated in relation to a treaty which are not reservations nor interpretative declarations are outside the scope of the present Guide to Practice.

1.4.1 [1.1.5]   *Statements purporting to undertake unilateral commitments*

A unilateral statement formulated by a State or an international organization in relation to a treaty, whereby its author purports to undertake obligations going beyond those imposed on it by the treaty constitutes a unilateral commitment which is outside the scope of the present Guide to Practice.

1.4.2 [1.1.6]   *Unilateral statements purporting to add further elements to a treaty*

A unilateral statement whereby a State or an international organization purports to add further elements to a treaty constitutes a proposal to modify the content of the treaty which is outside the scope of the present Guide to Practice.

1.4.3 [1.1.7]   *Statements of non-recognition*

A unilateral statement by which a State indicates that its participation in a treaty does not imply recognition of an entity which it does not recognize constitutes a statement of non-recognition which is outside the scope of the present Guide to Practice even if it purports to exclude the application of the treaty between the declaring State and the non-recognized entity.

1.4.4 [1.2.5]   *General statements of policy*

A unilateral statement formulated by a State or by an international organization whereby that State or that organization expresses its views on a treaty or on the subject matter covered by the treaty, without purporting to produce a legal effect on the treaty, constitutes a general statement of policy which is outside the scope of the present Guide to Practice.

1.4.5 [1.2.6]   *Statements concerning modalities of implementation of a treaty at the internal level*

A unilateral statement formulated by a State or an international organization whereby that State or that organization indicates the manner in which it intends to implement a treaty at the internal level, without purporting as such to affect its rights and obligations towards the other contracting parties, constitutes an informative statement which is outside the scope of the present Guide to Practice.

1.4.6. [1.4.6, 1.4.7]   *Unilateral statements made under an optional clause*

1. A unilateral statement made by a State or by an international organization, in accordance with a clause in a treaty expressly authorizing the parties to accept an obligation that is not otherwise imposed by the treaty, is outside the scope of the present Guide to Practice.

2. A restriction or condition contained in such statement does not constitute a reservation within the meaning of the present Guide to Practice.

1.4.7 [1.4.8]   *Unilateral statements providing for a choice between the provisions of a treaty*

A unilateral statement made by a State or an international organization, in accordance with a clause in a treaty that expressly requires the parties to choose between two or more provisions of the treaty, is outside the scope of the present Guide to Practice.

1.5   *Unilateral statements in respect of bilateral treaties*

1.5.1 [1.1.9]   *"Reservations" to bilateral treaties*

A unilateral statement, however phrased or named, formulated by a State or an international organization after initialling or signature but prior to entry into force of a bilateral treaty, by which that State or that organization purports to obtain from the other party a modification of the provisions of the treaty to which it is subjecting the expression of its final consent to be bound, does not constitute a reservation within the meaning of the present Guide to Practice.

1.5.2 [1.2.7]   *Interpretative declarations in respect of bilateral treaties*

Draft guidelines 1.2 and 1.2.1 are applicable to interpretative declarations in respect of multilateral as well as bilateral treaties.

1.5.3 [1.2.8]   *Legal effect of acceptance of an interpretative declaration made in respect of a bilateral treaty by the other party*

The interpretation resulting from an interpretative declaration made in respect of a bilateral treaty by a State or an international organization party to the treaty and accepted by the other party constitutes the authentic interpretation of that treaty.

1.6   *Scope of definitions*[67]

The definitions of unilateral statements included in the present chapter of the Guide to Practice are without prejudice to the validity and effects of such statements under the rules applicable to them.

1.7   *Alternatives to reservations and interpretative declarations*

1.7.1 [1.7.1, 1.7.2, 1.7.3, 1.7.4]   *Alternatives to reservations*

In order to achieve results comparable to those effected by reservations, States or international organizations may also have recourse to alternative procedures, such as:

(*a*) the insertion in the treaty of restrictive clauses purporting to limit its scope or application;

(*b*) the conclusion of an agreement, under a specific provision of a treaty, by which two or more States or international organizations purport to exclude or modify the legal effects of certain provisions of the treaty as between themselves.

---

[67] This draft guideline was reconsidered and modified during the fifty-eighth session of the Commission, in 2006. For the new commentary, see *Yearbook ... 2006*, vol. II (Part Two), chapter VIII, section C.2, pp. 156–157.

1.7.2 [1.7.5] *Alternatives to interpretative declarations*

In order to specify or clarify the meaning or scope of a treaty or certain of its provisions, States or international organizations may also have recourse to procedures other than interpretative declarations, such as:

(*a*) the insertion in the treaty of provisions purporting to interpret the same treaty;

(*b*) the conclusion of a supplementary agreement to the same end.

2. Procedure

2.1 Form and notification of reservations

2.1.1 Written form

A reservation must be formulated in writing.

2.1.2 Form of formal confirmation

Formal confirmation of a reservation must be made in writing.

2.1.3 Formulation of a reservation at the international level

1. Subject to the customary practices in international organizations which are depositaries of treaties, a person is considered as representing a State or an international organization for the purpose of formulating a reservation if:

(*a*) that person produces appropriate full powers for the purposes of adopting or authenticating the text of the treaty with regard to which the reservation is formulated or expressing the consent of the State or organization to be bound by the treaty; or

(*b*) it appears from practice or other circumstances that it was the intention of the States and international organizations concerned to consider that person as competent for such purposes without having to produce full powers.

2. By virtue of their functions and without having to produce full powers, the following are considered as representing a State for the purpose of formulating a reservation at the international level:

(*a*) Heads of State, Heads of Government and Ministers for Foreign Affairs;

(*b*) representatives accredited by States to an international conference for the purpose of formulating a reservation to a treaty adopted at that conference;

(*c*) representatives accredited by States to an international organization or one of its organs, for the purpose of formulating a reservation to a treaty adopted by that organization or body;

(*d*) heads of permanent missions to an international organization, for the purpose of formulating a reservation to a treaty between the accrediting States and that organization.

2.1.4 [2.1.3 *bis*, 2.1.4] *Absence of consequences at the international level of the violation of internal rules regarding the formulation of reservations*

1. The determination of the competent authority and the procedure to be followed at the internal level for formulating a reservation is a matter for the internal law of each State or relevant rules of each international organization.

2. A State or an international organization may not invoke the fact that a reservation has been formulated in violation of a provision of the internal law of that State or the rules of that organization regarding competence and the procedure for formulating reservations as invalidating the reservation.

2.1.5 Communication of reservations

1. A reservation must be communicated in writing to the contracting States and contracting organizations and other States and international organizations entitled to become parties to the treaty.

2. A reservation to a treaty in force which is the constituent instrument of an international organization or to a treaty which creates an organ that has the capacity to accept a reservation must also be communicated to such organization or organ.

2.1.6 [2.1.6, 2.1.8] *Procedure for communication of reservations*

1. Unless otherwise provided in the treaty or agreed by the contracting States and contracting organizations, a communication relating to a reservation to a treaty shall be transmitted:

(*a*) if there is no depositary, directly by the author of the reservation to the contracting States and contracting organizations and other States and international organizations entitled to become parties to the treaty; or

(*b*) if there is a depositary, to the latter, which shall notify the States and organizations for which it is intended as soon as possible.

2. A communication relating to a reservation shall be considered as having been made by the author of the reservation only upon receipt by the State or by the organization to which it was transmitted or, as the case may be, upon its receipt by the depositary.

3. The period during which an objection to a reservation may be raised starts at the date on which a State or an international organization received notification of the reservation.

4. Where a communication relating to a reservation to a treaty is made by electronic mail or by facsimile, it must be confirmed by diplomatic note or depositary notification. In such a case the communication is considered as having been made at the date of the electronic mail or the facsimile.

2.1.7 Functions of depositaries

1. The depositary shall examine whether a reservation to a treaty formulated by a State or an international organization is in due and proper form and, if need be, bring the matter to the attention of the State or international organization concerned.

2. In the event of any difference appearing between a State or an international organization and the depositary as to the performance of the latter's functions, the depositary shall bring the question to the attention of:

(*a*) the signatory States and organizations and the contracting States and contracting organizations; or

(*b*) where appropriate, the competent organ of the international organization concerned.

2.1.8 [2.1.7 *bis*] *Procedure in case of manifestly invalid reservations*[68]

1. Where, in the opinion of the depositary, a reservation is manifestly invalid, the depositary shall draw the attention of the author of the reservation to what, in the depositary's view, constitutes the grounds for the invalidity of the reservation.

2. If the author of the reservation maintains the reservation, the depositary shall communicate the text of the reservation to the signatory States and international organizations and to the contracting States and international organizations and, where appropriate, the competent organ of the international organization concerned, indicating the nature of legal problems raised by the reservation.

2.2.1 *Formal confirmation of reservations formulated when signing a treaty*

If formulated when signing a treaty subject to ratification, act of formal confirmation, acceptance or approval, a reservation must be formally confirmed by the reserving State or international organization when expressing its consent to be bound by the treaty. In such a case the reservation shall be considered as having been made on the date of its confirmation.

---

[68] *Idem.*

2.2.2 [2.2.3] *Instances of non-requirement of confirmation of reservations formulated when signing a treaty*

A reservation formulated when signing a treaty does not require subsequent confirmation when a State or an international organization expresses by its signature the consent to be bound by the treaty.

2.2.3 [2.2.4] *Reservations formulated upon signature when a treaty expressly so provides*

A reservation formulated when signing a treaty, where the treaty expressly provides that a State or an international organization may make such a reservation at that time, does not require formal confirmation by the reserving State or international organization when expressing its consent to be bound by the treaty.

...[69]

2.3.1 *Late formulation of a reservation*

Unless the treaty provides otherwise, a State or an international organization may not formulate a reservation to a treaty after expressing its consent to be bound by the treaty except if none of the other contracting parties objects to the late formulation of the reservation.

2.3.2 *Acceptance of late formulation of a reservation*

Unless the treaty provides otherwise or the well-established practice followed by the depositary differs, late formulation of a reservation shall be deemed to have been accepted by a contracting party if it has made no objections to such formulation after the expiry of the 12-month period following the date on which notification was received.

2.3.3 *Objection to late formulation of a reservation*

If a contracting party to a treaty objects to late formulation of a reservation, the treaty shall enter into or remain in force in respect of the reserving State or international organization without the reservation being established.

2.3.4 *Subsequent exclusion or modification of the legal effect of a treaty by means other than reservations*

A contracting party to a treaty may not exclude or modify the legal effect of provisions of the treaty by:

(*a*) interpretation of a reservation made earlier; or

(*b*) a unilateral statement made subsequently under an optional clause.

2.3.5 *Widening of the scope of a reservation*

The modification of an existing reservation for the purpose of widening its scope shall be subject to the rules applicable to the late formulation of a reservation. However, if an objection is made to that modification, the initial reservation remains unchanged.

2.4 *Procedure for interpretative declarations*

2.4.1 *Formulation of interpretative declarations*

An interpretative declaration must be formulated by a person who is considered as representing a State or an international organization for the purpose of adopting or authenticating the text of a treaty or expressing the consent of the State or international organization to be bound by a treaty.

[2.4.2 [2.4.1 *bis*] *Formulation of an interpretative declaration at the internal level*

1. The determination of the competent authority and the procedure to be followed at the internal level for formulating an interpretative declaration is a matter for the internal law of each State or relevant rules of each international organization.

2. A State or an international organization may not invoke the fact that an interpretative declaration has been formulated in violation of a provision of the internal law of that State or the rules of that organization regarding competence and the procedure for formulating interpretative declarations as invalidating the declaration.]

2.4.3 *Time at which an interpretative declaration may be formulated*

Without prejudice to the provisions of guidelines 1.2.1, 2.4.6 [2.4.7] and 2.4.7 [2.4.8], an interpretative declaration may be formulated at any time.

2.4.4 [2.4.5] *Non-requirement of confirmation of interpretative declarations made when signing a treaty*

An interpretative declaration made when signing a treaty does not require subsequent confirmation when a State or an international organization expresses its consent to be bound by the treaty.

2.4.5 [2.4.4] *Formal confirmation of conditional interpretative declarations formulated when signing a treaty*

If a conditional interpretative declaration is formulated when signing a treaty subject to ratification, act of formal confirmation, acceptance or approval, it must be formally confirmed by the declaring State or international organization when expressing its consent to be bound by the treaty. In such a case the interpretative declaration shall be considered as having been made on the date of its confirmation.

2.4.6 [2.4.7] *Late formulation of an interpretative declaration*

Where a treaty provides that an interpretative declaration may be made only at specified times, a State or an international organization may not formulate an interpretative declaration concerning that treaty subsequently except if none of the other contracting parties objects to the late formulation of the interpretative declaration.

[2.4.7 [2.4.2, 2.4.9] *Formulation and communication of conditional interpretative declarations*

1. A conditional interpretative declaration must be formulated in writing.

2. Formal confirmation of a conditional interpretative declaration must also be made in writing.

3. A conditional interpretative declaration must be communicated in writing to the contracting States and contracting organizations and other States and international organizations entitled to become parties to the treaty.

4. A conditional interpretative declaration regarding a treaty in force which is the constituent instrument of an international organization or a treaty which creates an organ that has the capacity to accept a reservation must also be communicated to such organization or organ.]

2.4.8 *Late formulation of a conditional interpretative declaration*[70]

A State or an international organization may not formulate a conditional interpretative declaration concerning a treaty after expressing its consent to be bound by the treaty except if none of the other contracting parties objects to the late formulation of the conditional interpretative declaration.

2.4.9 *Modification of an interpretative declaration*

Unless the treaty provides that an interpretative declaration may be made or modified only at specified times, an interpretative declaration may be modified at any time.

2.4.10 *Limitation and widening of the scope of a conditional interpretative declaration*

The limitation and the widening of the scope of a conditional interpretative declaration are governed by the rules respectively

---

[69] Section 2.3 proposed by the Special Rapporteur deals with the late formulation of reservations.

[70] This draft guideline (formerly 2.4.7 [2.4.8]) was renumbered as a result of the adoption of new draft guidelines at the fifty-fourth session of the Commission, in 2002.

applicable to the partial withdrawal and the widening of the scope of reservations.

2.5 Withdrawal and modification of reservations and interpretative declarations

2.5.1 Withdrawal of reservations

Unless the treaty otherwise provides, a reservation may be withdrawn at any time and the consent of a State or of an international organization which has accepted the reservation is not required for its withdrawal.

2.5.2 Form of withdrawal

The withdrawal of a reservation must be formulated in writing.

2.5.3 Periodic review of the usefulness of reservations

1. States or international organizations which have made one or more reservations to a treaty should undertake a periodic review of such reservations and consider withdrawing those which no longer serve their purpose.

2. In such a review, States and international organizations should devote special attention to the aim of preserving the integrity of multilateral treaties and, where relevant, give consideration to the usefulness of retaining the reservations, in particular in relation to developments in their internal law since the reservations were formulated.

2.5.4 [2.5.5] Formulation of the withdrawal of a reservation at the international level

1. Subject to the usual practices in international organizations which are depositaries of treaties, a person is competent to withdraw a reservation made on behalf of a State or an international organization if:

(a) that person produces appropriate full powers for the purposes of that withdrawal; or

(b) it appears from practice or other circumstances that it was the intention of the States and international organizations concerned to consider that person as competent for such purposes without having to produce full powers.

2. By virtue of their functions and without having to produce full powers, the following are competent to withdraw a reservation at the international level on behalf of a State:

(a) Heads of State, Heads of Government and Ministers for Foreign Affairs;

(b) representatives accredited by States to an international organization or one of its organs, for the purpose of withdrawing a reservation to a treaty adopted by that organization or body;

(c) heads of permanent missions to an international organization, for the purpose of withdrawing a reservation to a treaty between the accrediting States and that organization.

2.5.5 [2.5.5 bis, 2.5.5 ter] Absence of consequences at the international level of the violation of internal rules regarding the withdrawal of reservations

1. The determination of the competent body and the procedure to be followed for withdrawing a reservation at the internal level is a matter for the internal law of each State or the relevant rules of each international organization.

2. A State or an international organization may not invoke the fact that a reservation has been withdrawn in violation of a provision of the internal law of that State or the rules of that organization regarding competence and the procedure for the withdrawal of reservations as invalidating the withdrawal.

2.5.6 Communication of withdrawal of a reservation

The procedure for communicating the withdrawal of a reservation follows the rules applicable to the communication of reservations contained in guidelines 2.1.5, 2.1.6 [2.1.6, 2.1.8] and 2.1.7.

2.5.7 [2.5.7, 2.5.8] Effect of withdrawal of a reservation

1. The withdrawal of a reservation entails the application as a whole of the provisions on which the reservation had been made in the relations between the State or international organization which withdraws the reservation and all the other parties, whether they had accepted the reservation or objected to it.

2. The withdrawal of a reservation entails the entry into force of the treaty in the relations between the State or international organization which withdraws the reservation and a State or international organization which had objected to the reservation and opposed the entry into force of the treaty between itself and the reserving State or international organization by reason of that reservation.

2.5.8 [2.5.9] Effective date of withdrawal of a reservation

Unless the treaty otherwise provides, or it is otherwise agreed, the withdrawal of a reservation becomes operative in relation to a contracting State or a contracting organization only when notice of it has been received by that State or that organization.

Model clauses

A. Deferment of the effective date of the withdrawal of a reservation

A contracting party which has made a reservation to this treaty may withdraw it by means of notification addressed to [the depositary]. The withdrawal shall take effect on the expiration of a period of X [months] [days] after the date of receipt of the notification by [the depositary].

B. Earlier effective date of withdrawal of a reservation

A contracting party which has made a reservation to this treaty may withdraw it by means of a notification addressed to [the depositary]. The withdrawal shall take effect on the date of receipt of such notification by [the depositary].

C. Freedom to set the effective date of withdrawal of a reservation

A contracting party which has made a reservation to this treaty may withdraw it by means of a notification addressed to [the depositary]. The withdrawal shall take effect on the date set by that State in the notification addressed to [the depositary].

2.5.9 [2.5.10] Cases in which a reserving State or international organization may unilaterally set the effective date of withdrawal of a reservation

The withdrawal of a reservation takes effect on the date set by the withdrawing State or international organization where:

(a) that date is later than the date on which the other contracting States or international organizations received notification of it; or

(b) the withdrawal does not add to the rights of the withdrawing State or international organization, in relation to the other contracting States or international organizations.

2.5.10 [2.5.11] Partial withdrawal of a reservation

1. The partial withdrawal of a reservation limits the legal effect of the reservation and achieves a more complete application of the provisions of the treaty, or of the treaty as a whole, to the withdrawing State or international organization.

2. The partial withdrawal of a reservation is subject to the same formal and procedural rules as a total withdrawal and takes effect on the same conditions.

2.5.11 [2.5.12]   *Effect of a partial withdrawal of a reservation*

1. The partial withdrawal of a reservation modifies the legal effect of the reservation to the extent of the new formulation of the reservation. Any objection made to the reservation continues to have effect as long as its author does not withdraw it, insofar as the objection does not apply exclusively to that part of the reservation which has been withdrawn.

2. No objection may be made to the reservation resulting from the partial withdrawal, unless that partial withdrawal has a discriminatory effect.

2.5.12   *Withdrawal of an interpretative declaration*

An interpretative declaration may be withdrawn at any time by the authorities competent for that purpose, following the same procedure applicable to its formulation.

2.5.13   *Withdrawal of a conditional interpretative declaration*

The withdrawal of a conditional interpretative declaration is governed by the rules applying to the withdrawal of reservations.

2.6.1   *Definition of objections to reservations*

"Objection" means a unilateral statement, however phrased or named, made by a State or an international organization in response to a reservation to a treaty formulated by another State or international organization, whereby the former State or organization purports to exclude or to modify the legal effects of the reservation, or to exclude the application of the treaty as a whole, in relations with the reserving State or organization.

2.6.2   *Definition of objections to the late formulation or widening of the scope of a reservation*

"Objection" may also mean a unilateral statement whereby a State or an international organization opposes the late formulation of a reservation or the widening of the scope of a reservation.

3.   *Validity of reservations and interpretative declarations*

3.1   *Permissible reservations*

A State or an international organization may, when signing, ratifying, formally confirming, accepting, approving or acceding to a treaty, formulate a reservation unless:

   (a)   the reservation is prohibited by the treaty;

   (b)   the treaty provides that only specified reservations, which do not include the reservation in question, may be made; or

   (c)   in cases not falling under subparagraphs (a) and (b), the reservation is incompatible with the object and purpose of the treaty.

3.1.1   *Reservations expressly prohibited by the treaty*

A reservation is expressly prohibited by the treaty if it contains a particular provision:

   (a)   prohibiting all reservations;

   (b)   prohibiting reservations to specified provisions and a reservation in question is formulated to one of such provisions; or

   (c)   prohibiting certain categories of reservations and a reservation in question falls within one of such categories.

3.1.2   *Definition of specified reservations*

For the purposes of guideline 3.1, the expression "specified reservations" means reservations that are expressly envisaged in the treaty to certain provisions of the treaty or to the treaty as a whole with respect to certain specific aspects.

3.1.3   *Permissibility of reservations not prohibited by the treaty*

Where the treaty prohibits the formulation of certain reservations, a reservation which is not prohibited by the treaty may be formulated by a State or an international organization only if it is not incompatible with the object and purpose of the treaty.

3.1.4   *Permissibility of specified reservations*

Where the treaty envisages the formulation of specified reservations without defining their content, a reservation may be formulated by a State or an international organization only if it is not incompatible with the object and purpose of the treaty.

3.1.5   *Incompatibility of a reservation with the object and purpose of the treaty*

A reservation is incompatible with the object and purpose of the treaty if it affects an essential element of the treaty that is necessary to its general thrust, in such a way that the reservation impairs the *raison d'être* of the treaty.

3.1.6   *Determination of the object and purpose of the treaty*

The object and purpose of the treaty is to be determined in good faith, taking account of the terms of the treaty in their context. Recourse may also be had in particular to the title of the treaty, the preparatory work of the treaty and the circumstances of its conclusion and, where appropriate, the subsequent practice agreed upon by the parties.

3.1.7   *Vague or general reservations*

A reservation shall be worded in such a way as to allow its scope to be determined, in order to assess in particular its compatibility with the object and purpose of the treaty.

3.1.8   *Reservations to a provision reflecting a customary norm*

1. The fact that a treaty provision reflects a customary norm is a pertinent factor in assessing the validity of a reservation although it does not in itself constitute an obstacle to the formulation of the reservation to that provision.

2. A reservation to a treaty provision which reflects a customary norm does not affect the binding nature of that customary norm which shall continue to apply as such between the reserving State or international organization and other States or international organizations which are bound by that norm.

3.1.9   *Reservations contrary to a rule of jus cogens*

A reservation cannot exclude or modify the legal effect of a treaty in a manner contrary to a peremptory norm of general international law.

3.1.10   *Reservations to provisions relating to non-derogable rights*

A State or an international organization may not formulate a reservation to a treaty provision relating to non-derogable rights unless the reservation in question is compatible with the essential rights and obligations arising out of that treaty. In assessing that compatibility, account shall be taken of the importance which the parties have conferred upon the rights at issue by making them non-derogable.

3.1.11   *Reservations relating to internal law*

A reservation by which a State or an international organization purports to exclude or to modify the legal effect of certain provisions of a treaty or of the treaty as a whole in order to preserve the integrity of specific norms of the internal law of that State or rules of that organization may be formulated only insofar as it is compatible with the object and purpose of the treaty.

3.1.12   *Reservations to general human rights treaties*

To assess the compatibility of a reservation with the object and purpose of a general treaty for the protection of human rights, account shall be taken of the indivisibility, interdependence and interrelatedness of the rights set out in the treaty as well as the importance that the right or provision which is the subject of the reservation has within the general thrust of the treaty, and the gravity of the impact the reservation has upon it.

3.1.13 *Reservations to treaty provisions concerning dispute settlement or the monitoring of the implementation of the treaty*

A reservation to a treaty provision concerning dispute settlement or the monitoring of the implementation of the treaty is not, in itself, incompatible with the object and purpose of the treaty, unless:

(*a*) the reservation purports to exclude or modify the legal effect of a provision of the treaty essential to its *raison d'être*; or

(*b*) the reservation has the effect of excluding the reserving State or international organization from a dispute settlement or treaty implementation monitoring mechanism with respect to a treaty provision that it has previously accepted, if the very purpose of the treaty is to put such a mechanism into effect.

2. TEXT OF THE DRAFT GUIDELINES ON RESERVATIONS TO TREATIES AND COMMENTARIES THERETO PROVISIONALLY ADOPTED BY THE COMMISSION AT ITS FIFTY-NINTH SESSION

154. The text of the draft guidelines with commentaries thereto adopted by the Commission at its fifty-ninth session is reproduced below.

3.1.5 *Incompatibility of a reservation with the object and purpose of the treaty*

A reservation is incompatible with the object and purpose of the treaty if it affects an essential element of the treaty that is necessary to its general thrust, in such a way that the reservation impairs the *raison d'être* of the treaty.

Commentary

(1) The compatibility of a reservation with the object and purpose of the treaty constitutes, in the terms of article 19 (*c*) of the Vienna Convention, reflected in guideline 3.1, subparagraph (*c*), the fundamental criterion for the permissibility of a reservation. It is also the criterion that poses the most difficulties.

(2) In fact the concept of the object and purpose of the treaty is far from being confined to reservations. In the Vienna Convention, it occurs in eight provisions,[71] only two of which—articles 19 (*c*) and 20, paragraph 2—concern reservations. However, none of them defines the concept of the object and purpose of the treaty or provides any particular "clues" for this purpose.[72] At most, one can infer that a fairly general approach is required: it is not a

question of "dissecting" the treaty in minute detail and examining its provisions one by one, but of extracting the "essence", the overall "mission" of the treaty:

– It is unanimously accepted that article 18, paragraph (*a*), of the Vienna Convention does not oblige a signatory State to *respect* the treaty, but merely to refrain from rendering the treaty inoperative prior to its expression of consent to be bound;[73]

– Article 58, paragraph 1 (*b*) (ii), is drafted in the same spirit: one can assume that it is not a case of compelling respect for the treaty, the very object of this provision being to determine the conditions in which the operation of the treaty may be suspended, but rather of preserving what is essential in the eyes of the contracting parties;

– Article 41, paragraph 1 (*b*) (ii), is also aimed at safeguarding the "effective execution ... of the treaty *as a whole*"[74] in the event that it is modified between certain of the contracting parties only;

– Likewise, article 60, paragraph 3 (*b*), defines a "material breach" of the treaty, in contrast to other breaches, as "[t]he violation of a[n *essential*[*]] provision"; and

– According to article 31, paragraph 1, and article 33, paragraph 4, the object and purpose of the treaty are supposed to clarify its overall meaning, thereby facilitating its interpretation.[75]

(3) There is little doubt that the expression "object and purpose of the treaty" has the same meaning in all of these provisions: one indication of this is that Waldock, who without exaggeration can be considered to be the father of the law of reservations to treaties in the Vienna Convention, referred to them[76] explicitly in order to justify the inclusion of this criterion in article 19, subparagraph (*c*), through a kind of *a fortiori* reasoning: since "the objects and purposes of the treaty ... are criteria of fundamental importance for the interpretation ... of a treaty" and since

the Commission has proposed that a State which has signed, ratified, acceded to, accepted or approved a treaty should, even before it comes into force, refrain from acts calculated to frustrate its objects... [i]t would seem somewhat strange if a freedom to make reservations incompatible with the objects and purposes of the treaty were to be recognized.[77]

---

[71] Cf. articles 18, 19 (*c*), 20, paragraph 2, 31, paragraph 1, 33, paragraph 4, 41, paragraph 1 (*b*) (ii), 58, paragraph 1 (*b*) (ii), and 60, paragraph 3 (*b*). A connection can be made with the provisions relating to the "essential bas[e]s" or "condition[s] of the consent to be bound" (P. Reuter, "Solidarité et divisibilité des engagements conventionnels", in Y. Dinstein (ed.), *International Law at a Time of Perplexity: Essays in Honour of Shabtai Rosenne*, Dordrecht, Martinus Nijhoff, 1989, p. 627; also reproduced in P. Reuter, *Le développement de l'ordre juridique international: Écrits de droit international*, Paris, Économica, 1995, p. 366.

[72] As Isabelle Buffard and Karl Zemanek have noted, the Commission's commentaries to the draft article in 1966 are virtually silent on the matter (see I. Buffard and K. Zemanek, "The 'object and purpose' of a treaty: an enigma?", *Austrian Review of International and European Law*, vol. 3, No. 3 (1998), pp. 311–343, at p. 322).

[73] See, for example, P. Reuter, *Introduction au droit des traités*, 3rd ed. revised and expanded by Ph. Cahier, Paris, Presses universitaires de France, 1995, p. 62, who defines the obligation arising from article 18 as an obligation of conduct, or Ph. Cahier, "L'obligation de ne pas priver un traité de son objet et de son but avant son entrée en vigueur", *Mélanges Fernand Dehousse*, Paris, Nathan, 1979, vol. I, p. 31.

[74] In this provision, the words "of the object and purpose", which are replaced by an ellipsis in the above quotation, obscure rather than clarify the meaning.

[75] See *The Pajzs, Csáky, Esterházy* Case, Judgment of 16 December 1936, P.C.I.J., Series A/B, No. 68, p. 30, at p. 60; see also S. Bastid, *Les traités dans la vie internationale—conclusion et effets*, Paris, Économica, 1985, p. 131, or S. Sur, *L'interprétation en droit international public*, Paris, Librairie générale de droit et de jurisprudence, 1974, pp. 227–230.

[76] More precisely, to (the current) articles 18 and 31.

[77] Fourth report of Special Rapporteur Sir Humphrey Waldock on the law of treaties, *Yearbook ... 1965*, vol. II, document A/CN.4/177 and Add.1–2, p. 51, para. 6.

However, this does not solve the problem: it simply demonstrates that there is a criterion, a unique and versatile criterion, but as yet no definition. As has been noted, "the object and purpose of a treaty are indeed something of an enigma".[78] Certainly, the attempt made in article 19, subparagraph (c), pursuant to the 1951 advisory opinion of the ICJ,[79] to introduce an element of objectivity into a largely subjective system is not entirely convincing:[80] "The claim that a particular reservation is contrary to object and purpose is easier made than substantiated."[81] In their joint opinion in 1951, the dissenting judges had criticized the solution retained by the majority in the advisory opinion on *Reservations to the Convention on the Prevention and Punishment of the Crime of Genocide*, emphasizing that it could not "produce final and consistent results",[82] and this had been one of the main reasons for the Commission's resistance to the flexible system adopted by the Court in 1951:

> Even if the distinction between provisions which do and those which do not form part of the object and purpose of a convention be regarded as one that it is intrinsically possible to draw, the Commission does not see how the distinction can be made otherwise than subjectively.[83]

(4)   Sir Humphrey Waldock himself still had hesitations in his all-important first report on the law of treaties in 1962:[84]

> [T]he principle applied by the Court is essentially subjective and unsuitable for use as a general test for determining whether a reserving State is or is not entitled to be considered a party to a multilateral treaty. The test is one which might be workable if the question of "compatibility with the object and purpose of the treaty" could always be brought to independent adjudication; but that is not the case ...

Nevertheless, the Court's criterion of "compatibility with the object and purpose of the convention" does express a valuable concept to be taken into account both by States formulating a reservation and by States deciding whether or not to consent to a reservation that has been formulated by another State. ... The Special Rapporteur, although also of the opinion that there is value in the Court's principle as a general concept, feels that there is a certain difficulty in using it as a *criterion* of a reserving State's status as a party to a treaty in combination with the objective criterion of the acceptance or rejection of the reservation by other States.[85]

No doubt, this was a case of tactical caution, for the "conversion" of the self-same Special Rapporteur to compatibility with the object and purpose of the treaty, not only as a test of the validity of reservations, but also as a key element to be taken into account in interpretation,[86] was swift.[87]

(5)   This criterion has considerable merit. Notwithstanding the inevitable "margin of subjectivity"—which is limited, however, by the general principle of good faith—article 19, subparagraph (c), is undoubtedly a useful guideline capable of resolving in a reasonable manner most problems that arise.

(6)   The preparatory work on this provision is of little assistance in determining the meaning of the expression.[88] As has been noted,[89] the commentary to draft article 16, adopted by the usually more prolix Commission in 1966, is confined to a single paragraph and does not even allude to the difficulties involved in defining the object and

---

[78] I. Buffard and K. Zemanek, *loc. cit.* (footnote 72 above), p. 342. The uncertainties surrounding this criterion have been noted (and criticized with varying degrees of harshness) in all the scholarly writing: see, for example, A. Aust, *Modern Treaty Law and Practice*, 2nd ed., Cambridge University Press, 2007, p. 111; P. -M. Dupuy, *Droit international public*, 8th ed., Paris, Dalloz, 2006, p. 286; G. G. Fitzmaurice, "Reservations to multilateral conventions", *International and Comparative Law Quarterly*, vol. 2 (January 1953), p. 12; M. Rama-Montaldo, "Human rights conventions and reservations to treaties", in *Héctor Gros Espiell Amicorum Liber: Human Person and International Law*, vol. II, Brussels, Bruylant, 1997, p. 1265; Ch. Rousseau, *Droit international public*, vol. I, *Introduction et sources*, Paris, Sirey, 1970, p. 126; or G. Teboul, "Remarques sur les réserves aux traités de codification", *Revue générale de droit international public*, vol. 86 (1982), pp. 695–696. See also the first report of the Special Rapporteur on the law and practice relating to reservations to treaties (footnote 12 above), p. 143, para. 109.

[79] See *Reservations to the Convention on the Prevention and Punishment of the Crime of Genocide* (footnote 26 above): "It follows that it is the compatibility of a reservation with the object and purpose of the Convention that must furnish the criterion for the attitude of a State in making the reservation on accession as well as for the appraisal by a State in objecting to the reservation. Such is the rule of conduct which must guide every State in the appraisal which it must make, individually and from its own standpoint, of the admissibility of any reservation."

[80] According to Jean Kyongun Koh, "[t]he International Court thereby introduced purposive words into the vocabulary of reservations which had previously been dominated by the term 'consent' " (J. K. Koh, "Reservations to multilateral treaties: how international legal doctrine reflects world vision", *Harvard International Law Journal*, vol. 23 (1982–1983), p. 85).

[81] L. Lijnzaad, *Reservations to UN-Human Rights Treaties: Ratify and Ruin?*, T.M.C. Asser Instituut, Dordrecht, Martinus Nijhoff, 1994, pp. 82–83.

[82] *Reservations to the Convention on the Prevention and Punishment of the Crime of Genocide* (see footnote 26 above), p. 44.

[83] Report of the Commission covering the work of its third session, *Yearbook ... 1951*, vol. II, document A/1858, p. 123, at p. 128, para. 24.

[84] It was this report that introduced the "flexible system" to the Commission and vigorously defended it, *Yearbook ... 1962*, vol. II, document A/CN.4/144 and Add.1, pp. 72–74).

[85] *Ibid.*, pp. 65–66, para. 10; along the same lines, see Waldock's oral statement, *ibid.*, vol. I, 651st meeting, 25 May 1962, p. 139, paras. 4–6; however, during the discussion the Special Rapporteur did not hesitate to characterize the principle of compatibility as a "test" (*ibid.*, p. 145, para. 85—this paragraph also shows that, from the outset, in Waldock's mind, this test was decisive as far as the formulation of reservations was concerned (in contrast to objections, for which the consensual principle alone appeared practicable to him)). The wording used in draft article 17, paragraph 2 (*a*), which was proposed by the Special Rapporteur, reflects this uncertainty: "When formulating a reservation under the provisions of paragraph 1 (*a*) of this article [with respect to this provision, see the commentary to draft guideline 3.1.1, paragraph 3, *Yearbook ... 2006*, vol. II (Part Two), chapter VIII, section C.2], a State shall have regard to the compatibility of the reservation with the object and purpose of the treaty" (*Yearbook ... 1962*, vol. II, p. 60). This principle met with general approval during the Commission's debates in 1962 (see, in particular, Briggs, *ibid.*, vol. I, 651st meeting, p. 140, para. 23; Lachs. p. 142, para. 54; Rosenne, pp. 144–145, para. 79, who had no hesitation in speaking of a "test" (see also para. 82, and 653rd meeting, 29 May 1962, p. 156, para. 27; and Castrén, 652nd meeting, 28 May 1962, p. 148, para. 25), and in 1965 (see Yasseen, *Yearbook ... 1965*, vol. I, 797th meeting, 8 June 1965, pp. 149–150, para. 20; Tunkin, p. 150, para. 25); see, however, the objections by de Luna, *Yearbook ... 1962*, vol. I, 652nd meeting, p. 148, para. 18, and 653rd meeting, p. 160, para. 67; Gros, 652nd meeting, p. 150, paras. 47–51; or Ago, 653rd meeting, p. 157, para. 34; or, during the debate in 1965, those of Ruda, *Yearbook ... 1965*, vol. I, 796th meeting, 4 June 1965, p. 147, para. 55, and 797th meeting, p. 154, para. 69; and Ago, 798th meeting, 9 June 1965, p. 161, para. 71). To the end, Tsuruoka opposed subparagraph (c) and, for that reason, abstained in the voting on draft article 18 as a whole (adopted by 16 votes to none with one abstention on 2 July 1965, *ibid.*, 816th meeting, 2 July 1965, p. 283, para. 42).

[86] See article 31, paragraph 1, of the 1969 Vienna Convention.

[87] See Buffard and Zemanek, *loc. cit.* (footnote 72 above), pp. 320–321.

[88] *Ibid.*, pp. 319–321.

[89] C. Redgwell, "The law of reservations in respect of multilateral conventions", in J. P. Gardner (ed.), *Human Rights as General Norms and a State's Right to Opt Out: Reservations and Objections to Human Rights Conventions*, London, British Institute of International and Comparative Law, 1997, p. 7.

purpose of the treaty, other than very indirectly, through a simple reference to draft article 17:[90] "The admissibility or otherwise of a reservation under paragraph (*c*) ... is in every case very much a matter of the appreciation of the acceptability of the reservation by the other contracting States."[91]

(7) The discussion of subparagraph (*c*) in the Commission[92] and subsequently at the United Nations Conference on the Law of Treaties[93] does not shed any more light on the meaning of the expression "object and purpose of the treaty" for the purposes of this provision. Nor does international jurisprudence enable us to define it, even though it is in common use.[94] There are, however, some helpful hints, particularly in the 1951 advisory opinion of the ICJ on *Reservations to the Convention on the Prevention and Punishment of the Crime of Genocide.*

(8) The expression seems to have been used for the first time in its current form[95] in the advisory opinion of the PCIJ of 31 July 1930 on the *Greco-Bulgarian "Communities"* case.[96] However, it was not until 1986 in the *Military and Paramilitary Activities ... in and against Nicaragua* case[97] that the Court put an end to what has been described as "terminological chaos",[98] no doubt influenced by the 1969 Vienna Convention.[99] It is difficult,

however, to infer a great deal from this relatively abundant case law regarding the method to be followed for determining the object and purpose of a given treaty: the Court often proceeds by simple affirmations[100] and, when it seeks to justify its position, it does so empirically.[101]

(9) It has been asked whether, in order to get around the difficulties resulting from such uncertainty, there is a need to delink the concept of the "object and purpose of the treaty" by looking first for the object and then for the purpose. For example, during the discussion of draft article 55 concerning the rule of *pacta sunt servanda*, Reuter emphasized that "the object of an obligation was one thing and its purpose was another".[102] While the distinction is common in French (or francophone) doctrine,[103] it provokes scepticism among authors trained in the German or English systems.[104]

(10) However, one (French) author has shown convincingly that the question cannot be settled by reference

---

[90] Future article 20 of the 1969 Vienna Convention. The article in no way resolves the issue, which is left pending.

[91] *Yearbook ... 1966*, vol. II, p. 207, para. 17. The commentary to the corresponding provision adopted in 1962 (art. 18, para. 1 (*d*)) is no more forthcoming (see *Yearbook ... 1962*, vol. II, p. 180, para. 15).

[92] See footnote 85 above.

[93] It is significant that none of the amendments proposed to the Commission's draft article 16—including the most radical ones—called this principle into question. At most, the amendments by Colombia, Spain and the United States proposed adding the concept of the "nature" of the treaty or substituting it for that of the object (see paragraph 6 of the commentary to draft guideline 3.1.1, *Yearbook ... 2006*, vol. II (Part Two), chapter VIII, section C.2, p. 149, footnote 759).

[94] See Buffard and Zemanek, *loc. cit.* (footnote 72 above), pp. 312–319, and footnote 99 below.

[95] Buffard and Zemanek note (*loc. cit.* (footnote 72 above), p. 315) that the expression "the aim and the scope" had already been used in the advisory opinion of the PCIJ of 23 July 1926 on *Competence of the International Labour Organization to Regulate, Incidentally, the Personal Work of the Employer* in reference to Part XIII of the Treaty of Peace between the Allied and Associated Powers and Germany (Treaty of Versailles), *Advisory Opinion of 23 July 1926, P.C.I.J., Series B, No. 13*, p. 18. The same authors, after citing exhaustively the relevant decisions of the Court, describe the difficulty of establishing definitive terminology (especially in English) in the Court's case law (Buffard and Zemanek, *loc. cit.* (footnote 72 above), pp. 315–316).

[96] *The Greco-Bulgarian "Communities", Advisory Opinion of 31 July 1930, P.C.I.J., Series B, No. 17*. The terms are inverted, however: the Court bases itself on "the aim and object" of the Convention between Greece and Bulgaria respecting Reciprocal Emigration, signed at Neuilly-sur-Seine on 27 November 1919, (*ibid.*, p. 21). For the text of the Convention, *ibid.*, p. 37.

[97] *Military and Paramilitary Activities in and against Nicaragua (Nicaragua v. United States of America), Merits, Judgment, I.C.J. Reports 1986*, p. 14, at pp. 135–137, paras. 271–273, p. 138, para. 275, or pp. 140–141, para. 280.

[98] Buffard and Zemanek, *loc. cit.*, p. 316.

[99] Henceforth, the terminology used by the Court seems to have been firmly established; cf.: *Border and Transborder Armed Actions (Nicaragua v. Honduras), Jurisdiction and Admissibility, Judgment of 20 December 1988, I.C.J. Reports 1988*, p. 69, at p. 89, para. 46; *Maritime Delimitation in the Area between Greenland and Jan Mayen, Judgment of 14 June 1993, I.C.J. Reports 1993*, p. 38, at pp. 49–51, paras. 25–27; *Territorial Dispute (Libyan Arab Jamahiriya/Chad),*

Judgment of 3 February 1994, I.C.J. Reports 1994, p. 6, at pp. 25–26, para. 52; *Oil Platforms, Preliminary Objection, Judgment of 12 December 1996, I.C.J. Reports 1996*, p. 813, para. 27; *Gabčíkovo–Nagymaros Project (Hungary/Slovakia), Judgment of 25 September 1997, I.C.J. Reports 1997*, p. 7, at pp. 64–65, para. 104, and p. 67, para. 110; *Land and Maritime Boundary between Cameroon and Nigeria, Preliminary Objections, Judgment of 11 June 1998, I.C.J. Reports 1998*, p. 275, at p. 318, para. 98; *Kasikili/Sedudu Island (Botswana/Namibia), Judgment of 13 December 1999, I.C.J. Reports 1999*, p. 1045, at pp. 1072–1073, para. 43; *LaGrand (Germany v. United States of America), Judgment of 27 June 2001, I.C.J. Reports 2001*, p. 466, at pp. 502–503, para. 102; *Sovereignty over Pulau Ligitan and Pulau Sipadan (Indonesia/Malaysia), Merits, Judgment of 17 December 2002, I.C.J. Reports 2002*, p. 625, at p. 652, para. 51; *Avena and Other Mexican Nationals (Mexico v. the United States of America), Judgment of 31 March 2004, I.C.J. Reports 2004*, p. 12, at p. 48, para. 85; *Legal Consequences of the Construction of a Wall in the Occupied Palestinian Territory, Advisory Opinion of 9 July 2004, I.C.J. Reports 2004*, p. 136, at p. 179, para. 109; *Legality of Use of Force (Serbia and Montenegro v. Belgium), Preliminary Objections, Judgment of 15 December 2004, I.C.J. Reports 2004*, p. 279, at p. 319, para. 102; *Armed Activities on the Territory of the Congo (New Application: 2002) (Democratic Republic of the Congo v. Rwanda), Jurisdiction and Admissibility, Judgment of 3 February 2006, ICJ Reports 2006*, p. 6, at p. 32, paras. 66–67, and p. 35, para. 77; *Application of the Convention on the Prevention and Punishment of the Crime of Genocide (Bosnia and Herzegovina v. Serbia and Montenegro), Merits, Judgment of 26 February 2007*, p. 43, at pp. 109–110, para. 160, and p. 126, para. 198.

[100] See, for example, *Jurisdiction of the European Commission of the Danube between Galatz and Braila, Advisory Opinion of 8 December 1927, P.C.I.J., Series B, No. 14*: "It is obvious that the object of the Treaty of Paris [of 1856] ... has been to assure freedom of navigation" (p. 64); *International Status of South-West Africa*, Advisory Opinion of 11 July 1950, *I.C.J. Reports 1950*, p. 128, at pp. 136–137, and the following judgments cited in the previous note: *Maritime Delimitation in the Area between Greenland and Jan Mayen* (judgment of 14 June 1993), pp. 50–51, para. 27; *Gabčíkovo–Nagymaros Project (Hungary/Slovakia)* (judgment of 25 September 1997), p. 67, para. 110; *Land and Maritime Boundary between Cameroon and Nigeria, Preliminary Objections* (judgment of 11 June 1998), p. 318, para. 98; *LaGrand* (judgment of 27 June 2001), pp. 502–503, para. 102; and *Legality of Use of Force (Serbia and Montenegro v. Belgium)*, (judgment of 15 December 2004), p. 319, para. 102.

[101] See paragraph (3) of the commentary to draft guideline 3.1.6 below.

[102] *Yearbook ... 1964*, vol. I, 726th meeting, 19 May 1964, p. 26, para. 77. Elsewhere, however, the same author manifests a certain scepticism regarding the utility of the distinction (see Reuter, "Solidarité...", *loc. cit.* (footnote 71 above), p. 625 (also reproduced in Reuter, *Le développement ..., op. cit. (ibid.)*), p. 363).

[103] See Buffard and Zemanek, *loc. cit.* (footnote 72 above), pp. 325–327.

[104] *Ibid.*, pp. 322–325 and 327–328.

to international jurisprudence,[105] particularly since neither the object—defined as the actual content of the treaty[106]—still less the purpose (the outcome sought)[107] remain immutable over time, as the theory of emergent purpose advanced by Sir Gerald Fitzmaurice clearly demonstrates: "[T]he notion of object and purpose is itself not a fixed and static one, but is liable to change, or rather develop as experience is gained in the operation and working of the convention."[108] Thus, it is hardly surprising that the attempts made in scholarly writing to define a general method for determining the object and purpose of the treaty have proven to be disappointing.[109]

(11)   As Ago argued during the debate in the Commission on draft article 17 (now article 19 of the Vienna Convention):

> The question of the admissibility of reservations could only be determined by reference to the terms of the treaty as a whole. As a rule it was possible to draw a distinction between the essential clauses of a treaty, which normally did not admit of reservations, and the less important clauses, for which reservations were possible.[110]

---

[105] G. Teboul, *loc. cit.* (footnote 78 above), p. 696.

[106] See, for example, J.-P. Jacqué, *Éléments pour une théorie de l'acte juridique en droit international public*, Paris, Librairie générale de droit et de jurisprudence, 1972, p. 142: the object of an instrument resides in the rights and obligations to which it gives rise.

[107] *Ibid.*

[108] G. G. Fitzmaurice, "The law and procedure of the International Court of Justice 1951–4: treaty interpretation and other treaty points", BYBIL, vol. 33 (1957), p. 208. See also G. Teboul, *loc. cit.* (footnote 78 above), p. 697, or W. A. Schabas, "Reservations to the Convention on the rights of the child", *Human Rights Quarterly*, vol. 18 (1996), p. 479.

[109] The most successful method, devised by Buffard and Zemanek, would involve a two-stage process: in the first stage, one would have "recourse to the title, preamble and, if available, programmatic articles of the treaty"; in the second stage, the conclusion thus reached *prima facie* would have to be tested in the light of the text of the treaty, Buffard and Zemanek, *loc. cit.* (footnote 72 above), p. 333. However, the application of this apparently logical method (even though it reverses the order stipulated in article 31 of the Vienna Convention, under which the "terms of the treaty" are the starting point for any interpretation; see also the advisory opinion of the Inter-American Court of Human Rights on *Restrictions to the Death Penalty (arts. 4(2) and 4(4) American Convention on Human Rights), Advisory Opinion OC-3/83 of 8 September 1983, Series A, No. 3*, para. 50) to concrete situations turns out to be rather unconvincing: the authors admit that they are unable to determine objectively and simply the object and purpose of four out of five treaties or groups of treaties used to illustrate their method (the Charter of the United Nations, the Vienna Convention on Diplomatic Relations, the 1969 Vienna Convention, the general human rights conventions and the International Convention on the Elimination of All Forms of Discrimination against Women, as well as the other human rights treaties dealing with specific rights; the method proposed proves convincing only in the latter instance (Buffard and Zemanek, *loc. cit.* (footnote 72 above)) and conclude that the concept indeed remains an "enigma" (see above, paragraph (3) of the present commentary). Other scholarly attempts are scarcely more convincing, despite the fact that their authors are often categorical in defining the object and purpose of the treaty studied. Admittedly, they are often dealing with human rights treaties, which lend themselves easily to conclusions influenced by ideologically-oriented positions, one symptom of which is the insistence that all the substantive provisions of such treaties reflect their object and purpose (which, taken to its logical extremes, is tantamount to precluding any reservation from being valid)—for a critique of this extreme view, see Schabas, "Reservations to the Convention on the rights of the child", *loc. cit.* (footnote 108 above), pp. 476–477, or "Invalid reservations to the International Covenant on Civil and Political Rights: is the United States still a party?", *Brooklyn Journal of International Law*, vol. 21, No. 2 (1995–1996), pp. 291–293. On the position of the Human Rights Committee, see paragraph (2) of the commentary to draft guideline 3.1.12.

[110] *Yearbook ... 1962*, vol. I, 651st meeting, 25 May 1962, p. 141, para. 35.

These are the two fundamental elements: the object and purpose can only be determined by an examination of the treaty as a whole;[111] and, on that basis, reservations to the "essential"[112] clauses, and only to such clauses, are rejected.

(12)   In other words, it is the "*raison d'être*"[113] of the treaty, its fundamental core[114] that is to be preserved in order to avoid the "effectiveness"[115] of the treaty as a whole to be undermined. "It implies a distinction between all obligations in the treaty and the core obligations that are the treaty's *raison d'être*."[116]

(13)   Even if the general approach is fairly clear, it is no easy matter to reflect this in a simple formulation. In the view of some members of the Commission, the "threshold" has been set too high in draft guideline 3.1.5 and may well unduly facilitate the formulation of reservations. Most members, however, have taken the view that by definition any reservation "purports to exclude or modify the legal effect of certain provisions of a treaty or of the treaty as a whole with respect to certain specific aspects in their application" to the author of the reservation[117] and that the definition of the object and purpose of the treaty should not be so broad as to impair the capacity to formulate reservations. By limiting the incompatibility of the reservation with the object and purpose of the treaty to cases in which (*a*) it impairs an essential element, (*b*) necessary to the general thrust of the treaty, (*c*) thereby compromising the *raison d'être* of the treaty, the formulation in draft guideline 3.1.5 strikes an acceptable balance between the need to preserve the integrity of the treaty and the concern to facilitate the broadest possible participation in multilateral conventions.

(14)   Although a definition of each of these three inseparable elements is doubtless not possible, some clarification may be useful:

(*a*)   The term "essential element" is to be understood in terms of the object of the reservation as formulated by

---

[111] What is involved is an examination of whether the reservation is compatible "with the general tenor" of the treaty (Bartoš, *ibid.*, pp. 141–142, para. 40).

[112] And not those that "related to detail only" (Paredes, *ibid.*, p. 146, para. 90).

[113] *Reservations to the Convention on the Prevention and Punishment of the Crime of Genocide* (see footnote 26 above), p. 21: "none of the contracting parties is entitled to frustrate or impair ... the purpose and *raison d'être* of the convention".

[114] Statement by the representative of France to the Third Committee at the eleventh session of the General Assembly, *Official Records of the General Assembly, Eleventh Session, Third Committee, 703rd meeting*, 6 December 1956, quoted in A.-C. Kiss, *Répertoire de la pratique française en matière de droit international public*, Paris, Centre national de la recherche scientifique, 1962, vol. I, p. 277, No. 552.

[115] See *Loizidou v. Turkey, Preliminary Objections, Judgment of 23 March 1995, Application no. 15318/89, European Court of Human Rights, Series A: Judgments and Decisions, vol. 310*, p. 27, para. 75: acceptance of separate regimes of enforcement of the European Convention on Human Rights "would ... diminish the effectiveness of the convention as a constitutional instrument of European public order (*ordre public*)".

[116] Lijnzaad, *op. cit.* (see footnote 81 above), p. 83; see also p. 59 or L. Sucharipa-Behrmann, "The legal effects of reservations to multilateral treaties", *Austrian Review of International and European Law*, vol. 1, No. 1 (1996), p. 76.

[117] See draft guideline 1.1.1.

the author and is not necessarily limited to a specific provision. An "essential element" may be a norm, a right or an obligation which, interpreted in context,[118] is essential to the general thrust of the treaty and whose exclusion or amendment would compromise its *raison d'être*. This would generally be the case if a State sought to exclude or significantly amend a provision of the treaty which embodied the object and purpose of the treaty. Thus a reservation which excluded the application of a provision comparable to article I of the Treaty of Amity, Economic Relations and Consular Rights between the United States of America and the Islamic Republic of Iran, signed in Tehran on 15 August 1955[119] would certainly impair an "essential element" within the meaning of guideline 3.1.5, given that this provision "must be regarded as fixing an objective, in the light of which the other Treaty provisions are to be interpreted and applied";[120]

(*b*)   This "essential element" must thus be "necessary to the general thrust of the treaty", that is the balance of rights and obligations which constitute its substance or the general concept underlying the treaty.[121] While the Commission has had no difficulty in adopting, in French, the term "*économie générale du traité*", which seems to it to accurately reflect the concept that the essential nature of the point to which the reservation applies must be assessed in the context of the treaty as a whole, it has been somewhat more hesitant as regards the English expression to be used. After having vacillated between "general framework", "general structure" and "overall structure", it appeared to the Commission that the expression "general thrust" had the merit of placing the emphasis on the global nature of the assessment to be made and of not imposing too rigid an interpretation. Thus the ICJ has determined the object and purpose of a treaty by reference not only to its preamble, but also to its "structure", as represented by the provisions of the treaty taken as a whole;[122]

(*c*)   Similarly, in an endeavour to avoid too high a "threshold", the Commission chose the adjective "necessary" in preference to the stronger term "essential", and decided on the verb "impair" (rather than "vitiate") to qualify the "*raison d'être*" of the treaty, it being understood that this can be simple and unambiguous (the "*raison d'être*" of the 1948 Convention on the Prevention and Punishment of the Crime of Genocide is clearly defined by its title) or much more complex (in the case of a general human rights treaty[123] or an environmental protection convention or commitments relating to a broad range of questions) and that the question arises of whether it may change over time.[124]

---

[118] See draft guideline 3.1.6.

[119] United Nations, *Treaty Series*, vol. 284, No. 4132, p. 93.

[120] *Oil Platforms* (see footnote 99 above), p. 814, para. 28.

[121] Since not all treaties are necessarily or entirely based on a balance of rights and obligations (see in particular those treaties relating to "integral obligations", including the human rights treaties) (second report on the law of treaties of Special Rapporteur G. G. Fitzmaurice, *Yearbook ... 1957*, vol. II, document A/CN.4/107, pp. 54–55, paras. 125–128).

[122] See *Oil Platforms* (footnote 99 above), pp. 813–814, para. 27, and *Sovereignty over Pulau Ligitan and Pulau Sipadan (Indonesia/Malaysia)* (ibid.), p. 652, para. 51.

[123] See draft guideline 3.1.12.

[124] See paragraph (10) above and paragraph (7) of the commentary to draft guideline 3.1.6 below.

(15)   The fact remains that draft guideline 3.1.5 indicates a direction rather than establishing a clear criterion that can be directly applied in all cases. Accordingly, it seems appropriate to complement it in two ways: on the one hand, by seeking to specify means of determining the object and purpose of a treaty—as in draft guideline 3.1.6, and, on the other hand, by illustrating the methodology more clearly by means of a series of examples chosen from areas in which the question of permissible reservations frequently arises (draft guidelines 3.1.7 to 3.1.13).

3.1.6   *Determination of the object and purpose of the treaty*

The object and purpose of the treaty is to be determined in good faith, taking account of the terms of the treaty in their context. Recourse may also be had in particular to the title of the treaty, the preparatory work of the treaty and the circumstances of its conclusion and, where appropriate, the subsequent practice agreed upon by the parties.

Commentary

(1)   It is by no means easy to put together in a single formula all the elements to be taken into account, in each specific case, in determining the object and purpose of the treaty. Such a process undoubtedly requires more "*esprit de finesse*" than "*esprit de géométrie*",[125] like any act of interpretation, for that matter—and this process is certainly one of interpretation.

(2)   Given the great variety of situations and their susceptibility to change over time,[126] it would appear to be impossible to devise a single set of methods for determining the object and purpose of a treaty, and admittedly a certain amount of subjectivity is inevitable—however, that is not uncommon in law in general and in international law in particular.

(3)   In this context, it may be observed that the ICJ has deduced the object and purpose of a treaty from a number of highly disparate elements, taken individually or in combination:

—   from its title;[127]

---

[125] B. Pascal, *Pensées, Œuvres complètes*, Paris, Bibliothèque de la Pléiade, N. R. F.-Gallimard, 1954, p. 1091.

[126] See above paragraph (10) of the commentary to draft guideline 3.1.5. The question could also be raised whether the cumulative weight of separate reservations, each of which, taken alone, would be admissible, might not ultimately result in their incompatibility with the object and purpose of the treaty (see B. Clark, "The Vienna Convention reservations regime and the Convention on Discrimination Against Women", AJIL, vol. 85 (1991), p. 314, and or R. J. Cook, "Reservations to the Convention on the Elimination of All Forms of Discrimination Against Women", *Virginia Journal of International Law*, vol. 30 (1989–1990), pp. 706–707).

[127] See *Certain Norwegian Loans, Judgment of 6 July 1957, I.C.J. Reports 1957*, p. 9, at p. 24; but see *Military and Paramilitary Activities in and against Nicaragua, Merits, Judgment of 27 June 1986* (footnote 97 above), pp. 136–137, para. 273, and *Oil Platforms, Preliminary Objection* (see footnote 99 above), p. 814, para. 28.

– from its preamble;[128]

– from an article placed at the beginning of the treaty that "must be regarded as fixing an objective, in the light of which the other treaty provisions are to be interpreted and applied";[129]

– from an article of the treaty that demonstrates "the major concern of each contracting party" when it concluded the treaty;[130]

– from the preparatory works on the treaty;[131] and

– from its overall framework.[132]

(4)   It is difficult, however, to regard this as a "method" properly speaking: these disparate elements are taken into consideration, sometimes separately, sometimes together, and the Court forms a "general impression", in which subjectivity inevitably plays a considerable part.[133] Since, however, the basic problem is one of interpretation, it would appear to be legitimate, *mutatis mutandis*, to transpose the principles in articles 31 and 32 of the 1969 and 1986 Vienna Conventions applicable to the interpretation of treaties—the "general rule of interpretation" set forth in article 31 and the "supplementary means of interpretation" set forth in article 32[134]—and to adapt them to the determination of the object and purpose of the treaty.

---

[128] See the advisory opinion of the PCIJ on *The Greco-Bulgarian "Communities"* (footnote 96 above), p. 19, or the judgments of the ICJ in *Rights of nationals of the United States of America in Morocco, Judgment of 27 August 1952, I.C.J. Reports 1952*, p. 176, at p. 196; *Military and Paramilitary Activities in and against Nicaragua (Nicaragua v. United States of America), Merits, Judgment,* (footnote 97 above) p. 138, para. 275; *Territorial Dispute (Libyan Arab Jamahiriya/Chad)* (footnote 99 above), pp. 25–26, para. 52; and *Sovereignty over Pulau Ligitan and Pulau Sipadan* (*ibid.*), p. 652, para. 51; see also the dissenting opinion of Judge Anzilotti appended to the advisory opinion on the *Interpretation of the Convention of 1919 concerning Employment of Women During the Night, Advisory Opinion of 15 November 1932, P.C.I.J., Series A/B, No. 50*, p. 384.

[129] *Oil Platforms* (see footnote 99 above), p. 814, para. 28.

[130] *Kasikili/Sedudu Island, Judgment of 13 December 1999, I.C.J. Reports 1999* (see footnote 99 above), pp. 1072–1073, para. 43.

[131] Often, as a way of confirming an interpretation based on the text itself; see the judgments of the ICJ in *Territorial Dispute (Libyan Arab Jamahiriya/Chad)* (footnote 99 above), pp. 27–28, paras. 55–56; *Kasikili/Sedudu Island* (*ibid.*), pp. 1074–1075, para. 46; or *Legal Consequences of the Construction of a Wall in the Occupied Palestinian Territory* (*ibid.*), p. 179, para. 109; see also the dissenting opinion of Judge Anzilotti in *Interpretation of the Convention of 1919 concerning Employment of Women During the Night* (footnote 128 above), pp. 388–389. In its advisory opinion of 28 May 1951 on *Reservations to the Convention on the Prevention and Punishment of the Crime of Genocide* (see footnote 26 above), the ICJ gives some weight to the "origins" of the Convention (p. 23).

[132] See the advisory opinions of the PCIJ on *Competence of the International Labour Organization to Regulate, Incidentally, the Personal Work of the Employer* (footnote 95 above), p. 18, and *The Greco-Bulgarian "Communities"* (footnote 96 above), p. 20; or the judgments of the ICJ in *Oil Platforms* (see footnote 99 above), pp. 813–814, para. 27, and *Sovereignty over Pulau Ligitan and Pulau Sipadan* (*ibid.*), p. 652, para. 51.

[133] "One could just as well believe that it was simply by intuition" (Buffard and Zemanek, *loc. cit.* (footnote 72 above), p. 319).

[134] See the advisory opinion of 8 September 1983 of the Inter-American Court of Human Rights on *Restrictions to the Death Penalty* (footnote 109 above), para. 63; see also Sucharipa-Behrmann, *loc. cit.* (footnote 116 above), p. 76. While showing that it was aware that the rules on interpretation of treaties could not be directly transposed to unilateral statements formulated by the parties concerning a treaty (reservations and interpretative declarations), the Commission

(5)   The Commission is fully aware that this position is to some extent tautological,[135] since paragraph 1 of article 31 reads:

A treaty shall be interpreted in good faith in accordance with the ordinary meaning to be given to the terms of the treaty in their context and *in the light of its object and purpose*[*].

(6)   That said, however, the determination of the object and purpose of a treaty is indeed a question of interpretation, whereby the treaty must be interpreted as a whole, in good faith, in its entirety, in accordance with the ordinary meaning to be given to the terms of the treaty in their context, including the preamble, taking into account practice[136] and, when appropriate, the preparatory work of the treaty and the "circumstances of its conclusion".[137]

(7)   These are the parameters underlying draft guideline 3.1.6, which partly reproduces the terms of articles 31 and 32 of the Vienna Conventions, in that it highlights the need for determination in good faith based on the terms of the treaty in their context. Given that, for the purposes of interpretation,[138] this latter comprises the text, including the preamble, it was not deemed useful to reproduce it.[139] On the other hand, mention of the preparatory works and of the circumstances of the conclusion is of indisputably greater importance for the determination of the object and purpose of the treaty than for the interpretation of one of its provisions, as is the case with the title of the treaty, which is not mentioned in articles 31 and 32 of the Vienna Conventions but which is of importance in determining the treaty's object and purpose. As for the phrase "the subsequent practice agreed upon by the parties", this reflects paragraphs 2, 3 (*a*) and 3 (*b*) of article 31, since most members of the Commission were of the view that the object and purpose of a treaty was likely to evolve over time.[140] Furthermore, even though it was argued that this mention was redundant in subsequent practice, since objections, if there are any, must be made during the year following the formulation of the reservation, it was pointed out that the reservation could be assessed by third parties at any time, even years after its formulation.

(8)   In some cases, the application of these methodological guidelines raises no problems. It is obvious that a reservation to the Convention on the Prevention and Punishment of the Crime of Genocide, by which a State sought to reserve the right to commit some of the

---

recognized that those rules constituted useful guidelines in that regard (see draft guideline 1.3.1 (Method of implementation of the distinction between reservations and interpretative declarations) and the commentary thereto, adopted by the Commission at its fifty-first session, *Yearbook ... 1999*, vol. II (Part Two), pp. 107–109). This is true *a fortiori* when the aim is to assess the compatibility of a reservation with the object and purpose *of the treaty* itself.

[135] See W. A. Schabas, "Reservations to human rights treaties: time for innovation and reform", *The Canadian Yearbook of International Law 1994*, p. 48.

[136] See article 31, paragraph 3.

[137] Article 32.

[138] Article 31, paragraph 2.

[139] Mention of the text also appeared to suffice for the purposes of including the provisions setting out the general objects of the treaty; these objects might, however, be of particular significance in a determination of the "general thrust" of the treaty (see footnote 129 above).

[140] See above, paragraph (10) of the commentary to draft guideline 3.1.5, and paragraph (2) of the present commentary.

prohibited acts in its territory or in certain parts thereof, would be incompatible with the object and purpose of the Convention.[141]

(9)   Germany and a number of other European countries presented the following arguments in support of their objections to a reservation formulated by Viet Nam to the 1988 United Nations Convention against Illicit Traffic in Narcotic Drugs and Psychotropic Substances:

The reservation made in respect of article 6 is contrary to the principle '*aut dedere au iudicare*' which provides that offences are brought before the court or that extradition is granted to the requesting States.

The Government of the Federal Republic of Germany is therefore of the opinion that the reservation jeopardizes the intention of the Convention, as stated in article 2 paragraph 1, to promote cooperation among the parties so that they may address more effectively the international dimension of illicit drug trafficking.

The reservation may also raise doubts as to the commitment of the Government of the Socialist Republic of Viet Nam to comply with fundamental provisions of the Convention.[142]

(10)   It can also happen that the prohibited reservation relates to less central provisions but is nonetheless contrary to the object and purpose of the treaty because it makes its implementation impossible. That is the rationale behind the wariness the Vienna Convention displays towards reservations to constituent instruments of international organizations.[143] For example, the German Democratic Republic, when ratifying the 1984 Convention against Torture and Other Cruel, Inhuman or Degrading Treatment or Punishment, declared that it would only bear its share of the expenses of the Committee against Torture for activities for which it recognized that the Committee had competence.[144] Luxembourg objected to that "declaration" (which was actually a reservation), arguing, correctly, that the effect would be "to inhibit activities of the Committee in a manner incompatible with the purpose and the goal of the Convention".[145]

(11)   It is clearly impossible to draw up an exhaustive list of the potential problems that may arise concerning the compatibility of a reservation with the object and purpose of the treaty. It is also clear, however, that reservations to certain categories of treaties or treaty provisions or reservations having certain specific characteristics raise particular problems that should be examined, one by one, in an attempt to develop guidelines that would be helpful to States in formulating reservations of that kind or in responding to them knowledgeably. This is the intent of draft guidelines 3.1.7 to 3.1.13, the preparation of which was prompted by the relative frequency with which problems arise; these draft guidelines are of a purely illustrative nature.

3.1.7   *Vague or general reservations*

A reservation shall be worded in such a way as to allow its scope to be determined, in order to assess in particular its compatibility with the object and purpose of the treaty.

Commentary

(1)   Since, under article 19 (*c*) of the 1969 and 1986 Vienna Conventions, reproduced in draft guideline 3.1, a reservation must be compatible with the object and purpose of the treaty, and since other States are required, under article 20, to take a position on this compatibility, it must be possible for them to do so. This will not be the case if the reservation in question is worded in such a way as to preclude any determination of its scope, in other words, if it is vague or general, as indicated in the title of draft guideline 3.1.7. This is not, strictly speaking, a case in which the reservation is incompatible with the object and purpose of the treaty: rather, it is a hypothetical situation in which it is impossible to assess this compatibility. This shortcoming seemed sufficiently serious to the Commission for it to come up with particularly strong wording: "shall be worded" rather than "should be worded" or "is worded". Furthermore, use of the term "worded" highlights the fact that this is a requirement of substance and not merely one of form.

(2)   In any event, the requirement for precision in the wording of reservations is implicit in their very definition. It is clear from article 2, paragraph 1 (*d*), of the Vienna Conventions, from which the text in draft guideline 1.1 of the Guide to Practice is taken, that the object of reservations is to exclude or to modify "the legal effect of

[141] The question is particularly relevant with regard to the scope of the "colonial clause" in article XII of the Convention, a clause contested by the Soviet bloc countries, which had made reservations to it (see *Multilateral Treaties Deposited with the Secretary-General: Status as at 31 December 2005*, vol. I (United Nations publication, Sales No. E.06.V.2), pp. 126–134 (chap. IV.1)), but the focus here is on the validity of that quasi-reservation clause.

[142] *Ibid.*, p. 466 (chap. VI.19); in the same vein see also the objections of Belgium, Denmark, Greece, Ireland, Italy, the Netherlands, Portugal, Spain, Sweden and the United Kingdom, and the less explicitly justified objections of Austria and France, *ibid.*, pp. 466–468. See also the objection of Norway, and the less explicit objections of Germany and Sweden to the Tunisian declaration concerning the application of the 1961 Convention on the reduction of statelessness, *ibid.*, pp. 400–401 (chap V.4). Another significant example is provided by the declaration of Pakistan concerning the 1997 International Convention for the Suppression of Terrorist Bombings, which excluded from the application of the Convention "struggles, including armed struggle, for the realization of the right of self-determination launched against any alien or foreign occupation or domination, in accordance with the rules of international law", *ibid.*, vol. II, pp. 135–136 (chap. XVIII.9). A number of States considered that "declaration" to be contrary to the object and purpose of the Convention, which is "the suppression of terrorist bombings, irrespective of where they take place and of who carries them out"; see the objections of Australia, Austria, Canada, Denmark, Finland, France, Germany, India, Italy, Japan (with a particularly clear statement of reasons), the Netherlands, New Zealand, Norway, Spain, Sweden, the United Kingdom and the United States of America, *ibid.*, pp. 137–143. Similarly, Finland justified its objection to the reservation made by Yemen to article 5 of the 1966 International Convention on the Elimination of All Forms of Racial Discrimination by the argument that "provisions prohibiting racial discrimination in the granting of such fundamental political rights and civil liberties as the right to participate in public life, to marry and choose a spouse, to inherit and to enjoy freedom of thought, conscience and religion are central in a convention against racial discrimination", *ibid.*, vol. I, pp. 145–146 (chap. IV.2).

[143] Cf. article 20, paragraph 3: "When a treaty is a constituent instrument of an international organization and unless it otherwise provides, a reservation requires the acceptance of the competent organ of that organization."

[144] See *Multilateral Treaties ...*, vol. I (footnote 141 above), p. 308, (chap. IV.9); see also R. W. Edwards, Jr., "Reservations to treaties", *Michigan Journal of International Law*, vol. 10, No. 2 (1989), pp. 391–393 and 400.

[145] *Multilateral Treaties ...*, vol. I (see footnote 141 above), p. 309. Fifteen other States raised objections on the same grounds.

certain provisions of the treaty in their application" to their authors.[146] Thus, it cannot be maintained that the effect of reservations could possibly be to prevent a treaty as a whole from producing its effects. And, although "across-the-board" reservations are common practice, they are, as specified in draft guideline 1.1.1 of the Guide to Practice,[147] valid only if they purport "to exclude or modify the legal effect ... of the treaty as a whole with respect to certain specific aspects".

(3) Furthermore, it follows from the inherently consensual nature of the law of treaties in general,[148] and the law of reservations in particular,[149] that, although States are free to formulate (not to make[150]) reservations, the other parties must be entitled to react by accepting the reservation or objecting to it. That is not the case if the text of the reservation does not allow its scope to be assessed.

(4) This is often the case when a reservation invokes the internal law of the State which has formulated it without identifying the provisions in question or specifying whether they are to be found in its constitution or its civil or criminal code. In these cases, the reference to

the domestic law of the reserving State is not *per se* the problem,[151] but the frequent vagueness and generality of the reservations referring to domestic law, which make it impossible for the other States parties to take a position on them. That was the thinking behind an amendment submitted by Peru at the United Nations Conference on the Law of Treaties seeking to add the following subparagraph (*d*) to future article 19 of the Convention:

(*d*) The reservation renders the treaty inoperative by making its application subject, in a general and indeterminate manner, to national law.[152]

(5) Finland's objections to the reservations of several States parties to the 1989 Convention on the rights of the child are certainly more solidly reasoned on that ground than by a reference to article 27 of the 1969 Vienna Convention;[153] for instance, in response to the reservation by Malaysia, which had accepted a number of the provisions of the Convention on the rights of the child "only if they are in conformity with the Constitution, national laws and national policies of the Government of Malaysia",[154] Finland considered that the "broad nature" of that reservation left open "to what extent Malaysia commits itself to the Convention and to the fulfilment of its obligations under the Convention".[155] Thailand's interpretative declaration to the effect that it "does not interpret and apply the provisions of this Convention [the International Convention on the Elimination of All Forms of Racial Discrimination] as imposing upon the Kingdom of Thailand any obligation beyond the confines of [its] Constitution and [its] laws"[156] also prompted an objection on the part of Sweden that, in so doing, Thailand was making the application of the Convention subject to a general

---

[146] See the comments of the Government of Israel on the Commission's first draft on the law of treaties, which caused the English text of the definition of reservations to be brought into line with the French text by changing the word "some" to "certain" (fourth report of the Special Rapporteur, Sir Humphrey Waldock, on the law of treaties (footnote 77 above), p. 15); see also Chile's statement at the United Nations Conference on the Law of Treaties, *Official Records of the United Nations Conference on the Law of Treaties, first session, Vienna, 26 March–24 May 1968, Summary records of plenary meetings and of the meetings of the Committee of the Whole* (A/CONF.39/11, United Nations publication, Sales No. E.68.V.7), Committee of the Whole, fourth meeting, 29 March 1968: "the words 'to vary the legal effect of certain provisions of the treaty' (subparagraph (*d*)) meant that the reservation must state clearly what provisions it related to. Imprecise reservations must be avoided" (p. 21, para. 5).

[147] *Yearbook ... 1999*, vol. II (Part Two), pp. 93–95. See also the remarks by Rosa Riquelme Cortado in *Las reservas a los tratados: Lagunas y ambigüedades del Régimen de Viena*, Universidad de Murcia, 2004, p. 172.

[148] See P. Reuter, *Introduction au droit des traités, op. cit.* (footnote 73 above), pp. 20–21; C. Tomuschat, "Admissibility and legal effects of reservations to multilateral treaties: comments on arts. 16 and 17 of the ILC's draft articles on the law of treaties", *Zeitschrift für ausländisches öffentliches Recht und Völkerrecht/Heidelberg Journal of International Law*, vol. 27 (1967), p. 466. See also, for example, the judgment of PCIJ of 17 August 1923 in *SS "Wimbledon", Judgments, 1923, P.C.I.J., Series A, No. 1*, p. 25, or the advisory opinion of the ICJ of 11 July 1950 on *International Status of South-West Africa* (footnote 100 above), p. 139.

[149] The ICJ specified in this connection in its advisory opinion of 1951 on *Reservations to the Convention on the Prevention and Punishment of the Crime of Genocide* (see footnote 26 above) that "[i]t is well established that in its treaty relations a State cannot be bound without its consent, and that consequently no reservation can be effective against any State without its agreement thereto" (p. 21). The authors of the joint dissenting opinion accompanying the advisory opinion expressed this idea still more strongly: "The consent of the parties is the basis of treaty obligations. The law governing reservations is only a particular application of this fundamental principle, whether the consent of the parties to a reservation is given in advance of the proposal of the reservation or at the same time or later" (*ibid.*, pp. 31–32). See also the arbitral award of 30 June 1977 in the *Case concerning the delimitation of the continental shelf between the United Kingdom of Great Britain and Northern Ireland, and the French Republic* (also known as the *English Channel* case), in UNRIAA, vol. XVIII (Sales No. E/F.80.V.7), pp. 41–42, paras. 60–61; and W. W. Bishop, Jr., "Reservations to treaties", *Recueil des Cours de l'Académie de Droit International*, vol. 103 (1961-II), p. 255.

[150] See paragraph (6) of the commentary to draft guideline 3.1, *Yearbook ... 2006*, vol. II (Part Two), chap. VIII, sect. C.2.

[151] See below paragraph (4) of the commentary to draft guideline 3.1.11.

[152] *Official Records of the United Nations Conference on the Law of Treaties, first and second sessions, Vienna, 26 March–24 May 1968 and 9 April–22 May 1969, Documents of the Conference* (A/CONF.39/11/Add.2, United Nations publication, Sales No. E.70.V.5), Report of the Committee of the Whole, A/CONF.39/14, pp. 133–134, para. 177; see the explanations of the representative of Peru at the 21st plenary meeting of the Conference, on 10 April 1968, *Official Records of the United Nations Conference on the Law of Treaties, first session...* (footnote 146 above), p. 109, para. 25. The amendment was rejected by 44 votes to 16 with 26 abstentions (25th plenary meeting, 16 April 1968, *ibid.*, p. 135, para. 26); a reading of the debate gives little explanation for the rejection: no doubt a number of delegations, like Italy, considered it "unnecessary to state that case expressly, since it was a case of reservations incompatible with the object of the treaty" (22nd plenary meeting, 11 April 1968, *ibid.*, p. 120, para. 75); along these same lines, see R. Szafarz, "Reservations to multilateral treaties", *Polish Yearbook of International Law*, vol. 3 (1970), p. 302.

[153] See below paragraph (4) of the commentary to draft guideline 3.1.11. Similarly, the reason given by the Netherlands and the United Kingdom in support of their objections to the second reservation of the United States to the Convention on the Prevention and Punishment of the Crime of Genocide, namely, that it created "uncertainty as to the extent of the obligations the Government of the United States of America is prepared to assume with regard to the Convention" (*Multilateral Treaties Deposited with the Secretary-General*, vol. I (see footnote 141 above), pp. 130–132 (chap. IV.1)) is more convincing than the argument based on an invocation of domestic law (see, below, the first two footnotes to paragraph (4) of the commentary to draft guideline 3.1.11).

[154] *Multilateral Treaties Deposited with the Secretary-General*, vol. I (see footnote 141 above), p. 326 (chap. IV.11).

[155] *Ibid.*, pp. 331–332. See also the objections by Finland and several other States parties to comparable reservations by several other States, *ibid.*, pp. 330–335.

[156] *Ibid.*, p. 142 (chap. IV.2).

reservation which made reference to the limits of national legislation, the content of which was not specified.[157]

(6) The same applies when a State reserves the general right to have its constitution prevail over a treaty,[158] as for instance in the reservation by the United States to the Convention on the Prevention and Punishment of the Crime of Genocide:

[N]othing in the Convention requires or authorizes legislation or other action by the United States of America prohibited by the Constitution of the United States as interpreted by the United States.[159]

(7) Some of the so-called "sharia reservations"[160] give rise to the same objection, a case in point being the reservation by which Mauritania approved the 1979 Convention on the Elimination of All Forms of Discrimination against Women "in each and every one of its parts which are not contrary to Islamic Sharia".[161] Here again, the problem lies not in the very fact that Mauritania is invoking a law of religious origin which it applies,[162] but, rather that, as

Denmark noted, "the general reservations with reference to the provisions of Islamic law ... are of unlimited scope and undefined character".[163] Thus, as the United Kingdom put it, such a reservation "which consists of a general reference to national law without specifying its contents does not clearly define for the other States Parties to the Convention the extent to which the reserving State has accepted the obligations of the Convention".[164]

(8) Basically, it is the impossibility of assessing the compatibility of such reservations with the object and purpose of the treaty, and not the certainty that they are incompatible, which makes them fall within the purview of article 19 (*c*) of the 1969 Vienna Convention. As the Human Rights Committee pointed out:

Reservations must be specific and transparent, so that the Committee, those under the jurisdiction of the reserving State and other States parties may be clear as to what obligations of human rights compliance have or have not been undertaken. Reservations may thus not be general, but must refer to a particular provision of the [International Covenant on Civil and Political Rights] and indicate in precise terms its scope in relation thereto.[165]

(9) According to article 57 of the Convention for the Protection of Human Rights and Fundamental Freedoms (European Convention on Human Rights), "[r]eservations of a general character shall not be permitted". The European Court of Human Rights, in the *Belilos* case, declared invalid the interpretative declaration (equivalent to a reservation) by Switzerland on article 6, paragraph 1, of the European Convention on Human Rights because it was "couched in terms that are too vague or broad for it to be possible to determine their exact meaning and scope".[166] But it is unquestionably the European Commission on Human Rights that most clearly formulated the principle

---

[157] *Ibid.*, pp. 148–149. See the objections of Norway and Sweden of 15 March and 14 December 1999, respectively, which follow the same line of thinking with regard to Bangladesh's reservation to the Convention on the Political Rights of Women of 31 March 1953, *ibid.*, vol. II (footnote 142 above), pp. 85–86 (chap. XVI.1) or the objections by Finland to a reservation by Guatemala to the Vienna Convention on the Law of Treaties and by Austria, the Netherlands and Sweden to a comparable reservation by Peru to the same Convention, in *ibid.*, pp. 380–384 (chap. XXIII.1).

[158] See Pakistan's reservation to the Convention on the Elimination of All Forms of Discrimination against Women (*ibid.*, vol. I (footnote 141 above), p. 253 (chap. IV.8)), and the objections made by Austria, Finland, Germany, the Netherlands and Norway (*ibid.*, pp. 256, 260–263, 264–265 and 267—272) and by Portugal (*ibid.*, p. 286, footnote 52).

[159] *Ibid.*, p. 128 (chap. IV.1).

[160] For a discussion of the various schools of thought, see especially A. Sassi, "General reservations to multilateral treaties" *Comunicazioni e Studi*, vol. 22 (2002), pp. 96–99. With regard specifically to the application of the reservation to the 1979 Convention on the Elimination of All Forms of Discrimination against Women, see Clark, *loc. cit.* (footnote 126 above), pp. 299–302 and pp. 310–311; J. Connors, "The Women's Convention in the Muslim world" in Gardner (ed.), *op. cit.* (footnote 89 above), pp. 85–103; Cook, *loc. cit.* (footnote 126 above), pp. 690–692; J. McBride, "Reservations and the capacity of States to implement human rights treaties" in Gardner (ed.), *op. cit.* (footnote 89 above), pp. 149–156 (with a great many examples) or Y. Tyagi, "The conflict of law and policy on reservations to human rights treaties", BYBIL, vol. 71 (2000), pp. 198–201 and, more specifically A. Jenefsky, "Permissibility of Egypt's reservations to the Convention on the Elimination of All Forms of Discrimination against Women", *Maryland Journal of International Law and Trade*, vol. 15 (1991), pp. 200–233.

[161] *Multilateral Treaties Deposited with the Secretary-General*, vol. I (see footnote 141 above), p. 251 (chap. IV.8). See also the reservations by Saudi Arabia, citing "the norms of islamic law" (*ibid.*, p. 253) and by Malaysia (*ibid.*, p. 250), or again the initial reservation by Maldives: "The Government of the Republic of Maldives will comply with the provisions of the Convention, except those which the Government may consider contradictory to the principles of the Islamic Sharia upon which the laws and traditions of the Maldives is founded" (*ibid.*, p. 284, footnote 43); the latter reservation having elicited several objections, the Government of the Maldives modified it in a more restrictive sense, but Germany once again objected to it and Finland criticized the new reservation (*ibid.*). Likewise, several States formulated objections to the reservation by Saudi Arabia to the 1966 International Convention on the Elimination of All Forms of Racial Discrimination, which made the application of its provisions subject to the condition that "these do not conflict with the precepts of the Islamic *Shariah*" (*ibid.*, pp. 141 and 144–149 (chap. IV.2)).

[162] The Holy See ratified the 1989 Convention on the rights of the child provided that "the application of the Convention be compatible in practice with the particular nature of the Vatican City State and of the sources of its objective law" (*ibid.*, pp. 324–325). As has been pointed

out (Schabas, "Reservations to the Convention on the rights of the child", *loc. cit.* (footnote 108 above), pp. 478–479), this text raises, *mutatis mutandis*, the same problems as the "sharia reservation".

[163] *Multilateral Treaties Deposited with the Secretary-General*, vol. I (see footnote 141 above), pp. 258–259 (chap. IV.8).

[164] *Ibid.*, pp. 277–278. See also the objections by Austria, Finland, Germany, Norway, the Netherlands, Portugal and Sweden (*ibid.*, pp. 256, 260–263, 264–265, 267–272 and 274–278). The reservations of many Islamic States to specific provisions of the Convention, on the grounds of their incompatibility with the sharia, are certainly less criticisable on that basis, although a number of them also drew objections from some States parties. (For example, whereas Clark, *op. cit.* (footnote 126 above), p. 300, observes that Iraq's reservation to article 16 of the Convention on the Elimination of All Forms of Discrimination against Women, based on the sharia, is specific and entails a regime more favourable than that of the Convention, this reservation nonetheless elicited the objections of Mexico, the Netherlands and Sweden, *Multilateral Treaties Deposited with the Secretary-General*, vol. I (see footnote 141 above), pp. 267–269 and 274–277 (chap. IV.8).)

[165] General Comment No. 24, Report of the Human Rights Committee, *Official Records of the General Assembly, Fiftieth Session, Supplement No. 40* (A/50/40), vol. I, Annex V, para. 19; see also paragraph 12, which links the issue of the invocation of domestic law to that of "widely formulated reservations".

[166] *Belilos v. Switzerland, Judgement of 29 April 1988, Application no. 10328/83, European Court of Human Rights, Series A: Judgments and Decisions*, vol. 132, p. 26, para. 55. See paragraph (8) of the commentary to draft guideline 3.1.2, *Yearbook ... 2006*, vol. II (Part Two), chap. VIII, sect. C.2. For a detailed analysis of the condition of generality raised by article 57 of the Convention, see especially I. Cameron and F. Horn, "Reservations to the European Convention on Human Rights: the Belilos case", *German Yearbook of International Law*, vol. 33 (1990), pp. 97–109, and R. St. J. MacDonald, "Reservations under the European Convention on Human Rights", *Revue belge de droit international*, vol. 21 (1988), pp. 433–438 and 443–448.

applicable here when it judged that "a reservation is of a general nature ... when it is worded in such a way that it does not allow its scope to be determined".[167]

(10)   Draft guideline 3.1.7 reflects this fundamental notion. Its title gives an indication of the (alternative) characteristics which a reservation needs to exhibit to come within its scope: it applies to reservations which are either "vague" or "general". The former might be a reservation which leaves some uncertainty as to the circumstances in which it might be applicable[168] or to the extent of the obligations effectively entered into by its author. The latter corresponds to the examples enumerated above.[169]

(11)   Although the present commentary may not be the right place for a discussion of the effects of vague or general reservations, it must still be noted that they raise particular problems. It would seem difficult, at the very outset, to maintain that they are invalid *ipso jure*: the main criticism that can be levelled against them is that they make it impossible to assess whether or not the conditions for their substantive validity have been fulfilled.[170] For that reason, they should lend themselves particularly well to a "reservations dialogue".

3.1.8   *Reservations to a provision reflecting a customary norm*

1.   The fact that a treaty provision reflects a customary norm is a pertinent factor in assessing the validity of a reservation although it does not in itself constitute an obstacle to the formulation of the reservation to that provision.

2.   A reservation to a treaty provision which reflects a customary norm does not affect the binding nature of that customary norm which shall continue to apply as such between the reserving State or international organization and other States or international organizations which are bound by that norm.

Commentary

(1)   Draft guideline 3.1.8 relates to a problem which arises fairly often in practice: that of the validity of a reservation to a provision which is restricted to reflecting a customary norm—the word "reflect" is preferred here to "enunciate" in order to demonstrate that the process of enshrining the norm in question in a treaty has no effect on its continued operation as a customary norm. This

principle of the persistence of customary norms (and of the obligations flowing therefrom for the States or international organizations bound by them) is also reflected in paragraph 2 of the draft guideline, which recalls that the author of a reservation to a provision of this type may not be relieved of his obligations thereunder by formulating a reservation. Paragraph 1, meanwhile, underlines the principle that a reservation to a treaty rule which reflects a customary norm is not *ipso jure* incompatible with the object and purpose of the treaty, even if due account must be taken of that element in assessing such compatibility.

(2)   In some cases, States parties to a treaty have objected to reservations and challenged their compatibility with its object and purpose under the pretext that they were contrary to well-established customary norms. Thus, Austria declared, in cautious terms, that it was

> of the view that the Guatemalan reservations [to the 1969 Vienna Convention on the Law of Treaties] refer almost exclusively to general rules of [the said Convention] many of which are solidly based on international customary law. The reservations could call into question well-established and universally accepted norms. Austria is of the view that the reservations also raise doubts as to their compatibility with the object and purpose of the [said Convention] ... .[171]

For its part, the Netherlands objected to the reservations formulated by several States in respect of various provisions of the 1961 Vienna Convention on Diplomatic Relations and took "the view that this provision remains in force in relations between it and [the said States in accordance] with international customary law".[172]

(3)   It has often been thought that this inability to formulate reservations to treaty provisions which codify customary norms could be deduced from the judgment of the ICJ in the *North Sea Continental Shelf* cases:[173]

> speaking generally, it is a characteristic of purely conventional rules and obligations that, in regard to them, some faculty of making unilateral reservations may, within certain limits, be admitted;—whereas this cannot be so in the case of general or customary law rules and obligations which, by their very nature, must have equal force for all members of the international community, and cannot therefore be the subject of any right of unilateral exclusion exercisable at will by any one of them in its own favour.[174]

---

[167] *Temeltasch* v. *Switzerland, Application No. 9116/80,* Council of Europe, European Commission of Human Rights, *Decisions and Reports,* vol. 31, 1983, p. 120, para. 90. See P.-H. Imbert, "Les réserves à la Convention européenne des droits de l'homme devant la Commission de Strasbourg (Affaire *Temeltasch*)", *Revue générale de droit international public,* vol. 87 (1983), pp. 580–625.

[168] See Malta's reservation to the 1966 International Covenant on Civil and Political Rights: "While the Government of Malta accepts the principle of compensation for wrongful imprisonment, it is not possible at this time to implement such a principle in accordance with article 14, paragraph 6, of the Covenant" (*Multilateral Treaties Deposited with the Secretary-General,* vol. I (see footnote 141 above), pp. 182–183 (chap. IV.4)).

[169] See paragraphs (5)–(9) of the present commentary.

[170] See paragraphs (1) and (4) above.

[171] *Multilateral Treaties Deposited with the Secretary-General,* vol. II (see footnote 142 above), p. 380 (chap. XXIII.1); see also the objections formulated in similar terms by Belgium, Denmark, Finland, Germany, Sweden and the United Kingdom (*ibid.,* pp. 381 and 383–385). In the *Case concerning the delimitation of the continental shelf between the United Kingdom of Great Britain and Northern Ireland, and the French Republic* (footnote 149 above), the United Kingdom maintained that France's reservation to article 6 of the Convention on the Continental Shelf was aimed at "the rules of customary international law" and was "inadmissible as a reservation to Article 6" (p. 38, para. 50).

[172] *Multilateral Treaties Deposited with the Secretary-General,* vol. I (see footnote 141 above), p. 96 (chap. III.3); in reality, it is not the provisions in question that remain in force, but rather the rules of customary law that they express (see below, paragraphs (13)–(16) of the present commentary). See also Poland's objections to the reservations of Bahrain and the Libyan Arab Jamahiriya (*ibid.,* p. 96) and D. W. Greig, "Reservations: equity as a balancing factor?", *Australian Year Book of International Law,* vol. 16 (1995), p. 88.

[173] *North Sea Continental Shelf, Judgment, I.C.J. Reports 1969,* p. 3. See the dissenting opinion of Judge Morelli, appended to the judgment (pp. 198–199) and the many commentaries cited in P.-H. Imbert, *Les réserves aux traités multilatéraux,* Paris, Pedone, 1978, p. 244, footnote 20; see also G. Teboul, *loc. cit.* (footnote 78 above), p. 685.

[174] *North Sea Continental Shelf* (see footnote 173 above), pp. 38–39, para. 63.

(4) While the wording adopted by the Court is certainly not the most felicitous, the conclusion that some have drawn from it seems incorrect if this passage is put back into its context. The Court goes on to exercise caution in respect of the deductions called for by the exclusion of certain reservations. Noting that the faculty of reservation to article 6 of the 1958 Convention on the Continental Shelf (delimitation) was not excluded by article 12 on reservations,[175] as it was in the case of articles 1 to 3, the Court considered it "normal" and "a legitimate inference that it was considered to have a different and less fundamental status and not, like those Articles, to reflect pre-existing or emergent customary law".[176]

(5) Thus, it is not true that the Court affirmed the inadmissibility of reservations in respect of customary law;[177] it simply stated that, in the case under consideration, the different treatment which the authors of the Convention accorded to articles 1 to 3, on the one hand, and article 6, on the other, suggested that they did not consider that the latter codified a customary norm which, moreover, confirms the Court's own conclusion.

(6) Furthermore, the judgment itself states, in an often-neglected dictum, that "no reservation could release the reserving party from obligations of general maritime law existing outside and independently of the Convention [on the Continental Shelf]".[178] Judge Morelli, dissenting, does not contradict this when he writes: "Naturally the power to make reservations affects only the contractual obligation flowing from the convention ... It goes without saying that a reservation has nothing to do with the customary rule as such. If that rule exists, it exists also for the State which formulated the reservation, in the same way as it exists for those States which have not ratified."[179] This clearly implies that the customary nature of the norm reflected in a treaty provision in respect of which a reservation is formulated does not in itself constitute grounds for invalidating the reservation: "the faculty of making reservations to a treaty provision has no necessary connection with the question whether or not the provision can be considered as expressing a generally recognized rule of law".[180]

(7) Moreover, although this principle is sometimes challenged,[181] it is recognized in the preponderance of doctrine,[182] and rightly so:

– Customary norms are binding on States, independently of their expression of consent to a conventional rule[183] but, unlike the case of peremptory norms, States may opt out by agreement *inter se*; it is not clear why they could not do so through a reservation[184]—providing that the latter is valid—but this is precisely the question raised;

– A reservation concerns only the expression of the norm in the context of the treaty, not its existence as a customary norm, even if, in some cases, it may cast doubt on the norm's general acceptance "as of right";[185] as the United Kingdom remarked in its observations on General Comment No. 24 of the Human Rights Committee, "there is a clear distinction between choosing not to enter into treaty obligations and trying to opt out of customary international law";[186]

– If this nature is clear, States remain bound by the customary norm, independently of the treaty;[187]

– Appearances to the contrary, there may be an interest (and not necessarily a laudable one) involved—for example, that of avoiding application to the relevant obligations of the monitoring or dispute settlement

---

[175] See paragraph (5) of the commentary to draft guideline 3.1.2, *Yearbook ... 2006*, vol. II (Part Two), chap. VIII, sect. C.2, pp. 150–151.

[176] *North Sea Continental Shelf* (see footnote 173 above), p. 40, para. 66; see also pp. 38–39, para. 63. In support of this position, see the individual opinion of Judge Padilla Nervo, *ibid.*, p. 89; against it, see the dissenting opinion of Vice-President Koretsky, *ibid.*, p. 163.

[177] P.-H. Imbert, *Les réserves aux traités multilatéraux*, op. cit. (footnote 173 above), p. 244, and, in the same vein, A. Pellet, "La C.I.J. et les réserves aux traités—Remarques cursives sur une révolution jurisprudentielle", in N. Ando, E. McWhinney and R. Wolfrum (eds.), Liber Amicorum *Judge Shigeru Oda*, vol. 1, The Hague, Kluwer Law International, 2002, pp. 507–508. In his dissenting opinion, Judge Tanaka takes the opposing position with respect to "the application of the provision for settlement by agreement, since this is required by general international law, notwithstanding the fact that Article 12 of the Convention does not expressly exclude Article 6, paragraphs 1 and 2, from the exercise of the reservation faculty" (*North Sea Continental Shelf* (see footnote 173 above), p. 182); this confuses the question of the faculty to make a reservation with that of the reservation's effects, where the provision that the reservation concerns is of a customary, and even a peremptory, nature. (Strangely, Judge Tanaka considers that the equidistance principle "must be recognized as *jus cogens*" (*ibid.*).)

[178] *Ibid.*, p. 40, para. 65.

[179] *Ibid.*, p. 198.

[180] Dissenting opinion of *ad hoc* Judge Sørensen, *ibid.*, p. 248.

[181] See the position taken by Briggs in the declaration which he attached to the arbitral award of 30 June 1977 in the *Case concerning the delimitation of the continental shelf between the United Kingdom of Great Britain and Northern Ireland, and the French Republic* (footnote 149 above), p. 123.

[182] See M. Coccia, "Reservations to multilateral treaties on human rights", *California Western International Law Journal*, vol. 15 (1985), pp. 31–32; G. Gaja, "Le riserve al Patto sui diritti civili e politici e il diritto consuetudinario", *Rivista di diritto internazionale*, vol. 79 (1996), pp. 451–452; P.-H. Imbert, "La question des réserves dans la décision arbitrale du 30 juin 1977 relative à la délimitation du plateau continental entre la République française et le Royaume-Uni de Grande-Bretagne et d'Irlande du Nord", *Annuaire français de droit international*, vol. 24 (1978), p. 48; Riquelme Cortado, *op. cit.* (footnote 147 above), pp. 159–171; and Sucharipa-Behrmann, *loc. cit.* (footnote 116 above), pp. 76–77.

[183] See Finland's objection to Yemen's reservations to article 5 of the 1966 Convention on the Elimination of All Forms of Racial Discrimination: "By making a reservation a State cannot contract out from universally binding human rights standards [but this is true as a general rule]" (*Multilateral Treaties Deposited with the Secretary-General*, vol. I (see footnote 141 above), p. 145 (chap. IV.2)).

[184] In that regard, see the dissenting opinion of *ad hoc* Judge Sørenson in the *North Sea Continental Shelf* cases (footnote 173 above), p. 248; see also M. Coccia, *loc. cit.* (footnote 182 above), p. 32. See, however, below, paragraph (3) of the commentary to draft guideline 3.1.9.

[185] See article 38, paragraph 1 (*b*), of the Statute of the International Court of Justice. In that regard, see R. R. Baxter, "Treaties and customs", *Collected Courses of the Hague Academy of International Law*, vol. 129 (1970-I), p. 50; M. Coccia, *loc. cit.* (footnote 182 above), p. 31; G. Gaja, *loc. cit.* (*ibid.*), p. 451; and G. Teboul, *loc. cit.* (footnote 78 above), pp. 711–714. Under certain (but not all) circumstances, the same may be true of the existence of a reservation clause (see Imbert, *Les réserves aux traités multilatéraux*, op. cit. (footnote 173 above), p. 246, and Reuter, "Solidarité...", *loc. cit.* (footnote 71 above), p. 631, footnote 16 (also reproduced in Reuter, *Le développement...*, *op. cit.* (*ibid.*), pp. 370–371)).

[186] *Official Records of the General Assembly, Fiftieth session, Supplement No. 40* (see footnote 165 above), pp. 131–132, para. 7.

[187] See below paragraphs (13)–(16) of the present commentary.

mechanisms envisaged in the treaty or of limiting the role of domestic judges, who may have different competences with respect to conventional rules, on the one hand, and customary rules, on the other;[188]

– Furthermore, as noted by France in its observations on General Comment No. 24 of the Human Rights Committee, "the State's duty to observe a general customary principle should [not] be confused with its agreement to be bound by the expression of that principle in a treaty, especially with the developments and clarifications that such formalization involves";[189]

– And, lastly, a reservation may be the means by which a "persistent objector" manifests the persistence of its objection; the objector may certainly reject the application, through a treaty, of a norm which cannot be invoked against it under general international law.[190]

(8) Here again, however, the question is whether this solution can be transposed to the field of human rights.[191] The Human Rights Committee challenged this view on the basis of the specific characteristics of human rights treaties:

> Although treaties that are mere exchanges of obligations between States allow them to reserve *inter se* application of rules of general international law, it is otherwise in human rights treaties, which are for the benefit of persons within their jurisdiction.[192]

(9) First, it should be noted that the Committee confirmed that reservations to customary norms are not excluded *a priori*. In arguing to the contrary in the specific case of human rights treaties, it simply notes that these instruments are designed to protect the rights of individuals. But this premise does not have the consequences that the Committee attributes to it[193] since, on the one hand, a reservation to a human rights treaty provision which reflects a customary norm in no way absolves the reserving State of its obligation to respect

the norm as such[194] and, on the other hand, in practice, it is quite likely that a reservation to such a norm (especially if the latter is peremptory) will be incompatible with the object and purpose of the treaty by virtue of the applicable general rules.[195] It is these considerations which led the Commission to indicate, at the outset, that: "[t]he fact that a treaty provision reflects a customary norm is a pertinent factor in assessing the validity of a reservation".

(10) On the more general issue of codification conventions, it might be wondered whether reservations to them are not incompatible with their object and purpose. There is no doubt that the desire to codify is normally accompanied by a concern to preserve the rule being affirmed:[196] if it were possible to formulate a reservation to a provision of customary origin in the context of a codification treaty, the codification treaty would fail in its objectives,[197] to the point that reservations and, in any case, multiple reservations, have been viewed as the very negation of the work of codification.[198]

---

[188] Such is the case in France, where treaties (under article 55 of the Constitution), but not customary norms, take precedence over laws; see the 20 October 1989 decision by the Assembly of the French Council of State in the *Nicolo* case, *Recueil des décisions du Conseil d'Etat, 1989*, p. 190, Frydman's conclusions, and the 6 June 1997 decision in the *Aquarone* case, *Recueil des décisions du Conseil d'Etat, 1997*, p. 206, Bachelier's conclusions.

[189] Report of the Human Rights Committee, *Official Records of the General Assembly, Fifty-first Session, Supplement No. 40* (A/51/40), vol. I, p. 104, para. 5; in the same vein, see the comment by the United States of America (*ibid., Fiftieth Session* (footnote 165 above), pp. 129–130. See also G. Cohen-Jonathan, "Les réserves dans les traités institutionnels relatifs aux droits de l'homme. Nouveaux aspects européens et internationaux", *Revue générale de droit international public*, vol. 100 (1996), pp. 932–933.

[190] See the final working paper submitted in 2004 by Ms. Françoise Hampson on reservations to human rights treaties (E/CN.4/Sub.2/2004/42), endnote 45.

[191] See the second report on reservations to treaties by Mr. Alain Pellet, Special Rapporteur (footnote 17 above), paras. 143–147.

[192] General Comment No. 24, *Official Records of the General Assembly, Fiftieth session, Supplement No. 40* (see footnote 165 above), para. 8.

[193] For an opposing view, see T. Giegerich, "Vorbehalte zu Menschenrechtsabkommen: Zulässigkeit, Gültigkeit und Prüfungskompetenzen von Vertragsgremien: Ein konstitutioneller Ansatz", *Zeitschrift für ausländisches öffentliches Recht und Völkerrecht/Heidelberg Journal of International Law*, vol. 55 (1995), p. 744 (English summary, pp. 778–782, at pp. 779–780).

[194] See above paragraph (7) of the present commentary. According to the Human Rights Committee, "a State may not reserve the right to engage in slavery, to torture, to subject persons to cruel, inhuman or degrading treatment or punishment, to arbitrarily deprive persons of their lives, to arbitrarily arrest and detain persons, to deny freedom of thought, conscience and religion, to presume a person guilty unless he proves his innocence, to execute pregnant women or children, to permit the advocacy of national, racial or religious hatred, to deny to persons of marriageable age the right to marry, or to deny to minorities the right to enjoy their own culture, profess their own religion, or use their own language" (General Comment No. 24, *Official Records of the General Assembly, Fiftieth session, Supplement No. 40* (see footnote 165 above), para. 8). This is certainly true, but it does not automatically mean that reservations to the relevant provisions of the International Covenant on Civil and Political Rights are prohibited; if these rights must be respected, it is because of their customary and, in some cases, peremptory nature, not because of their inclusion in the Covenant. For a similar view, see Gaja, *loc. cit.* (footnote 182 above), p. 452. Furthermore, the Human Rights Committee simply makes assertions; it does not justify its identification of customary rules attached to these norms; in another context, it has been said that "[t]he 'ought' merges with the 'is', the *lex ferenda* with the *lex lata*" (T. Meron, "The Geneva Conventions as customary norms", AJIL, vol. 81 (1987) p. 361; see also Schabas's well-argued critique concerning articles 6 and 7 of the Covenant ("Invalid reservations..." *loc. cit.* (footnote 109 above), pp. 296–310).

[195] In that regard, see Françoise Hampson's working paper on reservations to human rights treaties (E/CN.4/Sub.2/1999/28), para. 17, and her final working paper on that topic (footnote 190 above), para. 51: "In theory, a State may make a reservation to a treaty provision without necessarily calling into question the customary status of the norm or its willingness to be bound by the customary norm. Nevertheless, in practice, reservations to provisions which reflect customary international law norms are likely to be viewed with considerable suspicion."

[196] Imbert, *Les réserves aux traités multilatéraux, op. cit.* (footnote 173 above), p. 246; see also Teboul, *op. cit.* (footnote 78 above), p. 680, who notes that while both are useful, the concept of a reservation is incompatible with that of a codification convention; this study gives a clear overview of the whole question of reservations to codification conventions (pp. 679–717, *passim*).

[197] Reuter, "Solidarité...", *loc. cit.* (footnote 71 above), pp. 630–631 (also reproduced in Reuter, *Le développement..., op. cit.* (*ibid.*), p. 370). The author adds that, for this reason, the treaty would also give rise to a situation further from its object and purpose than if it had not existed, since the scope of application of a general rule would be restricted (*ibid*). This second statement is more debatable: it seems to assume that the reserving State, by virtue of its reservation, is exempt from the application of the rule; this is not the case (see below footnote 206).

[198] R. Ago in *Yearbook ... 1965*, vol. I, 797th meeting, 8 June 1965, p. 153, para. 58.

(11) This does not mean that, in essence, any reservation to a codification treaty is incompatible with its object and purpose:

– It is certain that reservations are hardly compatible with the desired objective of standardizing and clarifying customary law but, on reflection, the overall balance which the reservation threatens is not the object and purpose of the treaty itself, but the object and purpose of the negotiations which gave rise to the treaty;[199]

– The very concept of a "codification convention" is tenuous. As the Commission has often stressed, it is impossible to distinguish between the codification *stricto sensu* of international law and the progressive development thereof.[200] How many rules of customary origin must a treaty contain in order to be defined as a "codification treaty"?;[201]

– The status of the rules included in a treaty changes over time: a rule which falls under the heading of "progressive development" may become pure codification and a "codification convention" often crystallizes into a rule of general international law a norm which was not of this nature at the time of its adoption.[202]

(12) Thus, the nature of codification conventions does not, as such, constitute an obstacle to the formulation of reservations to some of their provisions on the same grounds (and with the same restrictions) as any other treaty and the arguments that can be put forward, in general terms, in support of the ability to formulate reservations to a treaty provision that sets forth a customary norm[203] are also fully transposable thereto. Furthermore, there is well-established practice in this area: there are more reservations to human rights treaties (which are, moreover, to a great extent codifiers of existing law) and codification treaties than to any other type of treaty.[204] And while some objections may have been based on the customary nature of the rules concerned,[205] the specific nature of these conventions seems never to have been invoked

in support of a declaration of incompatibility with their object and purpose.

(13) Nevertheless, the customary nature of a provision which is the object of a reservation has important consequences with respect to the effects produced by the reservation; once established, it prevents application of the conventional rule which is the object of the reservation in the reserving State's relations with the other parties to the treaty, but it does not eliminate that State's obligation to respect the customary norm (the content of which may be identical).[206] The reason for this is simple and appears quite clearly in the famous dictum of the ICJ in the *Military and Paramilitary Activities in and against Nicaragua* case:

> The fact that the above-mentioned principles [of general and customary international law], recognized as such, have been codified or embodied in multilateral conventions does not mean that they cease to exist and to apply as principles of customary law, even as regards countries that are parties to such conventions.[207]

(14) Thus, the United States of America rightly considered, in its objection to the Syrian Arab Republic's reservation to the Vienna Convention on the Law of Treaties, that

> the absence of treaty relations between the United States of America and the Syrian Arab Republic with regard to certain provisions in Part V will not in any way impair the duty of the latter to fulfil any obligation embodied in those provisions to which it is subject under international law independently of the Vienna Convention on the Law of Treaties.[208]

(15) In his dissenting opinion appended to the 1969 judgment of the ICJ in the *North Sea Continental Shelf* cases, *ad hoc* Judge Sørensen summarized the rules applicable to reservations to a declaratory provision of customary law as follows:

> the faculty of making reservations to a treaty provision has no necessary connection with the question whether or not the provision can be considered as expressing a generally recognized rule of law. To substantiate this opinion it may be sufficient to point out that a number of reservations have been made to provisions of the Convention on the High Seas, although this Convention, according to its preamble, is 'generally declaratory of established principles of international law'. Some of these reservations have been objected to by other contracting

---

[199] G. Teboul, *loc. cit.* (footnote 78 above), p. 700.

[200] See, for example, the Commission's reports on its eighth (1956) and forty-eighth (1996) sessions, *Yearbook ... 1956*, vol. II, pp. 255–256, para. 26, and *Yearbook ... 1996*, vol. II (Part Two), p. 86, paras. 156–157.

[201] Reuter, "Solidarité...", *loc. cit.* (footnote 71 above), p. 632 (also reproduced in Reuter, *Le développement ..., op. cit.* (*ibid.*), p. 371).

[202] See below paragraph (17) of the present commentary; on the issue of the death penalty from the point of view of articles 6 and 7 of the 1966 Covenant on Civil and Political Rights (taking a negative position), see Schabas, "Invalid reservations...", *loc. cit.* (footnote 109 above), pp. 308–310.

[203] See above paragraph (2) of the present commentary.

[204] For example, on 31 December 2003, the Vienna Convention on Diplomatic Relations was the object of 57 reservations or declarations (of which 50 are still in force) by 34 States parties (currently, 31 States have reservations still in force) (*Multilateral Treaties Deposited with the Secretary-General*, vol. I (see footnote 141 above), pp. 90–100 (chap. III.3)) and the 1969 Vienna Convention was the subject of 70 reservations or declarations (of which 60 are still in force) by 35 States (32 at present) (*ibid.*, vol. II (footnote 142 above), pp. 340–351. For its part, the 1966 Covenant on Civil and Political Rights, which (now, at least) seems primarily to codify the general international law currently in force, was the object of 218 reservations or declarations (of which 196 are still in force) by 58 States (*ibid.*, pp. 173-184).

[205] See above paragraph (2) of the present commentary.

[206] In support of this position, see *Oppenheim's International Law*, 9th ed., vol. I, *Peace*, R. Y. Jennings and A. D. Watts (eds.), Harlow, Longman, 1992, pp. 1243–1244; Teboul, *loc. cit.* (footnote 78 above), p. 711; and P. Weil, "Vers une normativité relative en droit international?", *Revue générale de droit international public*, vol. 86 (1982), pp. 43–44. See also the authors cited in footnote 185 above or Schabas, "Reservations to human rights treaties", *loc. cit.* (footnote 135 above), p. 56. Paul Reuter takes the opposing view, arguing that the customary norm no longer applies between the State that formulates a reservation and the parties that refrain from objecting to it since, through a conventional mechanism subsequent to the establishment of the customary rule, its application has been suspended (Reuter, "Solidarité...", *loc. cit.* (footnote 71 above), p. 631 (also reproduced in Reuter, *Le développement..., op. cit.* (*ibid.*), p. 370); for a similar argument, see Teboul, *loc. cit.*, pp. 690 and 708. There are serious objections to this view; see below paragraph (2) of guideline 3.1.9.

[207] *Military and Paramilitary Activities in and against Nicaragua (Nicaragua v. United States of America), Jurisdiction and Admissibility, Judgment of 26 November 1984, I.C.J. Reports 1984*, p. 392, at pp. 424–425, para. 73; see also Judge Morelli's dissenting opinion in the *North Sea Continental Shelf* cases (footnote 173 above), at p. 198.

[208] See *Multilateral Treaties Deposited with the Secretary-General*, vol. II (see footnote 142 above), p. 385 (chap. XXIII.1); see also the objections of the Netherlands and Poland, cited in paragraphs (6) and (7) above.

States, while other reservations have been tacitly accepted. The acceptance, whether tacit or express, of a reservation made by a contracting party does not have the effect of depriving the Convention as a whole, or the relevant article in particular, of its declaratory character. It only has the effect of establishing a special contractual relationship between the parties concerned within the general framework of the customary law embodied in the Convention. Provided the customary rule does not belong to the category of *jus cogens*, a special contractual relationship of this nature is not invalid as such. Consequently, there is no incompatibility between the faculty of making reservations to certain articles of the Convention on the Continental Shelf and the recognition of that Convention or the particular articles as an expression of generally accepted rules of international law.[209]

(16)   This means that the (customary) nature of the rule reflected in a treaty provision does not in itself constitute an obstacle to the formulation of a reservation, but that such a reservation can in no way call into question the binding nature of the rule in question in relations between the reserving State or international organization and other States or international organizations, whether or not they are parties to the treaty.

(17)   The customary nature of the rule "reflected" in the treaty provision pursuant to which a reservation is formulated must be determined at the moment of such formulation. Nor can it be excluded that the adoption of the treaty might have helped crystallize this nature, particularly if the reservation was formulated long after the conclusion of the treaty.[210]

(18)   The somewhat complicated wording of the last part of draft guideline 3.1.8, paragraph 2, may be explained by the diversity *ratione loci* of customary norms: some may be universal in application while others have only a regional scope[211] and may even be applicable only at the purely bilateral level.[212]

3.1.9   *Reservations contrary to a rule of* jus cogens

A reservation cannot exclude or modify the legal effect of a treaty in a manner contrary to a peremptory norm of general international law.

Commentary

(1)   Draft guideline 3.1.9 is a compromise between two opposing lines of argument which emerged during the Commission's debate. Some members held that the

peremptory nature of the norm to which the reservation related made the reservation in question invalid, while others maintained that the logic behind draft guideline 3.1.8, on reservations to a provision reflecting a customary norm, should apply and that it should be accepted that such a reservation was not invalid in itself, provided it concerned only some aspect of a treaty provision setting forth the rule in question and left the norm itself intact. Both groups agreed that a reservation should not have any effect on the content of the binding obligations stemming from the *jus cogens* norm as reflected in the provision to which it referred. This consensus is reflected in draft guideline 3.1.9; without adopting a position as to whether these opposing arguments are founded or unfounded, it establishes that a reservation should not permit a breach of a peremptory norm of general international law.

(2)   According to Paul Reuter, since a reservation, through acceptances by other parties, establishes a "contractual relationship" among the parties, a reservation to a treaty provision that sets forth a peremptory norm of general international law is inconceivable: the resulting agreement would automatically be null and void as a consequence of the principle established in article 53 of the Vienna Convention.[213]

(3)   This reasoning is not, however, axiomatic, but is based on one of the postulates of the "opposability" school, according to which the issue of the validity of reservations is left entirely to the subjective judgement of the contracting parties and depends only on the provisions of article 20 of the 1969 and 1986 Vienna Conventions.[214] Yet this reasoning is far from clear;[215] above all, it regards the reservations mechanism as a purely treaty-based process, whereas a reservation is a *unilateral* act; although linked to the treaty, it has no exogenous effects. By definition, it "purports to exclude or to modify the legal effect of *certain provisions of the treaty* in their application" to the reserving State[216] and, if it is accepted, those are indeed its consequences;[217] however, whether or not it is accepted, "neighbouring" international law remains intact; the legal situation of interested States is affected by it only in their *treaty relations*.[218] Other, more numerous authors assert the incompatibility of any reservation with a provision which reflects a peremptory norm of general international law, either without giving any explanation,[219] or arguing

[209] *North Sea Continental Shelf* (see footnote 173 above), p. 248.

[210] In its judgment of 20 February 1969 in the *North Sea Continental Shelf* cases (see footnote 173 above), the ICJ also recognized that "a norm-creating provision [may constitute] the foundation of, or [generate] a rule which, while only conventional or contractual in its origin, has since passed into the general corpus of international law, and is now accepted as such by the *opinio juris*, so as to have become binding even for countries which have never, and do not, become parties to the Convention. There is no doubt that this process is a perfectly possible one and does from time to time occur: it constitutes indeed one of the recognized methods by which new rules of customary international law may be formed" (p. 41, para. 71).

[211] See, in particular, the judgments of the ICJ in *Colombian-Peruvian asylum case, Judgment of 20 November 1950, I.C.J. Reports 1950*, p. 266, at pp. 27–277; *Fisheries (United Kingdom v. Norway), Judgment of 18 December 1951, I.C.J. Reports 1951*, p. 116, at pp. 136–139; and *Rights of Nationals of the United States of America in Morocco* (footnote 128 above), p. 200.

[212] See *Right of Passage over Indian Territory, Merits, Judgment of 12 April 1960, I.C.J. Reports 1960*, p. 6, at p. 39.

[213] See Reuter, "Solidarité...", *loc. cit.* (footnote 71 above), p. 625 (also reproduced in Reuter, *Le développement ..., op. cit.* (footnote 71 above), p. 363). See also Teboul, *loc. cit.* (footnote 78 above), pp. 691–692.

[214] "The validity of a reservation depends, under the Convention's system, on whether the reservation is or is not accepted by another State, not on the fulfilment of the condition for its admission on the basis of its compatibility with the object and purpose of the treaty" (J. M. Ruda, "Reservations to treaties", *Collected Courses of the Hague Academy of International Law, 1975-III*, vol. 146 (1977), p. 190).

[215] See the first report of Special Rapporteur Alain Pellet on the law and practice relating to reservations to treaties (footnote 12 above), paras. 100–105.

[216] Article 2, paragraph 1 (*d*), of the Vienna Conventions, reproduced in draft guideline 1.1; see also draft guideline 1.1.1.

[217] See article 21 of the Vienna Conventions.

[218] See above paragraph (13) of the commentary to draft guideline 3.1.8.

[219] See, for example, Riquelme Cortado, *op. cit.* (footnote 147 above), p. 147. See also the second report of Special Rapporteur Alain Pellet on reservations to treaties (footnote 17 above), paras. 141–142.

that such a reservation would, *ipso facto*, be contrary to the object and purpose of the treaty.[220]

(4) This is also the position of the Human Rights Committee in its General Comment No. 24: "Reservations that offend peremptory norms would not be compatible with the object and purpose of the Covenant."[221] This formulation is debatable[222] and, in any case, cannot be generalized: it is perfectly conceivable that a treaty might refer marginally to a rule of *jus cogens* without the latter being its object and purpose.

(5) It has, however, been asserted that the rule prohibiting derogation from a rule of *jus cogens* applies not only to treaty relations, but also to all legal acts, including unilateral acts.[223] This is certainly true and in fact constitutes the only intellectually convincing argument for not transposing to reservations to peremptory provisions the reasoning that would not exclude, in principle, the ability to formulate reservations to treaty provisions embodying customary rules.[224]

(6) Conversely, it should be noted that when formulating a reservation, a State may indeed seek to exempt itself from the rule to which the reservation itself relates, and in the case of a peremptory norm of general international law this is out of the question[225]—all the more so because it is inconceivable that a persistent objector

could thwart such a norm. The objectives of the reserving State, however, may be different: while accepting the content of the rule, it may wish to escape the consequences arising out of it, particularly in respect of monitoring,[226] and on this point there is no reason why the logic followed in respect of customary rules which are merely binding should not be transposed to peremptory norms.

(7) However, as regrettable as this may seem, reservations do not have to be justified, and in fact they seldom are. In the absence of clear justification, therefore, it is impossible for the other contracting parties or for monitoring bodies to verify the validity of the reservation, and it is best to adopt the principle that any reservation to a provision which formulates a rule of *jus cogens* is null and void *ipso jure*.

(8) Yet, even in the eyes of its advocates, this conclusion must be accompanied by two major caveats. First, this prohibition does not result from article 19 (*c*) of the Vienna Convention but, *mutatis mutandis*, from the principle set out in article 53. Secondly, there are other ways for States to avoid the consequences of the inclusion in a treaty of a peremptory norm of general international law: they may formulate a reservation not to the substantive provision concerned, but to "secondary" articles governing treaty relations (monitoring, dispute settlement, interpretation), even if this means restricting its scope to a particular substantive provision.[227]

(9) This dissociation is illustrated by the line of argument followed by the ICJ in *Armed Activities on the Territory of the Congo (Democratic Republic of the Congo v. Rwanda)*:

> In relation to the DRC's argument that the reservation in question [to article 22 of the International Convention on the Elimination of All Forms of Racial Discrimination] is without legal effect because, on the one hand, the prohibition on racial discrimination is a peremptory norm of general international law and, on the other, such a reservation is in conflict with a peremptory norm,

the Court referred

> to its reasoning when dismissing the DRC's similar argument in regard to Rwanda's reservation to Article IX of the Genocide Convention (see paragraphs 64–69 above [[228]]): the fact that a dispute concerns non-compliance with a peremptory norm of general international law cannot suffice to found the Court's jurisdiction to entertain such a dispute, and there exists no peremptory norm requiring States to consent to such jurisdiction in order to settle disputes relating to the Convention on Racial Discrimination.[229]

---

[220] See also the dissenting opinion of Judge Tanaka in the *North Sea Continental Shelf* cases (see footnote 173 above), p. 182.

[221] *Official Records of the General Assembly, Fiftieth session, Supplement No. 40* (see footnote 165 above), para. 8. In its comments, France argued that "[p]aragraph 8 of general comment No. 24 (52) is drafted in such a way as to link the two distinct legal concepts: of 'peremptory norms' and rules of 'customary international law' to the point of confusing them" (*Official Records of the General Assembly, Fifty-first Session, Supplement No. 40* (see footnote 189 above), vol. I, Annex VI, p. 104, para. 3).

[222] See the doubts expressed on this subject by the United States of America which, in its commentary on General Comment No. 24, transposes to provisions which set forth peremptory norms the solution that is essential for those norms that formulate rules of customary law: "[i]t is clear that a State cannot exempt itself from a peremptory norm of international law by making a reservation to the Covenant. It is not at all clear that a State cannot choose to exclude one means of enforcement of particular norms by reserving against inclusion of those norms in its Covenant obligations" (*Official Records of the General Assembly, Fiftieth Session, Supplement No. 40* (see footnote 165 above), vol. I, p. 132).

[223] Teboul, *loc. cit.* (footnote 78 above), p. 707, note 52, referring to J.-D. Sicault, "Du caractère obligatoire des engagements unilatéraux en droit international public", *Revue générale de droit international public*, vol. 83 (1979), p. 663, and the legal writings quoted therein.

[224] This is true *a fortiori* if one considers the reservation/acceptance "pair" as an agreement amending the treaty in the relations between the two States concerned. (See Coccia, *loc. cit.* (footnote 182 above), pp. 30–31; see also the position of Reuter referred to above in paragraph (2) of the present commentary); this analysis, however, is unconvincing (see paragraph (3) of the present commentary).

[225] There are, of course, few examples of reservations which are clearly contrary to a norm of *jus cogens*. See, however, the reservation formulated by Myanmar when it acceded, in 1993, to the 1989 Convention on the rights of the child. Myanmar reserved the right not to apply article 37 of the Convention and to exercise "powers of arrest, detention, imprisonment, exclusion, interrogation, enquiry and investigation" in respect of children, in order to "protect the supreme national interest" (*Multilateral Treaties Deposited with the Secretary-General*, vol. I (see footnote 141 above), p. 339, note 29 (chap. IV.11)); this reservation, to which four States expressed objections (on the basis of referral to domestic legislation, not the conflict of the reservation with a peremptory norm), was withdrawn in 1993 (*ibid.*).

[226] See paragraph (7) of the commentary to draft guideline 3.1.8.

[227] In this regard, see, for example, the reservations of Malawi and Mexico to the 1979 International Convention Against the Taking of Hostages, subjecting the application of article 16 (dispute settlement and jurisdiction of the Court) to the conditions of their optional declarations pursuant to article 36 (2) of the Statute of the International Court of Justice, *Multilateral Treaties Deposited with the Secretary-General*, vol. II (see footnote 142 above), p. 112 (chap. XVIII.5). There can be no doubt that such reservations are not prohibited in principle; see draft guideline 3.1.13 and the commentary thereto.

[228] On this aspect of the judgment, see below paragraphs (2) and (3) of the commentary to draft guideline 3.1.13.

[229] *Armed Activities on the Territory of the Congo (New Application: 2002) (Democratic Republic of the Congo v. Rwanda), Jurisdiction and Admissibility, Judgment of 3 February 2006* (see footnote 99 above), p. 35, para. 78.

In this case, it is clear that the Court found that the peremptory nature of the prohibition on racial discrimination did not invalidate the reservations relating not to the prohibitory norm itself but to the rules surrounding it.

(10) Since it proved impossible to opt for one or the other of these two opposing lines of argument, the Commission decided to tackle the question from a different angle, namely that of the legal effects which a reservation could (or could not) produce. Having its basis in the actual definition of reservations, draft guideline 3.1.9 states that a reservation cannot in any way exclude or modify the legal effect of a treaty in a manner contrary to *jus cogens*. For the sake of conciseness, it did not seem necessary to reproduce the texts of draft guidelines 1.1 and 1.1.1 in full, but the phrase "exclude or modify the legal effect of a treaty" must be understood to mean to exclude or modify both the "legal effect of certain provisions of the treaty" and "the legal effect ... of the treaty as a whole with respect to certain specific aspects in their application to the State or to the international organization which formulates the reservation".

(11) The draft guideline covers the case in which, although no rule of *jus cogens* was reflected in the treaty, a reservation would require that the treaty be applied in a manner conflicting with *jus cogens*. For instance, a reservation could be intended to exclude a category of persons from benefiting from certain rights granted under a treaty, on the basis of a form of discrimination that would be contrary to *jus cogens*.

(12) Some Commission members did not think that draft guideline 3.1.9 had a direct bearing on the questions examined in this part of the Guide to Practice and had to do more with the effects of reservations than with their validity. The same members also contended that the draft guideline did not answer the question, which was nevertheless significant, of the material validity of reservations to treaty provisions reflecting *jus cogens* norms.

3.1.10   *Reservations to provisions relating to non-derogable rights*

A State or an international organization may not formulate a reservation to a treaty provision relating to non-derogable rights unless the reservation in question is compatible with the essential rights and obligations arising out of that treaty. In assessing that compatibility, account shall be taken of the importance which the parties have conferred upon the rights at issue by making them non-derogable.

Commentary

(1) In appearance, the question of reservations to non-derogable obligations contained in human rights treaties, as well as in certain conventions on the law of armed conflict,[230] environmental protection[231] or diplomatic

relations,[232] is very similar to the question of reservations to treaty provisions reflecting peremptory norms of general international law. It could, however, be resolved in an autonomous manner.[233] States frequently justify their objections to reservations to such provisions on grounds of the treaty-based prohibition on suspending their application whatever the circumstances.[234]

(2) Clearly, to the extent that non-derogable provisions relate to rules of *jus cogens*, the reasoning applicable to the latter applies also to the former.[235] However, the two are not necessarily identical.[236] According to the Human Rights Committee:

> While there is no automatic correlation between reservations to non-derogable provisions and reservations which offend against the object and purpose of the Covenant, a State has a heavy onus to justify such a reservation.[237]

This last point is question-begging and is undoubtedly motivated by reasons of convenience, but is not based on any principle of positive law and could only reflect the progressive development of international law, rather than codification *stricto sensu*. Incidentally, it follows *a contrario* from this position that, in the Committee's view, if a non-derogable right is not a matter of *jus cogens*, it can in principle be the object of a reservation.

(3) The Inter-American Court on Human Rights declared in its advisory opinion of 8 September 1983 on *Restrictions to the Death Penalty*:

> Article 27 of the Convention allows the States Parties to suspend, in time of war, public danger, or other emergency that threatens their independence or security, the obligations they assumed by ratifying the Convention, provided that in doing so they do not suspend or

---

wastes and their disposal), they very often prohibit all reservations. See also article 311, paragraph 3, of the United Nations Convention on the Law of the Sea.

[232] See article 45 of the 1961 Vienna Convention on Diplomatic Relations. See also *United States Diplomatic and Consular Staff in Tehran, Judgment, I.C.J. Reports 1980*, p. 3, at p. 40, para. 86.

[233] On this issue, see Riquelme Cortado, *op. cit.* (footnote 147 above), pp. 147–159.

[234] See article 4, paragraph 2, of the 1966 International Covenant on Civil and Political Rights, article 15 (2) of the European Convention on Human Rights (see also article 3 of Protocol No. 6, article 4 (3) of Protocol No. 7 and article 2 of Protocol No. 13), and article 27 of the American Convention on Human Rights: "Pact of San José, Costa Rica". Neither the International Covenant on Economic, Social and Cultural Rights nor the African Charter on Human and Peoples' Rights contain clauses of this type (see F. Ouguergouz, "L'absence de clauses de dérogation dans certains traités relatifs aux droits de l'homme: les réponses du droit international général", *Revue générale de droit international public*, vol. 98 (1994), pp. 289–336.

[235] See the Human Rights Committee's General Comment No. 24: "some non-derogable rights, which in any event cannot be reserved because of their status as peremptory norms ... —the prohibition of torture and arbitrary deprivation of life are examples" (*Official Records of the General Assembly, Fiftieth Session, Supplement No. 40* (see footnote 165 above), para. 10).

[236] See General Comment No. 29 Report of the Human Rights Committee, *Official Records of the General Assembly, Fifty-sixth Session, Supplement No. 40* (A/56/40), vol. I, Annex VI, para. 11. See also Riquelme Cortado, *op. cit.* (footnote 147 above), pp. 153–155, or K. Teraya, "Emerging hierarchy in international human rights and beyond: from the perspective of non-derogable rights", *European Journal of International Law*, vol. 12, No. 5 (2001), pp. 917–941.

[237] General Comment No. 24, *Official Records of the General Assembly, Fiftieth Session, Supplement No. 40* (see footnote 165 above), para. 10.

---

[230] The principles set out in common article 3, paragraph 1, of the 1949 Geneva Conventions for the protection of war victims are non-derogable and must be respected "at any time and in any place".

[231] Although most environmental protection conventions contain rules considered to be non-derogable (see article 11 of the Basel Convention on the control of transboundary movements of hazardous

derogate from certain basic or essential rights, among them the right to life guaranteed by Article 4. It would follow therefrom that a reservation which was designed to enable a State to suspend any of the non-derogable fundamental rights must be deemed to be incompatible with the object and purpose of the Convention and, consequently, not permitted by it. The situation would be different if the reservation sought merely to restrict certain aspects of a non-derogable right without depriving the right as a whole of its basic purpose. Since the reservation referred to by the Commission in its submission does not appear to be of a type that is designed to deny the right to life as such, the Court concludes that to that extent it can be considered, in principle, as not being incompatible with the object and purpose of the Convention.[238]

(4)   In opposition to any possibility of formulating reservations to a non-derogable provision, it has been argued that, when any suspension of the obligations in question is excluded by the treaty, "with greater reason one should not admit any reservations, perpetuated in time until withdrawn by the State at issue; such reservations are … without any *caveat*, incompatible with the object and purpose of those treaties".[239] This argument is not persuasive: it is one thing to prevent derogations from a binding provision, but another thing to determine whether a State is bound by the provision at issue.[240] It is this second problem that needs to be resolved.

(5)   It must therefore be accepted that, while certain reservations to non-derogable provisions are certainly ruled out—either because they would hold in check a peremptory norm, assuming that such reservations are impermissible,[241] or because they would be contrary to the object and purpose of the treaty—this is not necessarily always the case.[242] The non-derogable nature of a right protected by a human rights treaty reveals the importance with which it is viewed by the contracting parties, and it follows that any reservation aimed purely and simply at preventing its implementation is without doubt contrary

to the object and purpose of the treaty.[243] It does not follow, however, that this non-derogable nature in itself prevents a reservation from being formulated to the provision setting out the right in question, provided that it applies only to certain limited aspects relating to the implementation of that right.

(6)   This balanced solution is well illustrated by Denmark's objection to the United States reservations to articles 6 and 7 of the 1966 International Covenant on Civil and Political Rights:

Denmark would like to recall article 4, para 2 of the Covenant according to which no derogation from a number of fundamental articles, *inter alia* 6 and 7, may be made by a State Party even in time of public emergency which threatens the life of the nation.

In the opinion of Denmark, reservation (2) of the United States with regard to capital punishment for crimes committed by persons below eighteen years of age as well as reservation (3) with respect to article 7 constitute general derogations from articles 6 and 7, while according to article 4, para 2 of the Covenant such derogations are not permitted.

Therefore, and taking into account that articles 6 and 7 are protecting two of the most basic rights contained in the Covenant, the Government of Denmark regards the said reservations incompatible with the object and purpose of the Covenant, and consequently Denmark objects to the reservations.[244]

Denmark objected not only because the reservations of the United States related to non-derogable rights, but also because their wording was such that they left essential provisions of the treaty empty of any substance. It should be noted that in certain cases, States parties formulated no objection to reservations relating to provisions in respect of which no derogation is permitted.[245]

(7)   Naturally, the fact that a provision may in principle be the object of a derogation does not mean that all reservations relating to it will be valid.[246] The criterion of compatibility with the object and purpose of the treaty also applies to them.

(8)   This leads to several observations:

–   First, different principles apply in evaluating the validity of reservations, depending on whether they relate to provisions setting forth rules of *jus cogens* or to non-derogable rules.

–   In the first case, questions persist as to whether it is possible to formulate a reservation to a treaty provision setting out a peremptory norm, because the reservation

---

[238] *Restrictions to the Death Penalty* (see footnote 109 above), para. 61.

[239] Separate opinion of Judge Antonio Augusto Cançado Trindade, appended to the decision of the Inter-American Court dated 22 January 1999 in *Blake (Reparations (Art. 63(1) of the American Convention on Human Rights), Judgement of 22 January 1999, Series C, No. 48*, para. 11; see the favourable comment by Riquelme Cortado, *op. cit.* (footnote 147 above), p. 155. To the same effect, see the objection by the Netherlands mentioning that the United States reservation to article 7 of the 1966 International Covenant on Civil and Political Rights "has the same effect as a general derogation from this article, while according to article 4 of the Covenant, no derogation, not even in times of public emergency, are permitted" (*Multilateral Treaties Deposited with the Secretary-General*, vol. I (see footnote 141 above), (chap. IV.4)).

[240] See the commentary by the United Kingdom on General Comment No. 24 of the Human Rights Committee: "Derogation from a formally contracted obligation and reluctance to undertake the obligation in the first place are not the same thing" (*Official Records of the General Assembly, Fiftieth session, Supplement No. 40* (see footnote 165 above) p. 131, para. 6).

[241] Regarding this ambiguity, see above draft guideline 3.1.9 and the commentary thereto.

[242] See the final working paper submitted in 2004 by Ms. Françoise Hampson on reservations to human rights treaties (footnote 190 above), para. 52; R. Higgins, "Human rights: some questions of integrity", *The Modern Law Review*, vol. 52, No. 1 (1989), p. 15; McBride, *loc. cit.* (footnote 160 above), pp. 163–164; J. Polakiewicz, *Treaty-Making in the Council of Europe*, Strasbourg, Council of Europe, 1999, p. 113, or C. J. Redgwell, "Reservations to treaties and Human Rights Committee General Comment No.24 (52)", *International and Comparative Law Quarterly*, vol. 46 (1997), p. 402; *contra*: Lijnzaad, *op. cit.* (footnote 81 above), p. 91.

[243] See above draft guideline 3.1.5: "A reservation is incompatible with the object and purpose of the treaty if it affects an essential element of the treaty …".

[244] *Multilateral Treaties Deposited with the Secretary-General*, vol. I (see footnote 141 above), p. 189 (chap. IV.4); see also, although they are less clearly based on the non-derogable nature of articles 6 and 7, the objections of Belgium, Finland, Germany, Italy, the Netherlands, mentioned above, and of Norway, Portugal or Sweden (*ibid.*, pp. 194–196).

[245] See the many examples given by Schabas relating to the 1966 International Covenant on Civil and Political Rights, the European Convention on Human Rights and the American Convention on Human Rights: "Pact of San José, Costa Rica", Schabas, "Reservations to human rights treaties...", *loc. cit.* (footnote 135 above), pp. 51–52, footnote 51.

[246] See Redgwell, *loc. cit.* (footnote 242 above), p. 402.

might threaten the integrity of the norm, the application of which (unlike that of customary rules, which permit derogations) must be uniform.

– In the second case, however, reservations remain possible provided they do not call into question the principle set forth in the treaty provision; in that situation, the methodological guidance contained in draft guideline 3.1.6[247] is fully applicable.

– Nevertheless, it is necessary to proceed with the utmost caution, and this is why the Commission has drafted the first sentence of draft guideline 3.1.10 in the negative ("A State or an international organization *may not* formulate a reservation … *unless* …"), as it has done on several occasions in the past when it wished to draw attention to the exceptional nature of certain behaviour in relation to reservations.[248]

– Moreover, in elaborating this draft guideline the Commission took care not to give the impression that it was introducing an additional criterion of permissibility with regard to reservations: the assessment of compatibility referred to in the second sentence of the provision concerns the reservation's relationship to "the essential rights and obligations arising out of [the] treaty", the effect on "an essential element of the treaty" being cited as one of the criteria for incompatibility with the object and purpose.[249]

3.1.11 *Reservations relating to internal law*

A reservation by which a State or an international organization purports to exclude or to modify the legal effect of certain provisions of a treaty or of the treaty as a whole in order to preserve the integrity of specific norms of the internal law of that State or rules of that organization may be formulated only insofar as it is compatible with the object and purpose of the treaty.

Commentary

(1) A reason frequently put forward by States in support of their formulation of a reservation relates to their desire to preserve the integrity of specific norms of their internal law.

(2) Although similar in certain respects, a distinction must be drawn between such reservations and those arising out of vague or general reservations. The latter are often formulated by reference to internal law in general or to whole sections of such law (such as constitutional, criminal or family law) without any further detail, thus making it impossible to assess the compatibility of the reservation in question with the object and purpose of the treaty. The question which draft guideline 3.1.11 seeks to

answer is a different one, namely whether the formulation of a reservation—clearly expressed and sufficiently detailed—could be justified by considerations arising from internal law.[250]

(3) Here again, in the Commission's view, a nuanced response is essential, and it is certainly not possible to respond categorically in the negative, as certain objections to reservations of this type would seem to suggest. For instance, several States have objected to the reservation made by Canada to the Convention on Environmental Impact Assessment in a Transboundary Context of 25 February 1991, on the grounds that the reservation "render[s] compliance with the provisions of the Convention dependent on certain norms of Canada's internal legislation".[251] Similarly, Finland objected to reservations made by several States to the 1989 Convention on the rights of the child on the "general principle of observance of treaties according to which a party may not invoke the provisions of its internal law as justification for failure to perform its treaty obligations".[252]

(4) This ground for objection is unconvincing. Doubtless, in accordance with article 27 of the Vienna Convention,[253] no party may invoke the provisions of its domestic law as justification for failure to apply a treaty.[254] The assumption, however, is that the problem is settled, in the sense that the provisions in question are applicable to the reserving States, but that is precisely the issue. As has been correctly pointed out, a State very often formulates a reservation *because* the treaty imposes on it obligations incompatible with its domestic law, which it is not in a position to amend,[255] at least initially.[256] Moreover,

[247] "Determination of the object and purpose of the treaty."

[248] See draft guidelines 2.3.1 ("Late formulation of a reservation"), 2.4.6 ("Late formulation of an interpretative declaration"), 2.4.8 ("Late formulation of a conditional interpretative declaration"), 2.5.11 ("Effect of a partial withdrawal of a reservation"), 3.1.3 ("Permissibility of reservations not prohibited by the treaty") and 3.1.4 ("Permissibility of specified reservations").

[249] See above draft guideline 3.1.5 and, in particular, paragraph (14) (*b*) of the commentary thereto.

[250] See above paragraphs (4) to (6) of the commentary to draft guideline 3.1.7.

[251] See the objection by Spain, as well as those by France, Norway, Ireland, Luxembourg and Sweden in *Multilateral Treaties Deposited with the Secretary-General*, vol. II (see footnote 142 above), pp. 495–498 (chap. XXVII.4).

[252] Objections by Finland to the reservations of Indonesia, Malaysia, Oman, Qatar and Singapore , *ibid.*, vol. I, pp. 331–332 (chap. IV.11). See also, for example, the objections of Denmark, Finland, Greece, Ireland, Mexico, Norway and Sweden to the second reservation of the United States to the Convention on the Prevention and Punishment of the Crime of Genocide, *ibid.*, pp. 130–131 (chap. IV.1); for the text of the reservation itself, see above paragraph (6) of the commentary to draft guideline 3.1.7; see also paragraph (4) of the same commentary.

[253] Expressly invoked, for instance, by Estonia and the Netherlands to support their objections to this same reservation by the United States, *ibid.*, pp. 130–131.

[254] In the words of article 27: "A party may not invoke the provisions of its internal law as justification for its failure to perform a treaty. This rule is without prejudice to article 46" (which has to do with "imperfect ratifications"). The rule set out in article 26 of the Convention concerns treaties in force, whereas, by definition, a reservation purports to exclude or to modify the legal effect of the provision in question in its application to the author of the reservation.

[255] See Schabas, "Reservations to the Convention on the rights of the child", *loc. cit.* (footnote 108 above), pp. 479–480 and also "Reservations to human rights treaties...", *loc. cit.* (footnote 135 above), p. 59.

[256] Sometimes the reserving State indicates the period of time it will need to bring its domestic law into line with the treaty (as in the case of Estonia's reservation to the application of article 6, or Lithuania's to article 5, paragraph 3, of the European Convention on Human Rights which gave one-year time limits (http://conventions.coe.int/)), or it indicates its intention to do so (as in the case of the reservations Cyprus and Malawi made upon accession to the 1979 Convention on the Elimination of All Forms of Discrimination against Women, commitments which were in fact kept—see *Multilateral Treaties Deposited with the Secretary-General*, vol. I (see footnote 141 above), p. 281, note 25,

article 57 of the European Convention on Human Rights does not simply authorize a State party to formulate a reservation where its internal law is not in conformity with a provision of the Convention, but restricts even that authority exclusively to instances where "a law ... in force in its territory is not in conformity with the provision".[257] Besides the European Convention on Human Rights, there are indeed reservations relating to the implementation of internal law that give rise to no objections and have in fact not met with objections.[258] On the other hand, this same article expressly prohibits "reservations of a general character".

(5)   What matters here is that the State formulating the reservation should not use its domestic law[259] as a cover for not actually accepting any new international obligation,[260] even though the treaty's aim is to change the practice of States parties to the treaty. While article 27 of the Vienna Conventions cannot rightly be said to apply to the case in point,[261] it should nevertheless be borne in mind that national laws are "merely facts" from the standpoint of international law[262] and that the very aim of a treaty can be to lead States to modify them.

(6)   The Commission preferred the term "particular norms of internal law" to the term "provisions of internal law", which ran the risk of suggesting that only the written rules of a constitutional, legislative or regulatory nature were involved, whereas draft guideline 3.1.11 applied also to customary norms or norms of jurisprudence. Similarly, the term "rules of the organization" means not only the "established practice of the organization" but also the constituent instruments and "decisions, resolutions and other acts taken by the organization in accordance with the constituent instruments".[263]

(7)   The Commission is aware that draft guideline 3.1.11 may, on first reading, seem to be merely a repetition of the principle set out in article 19 (c) of the Vienna Conventions and reproduced in draft guideline 3.1. Its function is important, nonetheless: it is to establish that, contrary to an erroneous but fairly widespread perception, a reservation is not invalid solely because it aims to preserve the integrity of particular norms of internal law—it being understood that, as in the case of any reservation, those made with such an objective must be compatible with the object and purpose of the treaty to which they relate.

(8)   A proposal was also made to create an additional draft guideline dealing with reservations to treaty clauses relating to the implementation of the treaty in internal law.[264] Without underestimating the potential significance of this issue, the Commission was of the view that it was premature to devote a separate draft article to it, given that, in practical terms, the problem did not seem to have arisen and that the purpose of draft articles 3.1.7 to 3.1.13 was to illustrate the general guidance given in draft guideline 3.1.5, with examples chosen on the basis of their

and p. 283, note 40 (chap. IV.8)); see also Indonesia's statement upon accession to the Basel Convention on the control of transboundary movements of hazardous wastes and their disposal of 22 March 1989, *ibid.* vol. II, p. 487 (chap. XXVII.3)). It is also not unusual for a State to withdraw a reservation made without any time indication after it has amended the provisions of its national law that had prompted the reservation: as in the case of withdrawal by France, Ireland and the United Kingdom of several reservations to the Convention on the Elimination of All Forms of Discrimination against Women (see *ibid.* vol. I, pp. 281–282, notes 28 and 32, and pp. 286–287, note 58 (chap. IV.8); see also the successive partial withdrawals (1996, 1998, 1999, 2001) by Finland of its reservations to article 6, paragraph 1, of the European Convention on Human Rights (http://conventions.coe.int/). Such practices are laudable and should definitely be encouraged (see draft guideline 2.5.3 in the Guide to Practice and the commentary thereto, *Yearbook ... 2003*, vol. II (Part Two), p. 76); yet they cannot be used as an argument for the invalidity of the principle of draft reservations on the grounds of domestic law.

[257] See paragraph (8) of the commentary to draft guideline 3.1.2, *Yearbook ... 2006*, vol. II (Part Two), chap. VIII, sect. C.2.

[258] See, for example, Mozambique's reservation to the International Convention against the taking of hostages of 17 December 1979, *Multilateral Treaties Deposited with the Secretary-General*, vol. II (see footnote 142 above), p. 112 (chap. XVIII.5). A reservation regarding the extradition of Mozambican nationals that reappears in connection with other treaties such as, for example, the International Convention for the Suppression of the Financing of Terrorism, *ibid.*, p. 167 (chap. XVIII.11), the reservations by Guatemala and the Philippines to the 1962 Convention on Consent for Marriage, Minimum Age for Marriage and Registration of Marriages, *ibid.*, p. 93 (chap. XVI.3); all the reservations by Colombia (made upon signature), Iran and the Netherlands (though very vague) to the United Nations Convention against Illicit Traffic in Narcotic Drugs and Psychotropic Substances, *ibid.*, vol. I, pp. 462–464 (chap. VI.19). France's reservation to article 5, paragraph 1, of the European Convention on Human Rights has given rise to more discussion: see N. Questiaux, "La Convention européenne des droits de l'homme et l'article 16 de la Constitution du 4 octobre 1958", *Revue des Droits Humains/Human Rights Journal*, vol. 3, No. 4 (1970), pp. 651–663; A. Pellet, "La ratification par la France de la Convention européenne des droits de l'homme", *Revue du droit public et de la science politique en France et à l'étranger*, vol. 90 (1974), pp. 1358–1365; or V. Coussirat-Coustère, "La réserve française à l'article 15 de la Convention européenne des droits de l'homme", *Journal du droit international*, vol. 102, No. 2 (1975), pp. 269–293.

[259] Or in the case of international organizations their "rules of the organization": the term is taken from articles 27 and 46 of the 1986 Vienna Convention. It also appears (and is defined) in article 4, paragraph 4, of the Commission's articles on responsibility of international organizations (see *Yearbook ... 2004*, vol. II (Part Two), p. 48). However, the reference to the rules of the organization may not raise a similar problem if the reservation only applies to the relations between the organization and its members.

[260] In its concluding observations of 6 April 1995 on the initial report of the United States of America on its implementation of the 1966 International Covenant on Civil and Political Rights, the Human Rights Committee "regrets the extent of the State party's reservations, declarations and understandings to the Covenant. It believes that, taken together, they intended to ensure that the United States has accepted only what is already the law of the United States. The Committee is also particularly concerned at reservations to article 6, paragraph 5, and article 7 of the Covenant, which it believes to be incompatible with the object and purpose of the Covenant" (*Official Records of the General Assembly, Fiftieth Session, Supplement No. 40* (see footnote 165 above), para. 279). See the analyses by Schabas, "Invalid reservations...", *loc. cit.* (footnote 109 above), pp. 277–325; and J. McBride, *loc. cit.* (footnote 160 above), p. 172.

[261] See above paragraph (4) of the present commentary.

[262] See *Certain German interests in Polish Upper Silesia, Merits, Judgment No. 7, 25 May 1926, P.C.I.J., Series A, No. 7*, p. 19; see also Arbitration Commission of the Conference on Yugoslavia, *Opinion No. 1 of 29 November 1991*, reproduced in ILM, vol. 31 (1992), p. 1494. The principle is confirmed in article 4 of the articles on responsibility of States for internationally wrongful acts adopted by the Commission at its fifty-third session, in 2001, *Yearbook ... 2001*, vol. II (Part Two) and corrigendum, pp. 40–42.

[263] *Yearbook ... 2004*, vol. II (Part Two), p. 48 (draft articles on responsibility of international organizations, art. 4, para. 4).

[264] See, for example, article I of the Convention relating to a uniform law on the formation of contracts for the international sale of goods (The Hague, 1 July 1964); article 1 of the European Convention providing a Uniform Law on Arbitration (Strasbourg, 20 January 1966); or articles 1 and 2 of the International Convention against the taking of hostages (New York, 17 December 1979).

practical importance for States.[265] The Commission in fact considers that reservations to provisions of this type would not be valid if they had the effect of hindering the effective implementation of the treaty.

3.1.12   *Reservations to general human rights treaties*

To assess the compatibility of a reservation with the object and purpose of a general treaty for the protection of human rights, account shall be taken of the indivisibility, interdependence and interrelatedness of the rights set out in the treaty as well as the importance that the right or provision which is the subject of the reservation has within the general thrust of the treaty, and the gravity of the impact the reservation has upon it.

Commentary

(1)   It is in the area of human rights that the most reservations have been made and the liveliest debates on their validity have taken place. Whenever necessary, the Commission has drawn attention to specific problems that could arise.[266] It was nonetheless deemed useful to have a specific draft guideline dealing with reservations made to general treaties such as the European, Inter-American and African conventions or the International Covenant on Economic, Social and Cultural Rights and the International Covenant on Civil and Political Rights.[267]

(2)   In the case of the latter, the Human Rights Committee stated in its General Comment No. 24 that:

> In an instrument which articulates very many civil and political rights, each of the many articles, and indeed their interplay, secures the objectives of the Covenant. The object and purpose of the Covenant is to create legally binding standards for human rights by defining certain civil and political rights and placing them in a framework of obligations which are legally binding for those States which ratify; and to provide an efficacious supervisory machinery for the obligations undertaken.[268]

Taken literally, this position would render invalid any general reservation bearing on any one of the rights protected by the Covenant.[269] That is not, however, the

position of States parties which have not systematically formulated objections to reservations of this type,[270] and the Committee itself does not go that far because, in the paragraphs following the statement of its position of principle, it sets out in greater detail the criteria it uses to assess whether reservations are compatible with the object and purpose of the Covenant:[271] it does not follow that, by its very nature, a general reservation bearing on one of the protected rights would be invalid as such.

(3)   Likewise, in the case of the 1989 Convention on the rights of the child, a great many reservations have been made to the provisions concerning adoption.[272] As has been noted, "[i]t would be difficult to conclude that this issue is so fundamental to the Convention as to render such reservations contrary to its object and purpose".[273]

(4)   In contrast with treaties relating to a particular human right, such as the conventions on torture or racial discrimination, the object and purpose of general human rights treaties is a complex matter. These treaties cover a wide range of human rights and are characterized by the global nature of the rights that they are intended to protect. Nevertheless, some of the protected rights may be more essential than others;[274] moreover, even in the case of essential rights, one cannot preclude the validity of a reservation dealing with certain limited aspects of the implementation of the right in question. In this respect reservations to general human rights treaties pose similar problems to reservations to provisions relating to non-derogable rights.[275]

---

[265] See above paragraph (15) of the commentary to draft guideline 3.1.5.

[266] With regard to guidelines on the permissibility of reservations, see in particular paragraphs (8) and (9) of the commentary to draft guideline 3.1.7 (Vague or general reservations), paragraphs (8) and (9) of the commentary to draft guideline 3.1.8 (Reservations to a provision reflecting a customary norm) or paragraph (4) of the commentary to draft guideline 3.1.9 (Reservations contrary to a rule of *jus cogens*) and the commentary to draft guideline 3.1.10 (*Reservations to provisions relating to non-derogable rights*), *passim*.

[267] These treaties are not the only ones covered by this draft guideline: a treaty such as the 1989 Convention on the rights of the child also seeks to protect a very wide range of rights. See also the 1979 International Convention on the Elimination of All Forms of Discrimination against Women or the 1990 International Convention on the Protection of the Rights of All Migrant Workers and Members of their Families.

[268] *Official Records of the General Assembly, Fiftieth Session, Supplement No. 40* (see footnote 165 above), para. 7. See the final working paper submitted in 2004 by Ms. Françoise Hampson on reservations to human rights treaties (footnote 190 above), para. 50.

[269] Some authors have maintained that the reservations regime is completely incompatible with human rights. See P.-H. Imbert, who does not share this radical view, "La question des réserves et les conventions en matière de droits de l'homme", *Actes du cinquième colloque international sur la Convention européenne des droits de l'homme,*

organisé conjointement par le Gouvernement de la République fédérale d'Allemagne et le secrétariat général du Conseil de l'Europe (Francfort, 9–12 avril 1980), Paris, Pedone, 1982, p. 99 (also in English: "Reservations and human rights conventions", *The Human Rights Review*, vol. 6, No. 1 (1981), p. 28) or *Les réserves aux traités multilatéraux, op. cit.* (footnote 173 above), p. 249. See also Coccia, *loc. cit.* (footnote 182 above), p. 16, or R. P. Anand, "Reservations to multilateral conventions", *The Indian Journal of International Law*, vol. 1, No. 1 (July 1960), p. 88; see also the commentaries on Human Rights Committee General Comment No. 24 (see footnote 165 above), by E. A. Baylis, "General Comment 24: confronting the problem of reservations to human rights treaties", *Berkeley Journal of International Law*, vol. 17 (1999), pp. 277–329; Redgwell, "Reservations to treaties...", *loc. cit.* (footnote 242 above), pp. 390–412; R. Higgins, "Introduction", in Gardner (ed.), *op. cit.* (footnote 89 above), pp. xvii–xxix; or K. Korkelia, "New challenges to the regime of reservations under the International Covenant on Civil and Political Rights", *European Journal of International Law*, vol. 13, No. 2 (2002), pp. 437–477.

[270] See, for example, the reservation of Malta to article 13 (on the conditions for the expulsion of aliens), to which no objection has been entered (see *Multilateral Treaties Deposited with the Secretary-General*, vol. I (see footnote 141 above), pp. 182–183 (chap. IV.4)). See also the reservation by Barbados to article 14, paragraph 3, or the reservation by Belize to the same provision (*ibid.*, p. 179); or the reservation by Mauritius to article 22 of the Convention on the rights of the child (*ibid.*, p. 326 (chap. IV.11)).

[271] General Comment No. 24 (see footnote 165 above); these criteria, beyond that of the compatibility of a reservation with the object and purpose of the Covenant, have to do with the customary, peremptory or non-derogable nature of the norm in question; see above draft guidelines 3.1.8–3.1.10.

[272] Articles 20 and 21; see *Multilateral Treaties Deposited with the Secretary-General*, vol. I (see footnote 141 above), pp. 321–335 (chap. IV.11).

[273] Schabas, "Reservations to the Convention on the rights of the child", *loc. cit.* (footnote 108 above), p. 480.

[274] See above paragraph (3) of the present commentary.

[275] See above draft guideline 3.1.10, and in particular paragraphs (4) to (8) of the commentary thereto.

(5) Draft guideline 3.1.12 attempts to strike a particularly delicate balance between these different considerations by combining three elements:

– "the indivisibility, interdependence and interrelatedness of the rights set out in the treaty";

– "the importance that the right or provision which is the subject of the reservation has within the general thrust of the treaty"; and

– "the gravity of the impact the reservation has upon it".

(6) The wording of the first element is taken from paragraph 5 of the Vienna Declaration and Programme of Action, adopted by the 1993 World Conference on Human Rights. It emphasizes the global nature of the protection afforded by general human rights treaties and is intended to prevent their dismantling.[276]

(7) The second element qualifies the previous one by recognizing—in keeping with practice—that certain rights protected by these instruments are no less important than other rights—and, in particular, non-derogable ones.[277] The wording used signals that the assessment must take into account both the rights concerned (substantive approach) and the provision of the treaty in question (formal approach), since it has been noted that one and the same right may be the subject of several provisions. As for the expression "general thrust of the treaty", it is taken up in draft guideline 3.1.5.[278]

(8) Lastly, the reference to "the gravity of the impact the reservation has upon" the right or the provision with respect to which it was made indicates that even in the case of essential rights, reservations are possible if they do not preclude protection of the rights in question and do not have the effect of excessively modifying their legal regime.

3.1.13 Reservations to treaty provisions concerning dispute settlement or the monitoring of the implementation of the treaty

A reservation to a treaty provision concerning dispute settlement or the monitoring of the implementation of the treaty is not, in itself, incompatible with the object and purpose of the treaty, unless:

(a) the reservation purports to exclude or modify the legal effect of a provision of the treaty essential to its raison d'être; or

(b) the reservation has the effect of excluding the reserving State or international organization from a dispute settlement or treaty implementation monitoring mechanism with respect to a treaty provision that it has previously accepted, if the very purpose of the treaty is to put such a mechanism into effect.

---

[276] Vienna Declaration and Programme of Action (A/CONF.157/24 (Part I), chap. III). This wording has since been regularly adopted—see in particular General Assembly resolutions on human rights, which systematically use the expression.

[277] See draft guideline 3.1.10 above.

[278] See in particular paragraph (14) (b) of the commentary to draft guideline 3.1.5 above.

Commentary

(1) In his first report on the law of treaties, Fitzmaurice categorically stated: "It is considered inadmissible that there should be parties to a treaty who are not bound by an obligation for the settlement of disputes arising under it, if this is binding on other parties."[279] His position, obviously inspired by the cold war debate on reservations to the Convention on the Prevention and Punishment of the Crime of Genocide, is too sweeping; moreover, it was rejected by the ICJ, which, in its orders of 2 June 1999 in response to Yugoslavia's requests for the indication of provisional measures against Spain and against the United States in the cases concerning *Legality of Use of Force*, clearly recognized the validity of the reservations made by those two States to article IX of the 1948 Convention on the Prevention and Punishment of the Crime of Genocide, which gives the Court jurisdiction to hear all disputes relating to the Convention,[280] even though some of the parties thought that such reservations were not compatible with the object and purpose of the Convention.[281]

(2) In its order on a request for the indication of provisional measures in the case concerning *Armed Activities on the Territory of the Congo (New Application: 2002)*, the ICJ came to the same conclusion with regard to the reservation of Rwanda to that same provision, stating that "that reservation does not bear on the substance of the law, but only on the Court's jurisdiction" and that "it therefore does not appear contrary to the object and purpose of the Convention".[282] It upheld that position in its judgment of 3 February 2006: in response to the Democratic Republic of the Congo, which had held that the Rwandan reservation to article IX of the Convention on the Prevention and Punishment of the Crime of Genocide "was invalid", after reaffirming the position it had taken in its advisory opinion of 28 May 1951 on *Reservations to the Convention on the Prevention and Punishment of the Crime of Genocide*,[283] according to which a reservation to that Convention would be permitted provided it was not incompatible with the object and purpose of the Convention, the Court concluded:

Rwanda's reservation to Article IX of the [Convention on the Prevention and Punishment of the Crime of Genocide] bears on the jurisdiction of the Court, and does not affect substantive obligations relating to acts of genocide themselves under that Convention. In the circumstances of the present case, the Court cannot conclude that the reservation of Rwanda in question, which is meant to exclude a particular method of settling a dispute relating to the interpretation,

---

[279] *Yearbook ... 1956*, vol. II, document A/CN.4/101, p. 127, para. 96; this was the purpose of draft article 37, paragraph 4, which the Special Rapporteur was proposing (*ibid.*, p. 115).

[280] See *Legality of Use of Force (Yugoslavia v. Spain), Provisional Measures, Order of 2 June 1999, I.C.J. Reports 1999*, p. 761, at p. 772, paras. 29–33, and *(Yugoslavia v. United States of America), ibid.*, p. 916, at pp. 923–924, paras. 21–25.

[281] See *Multilateral Treaties Deposited with the Secretary-General*, vol. I (see footnote 141 above), pp. 129–132 (chap. IV.1) (see in particular the clear objections to that effect of Brazil, China, Mexico and the Netherlands).

[282] *Armed Activities on the Territory of the Congo (New Application: 2002) (Democratic Republic of the Congo v. Rwanda), Provisional Measures, Order of 10 July 2002, I.C.J. Reports 2002*, p. 219, at p. 246, para. 72.

[283] See *I.C.J. Reports 1951*, p. 15.

application or fulfilment of the Convention, is to be regarded as being incompatible with the object and purpose of the Convention.[284]

The ICJ, confirming its prior case law, thus gave effect to Rwanda's reservation to article IX of the Convention on the Prevention and Punishment of the Crime of Genocide. This conclusion is corroborated by the very common nature of such reservations and the erratic practice followed in the objections to them.[285]

(3)   In their joint separate opinion, however, several judges stated the view that the principle applied by the Court in its judgment might not be absolute in scope. They stressed that there might be situations where reservations to clauses concerning dispute settlement could be contrary to the treaty's object and purpose: it depended on the particular case.[286]

(4)   The Human Rights Committee, meanwhile, felt that reservations to the 1966 International Covenant on Civil and Political Rights relating to guarantees of its implementation and contained both in the Covenant itself and in the Optional Protocol thereto could be contrary to the object and purpose of those instruments:

These guarantees provide the necessary framework for securing the rights in the Covenant and are thus essential to its object and purpose. ... The Covenant ... envisages, for the better attainment of its stated objectives, a monitoring role for the Committee. Reservations that purport to evade that essential element in the design of the Covenant, which is ... directed to securing the enjoyment of the rights, are ... incompatible with its object and purpose. A State may not reserve the right not to present a report and have it considered by the Committee. The Committee's role under the Covenant, whether under article 40 or under the Optional Protocols, necessarily entails interpreting the provisions of the Covenant and the development of a jurisprudence. Accordingly, a reservation that rejects the Committee's competence to interpret the requirements of any provisions of the Covenant would also be contrary to the object and purpose of that treaty.[287]

---

[284] *Armed Activities on the Territory of the Congo (New Application: 2002) (Democratic Republic of the Congo v. Rwanda), Jurisdiction and Admissibility, Judgment of 3 February 2006* (see footnote 99 above), para. 67.

[285] See in this connection Riquelme Cortado, *op. cit.* (footnote 147 above), pp. 192–202. As it happens, objections to reservations to dispute settlement clauses are rare. Apart from the objections raised to reservations to article IX of the Convention on the Prevention and Punishment of the Crime of Genocide, however, see the objections formulated by several States to the reservations to article 66 of the 1969 Vienna Convention, in particular the objections of Germany, Canada, Egypt, the United States of America (which argued that the reservation of the Syrian Arab Republic "is incompatible with the object and purpose of the Convention and undermines the principle of impartial settlement of disputes concerning the invalidity, termination, and suspension of the operation of treaties, which was the subject of extensive negotiation at the Vienna Conference" (*Multilateral Treaties Deposited with the Secretary-General*, vol. II (see footnote 142 above), p. 385 (chap. XXIII.1)), Japan, New Zealand, the Netherlands ("provisions regarding the settlement of disputes, as laid down in Article 66 of the Convention, are an important part of the Convention and ... cannot be separated from the substantive rules with which they are connected" (*ibid.*, p. 382)), the United Kingdom ("These provisions are inextricably linked with the provisions of Part V to which they relate. Their inclusion was the basis on which those parts of Part V which represent progressive development of international law were accepted by the Vienna Conference." (*ibid.*, p. 384)) and Sweden (espousing essentially the same position as the United Kingdom (*ibid.*, p. 383)).

[286] Joint separate opinion of Judges Higgins, Kooijmans, Elaraby, Owada and Simma to the judgment of 3 February 2006 referred to in footnote 284 above, para. 21.

[287] *Official Records of the General Assembly, Fiftieth Session, Supplement No. 40* (see footnote 165 above), para. 11; see also the final working paper submitted in 2004 by Ms. Françoise Hampson on reservations to human rights treaties (footnote 190 above), para. 55.

With respect to the Optional Protocol, the Committee adds:

A reservation cannot be made to the Covenant through the vehicle of the Optional Protocol but such a reservation would operate to ensure that the State's compliance with the obligation may not be tested by the Committee under the first Optional Protocol. And because the object and purpose of the first Optional Protocol is to allow the rights obligatory for a State under the Covenant to be tested before the Committee, a reservation that seeks to preclude this would be contrary to the object and purpose of the first Optional Protocol, even if not of the Covenant. A reservation to a substantive obligation made for the first time under the first Optional Protocol would seem to reflect an intention by the State concerned to prevent the Committee from expressing its views relating to a particular article of the Covenant in an individual case.[288]

Based on this reasoning, the Human Rights Committee, in the *Rawle Kennedy* case, held that a reservation made by Trinidad and Tobago excluding the Committee's competence to consider communications relating to a prisoner under sentence of death was not valid.[289]

(5)   The European Court of Human Rights, in the *Loizidou* case, concluded from an analysis of the object and purpose of the European Convention on Human Rights "that States could not qualify their acceptance of the optional clauses thereby effectively excluding areas of their law and practice within their 'jurisdiction' from supervision by the Convention institutions"[290] and that any restriction of its competence *ratione loci* or *ratione materiae* was incompatible with the nature of the Convention.[291]

(6)   This body of case law led the Commission to:

(*a*)   recall that the formulation of reservations to treaty provisions concerning dispute settlement or the monitoring of the implementation of the treaty is not in itself precluded; this is the purpose of the "*chapeau*" of draft guideline 3.1.13;

(*b*)   unless the regulation or monitoring in question is the purpose of the treaty instrument to which a reservation is being made; and

---

[288] *Official Records of the General Assembly, Fiftieth Session, Supplement No. 40* (see footnote 165 above), para. 13. In the following paragraph, the Committee "considers that reservations relating to the required procedures under the first Optional Protocol would not be compatible with its object and purpose".

[289] Communication No. 845/1999, *Rawle Kennedy* v. *Trinidad and Tobago*, Report of the Human Rights Committee, *Official Records of the General Assembly, Fifty-fifth Session, Supplement No. 40* (A/55/40), vol. II, Annex XI.A, para. 6.7. To justify its reservation Trinidad and Tobago argued that it accepted "the principle that States cannot use the Optional Protocol as a vehicle to enter reservations to the International Covenant on Civil and Political Rights itself, [but it] stresses that its Reservation to the Optional Protocol in no way detracts from its obligations and engagements under the Covenant" (*Multilateral Treaties Deposited with the Secretary-General*, vol. I (see footnote 141 above), p. 234 (chap. IV.5)). Seven States reacted with objections to the reservation, before Trinidad and Tobago finally denounced the Protocol as a whole (*ibid.*, pp. 236–237, note 3).

[290] *Loizidou* v. *Turkey* (see footnote 115 above), p. 28, para. 77.

[291] *Ibid.*, paras. 70–89; see in particular paragraph 79. See also the decision of 4 July 2001 of the Grand Chamber on the admissibility of Application no. 48787/99 in the case of *Ilie Ilaşcu* et al. v. *Moldova and the Russian Federation*, p. 20, or the judgment of the Grand Chamber of 8 April 2004 in the case of *Assanidze* v. *Georgia* (Application no. 71503/01), para. 140.

(*c*) nevertheless indicate that a State or an international organization cannot minimize its substantial prior treaty obligations by formulating a reservation to a treaty provision concerning dispute settlement or the monitoring of the implementation of the treaty at the time it accepts the provision.

(7) Although some members have disagreed, the Commission felt that there was no reason to draw a distinction between these two types of provisions: even if their purposes are somewhat different,[292] the reservations that can be formulated to both types give rise to the same type of problems, and splitting them into two separate draft guidelines would have entailed setting out the same rules twice.

---

[292] In part simply because the (non-binding) settlement of disputes could be one of the functions of a treaty monitoring body and could be part of its overall task of monitoring.

Chapter V

SHARED NATURAL RESOURCES

A. Introduction

155. The Commission, at its fifty-fourth session (2002), decided to include the topic "Shared natural resources" in its programme of work and appointed Mr. Chusei Yamada as Special Rapporteur.[293] A Working Group was also established to assist the Special Rapporteur in sketching out the general orientation of the topic in the light of the syllabus prepared in 2000.[294] The Special Rapporteur indicated his intention to deal with confined transboundary groundwaters, oil and gas in the context of the topic and proposed a step-by-step approach beginning with groundwaters.[295]

156. From its fifty-fifth (2003) to fifty-eighth (2006) sessions, the Commission received and considered three reports from the Special Rapporteur.[296] During this period, the Commission established three working groups: the first in 2004, chaired by the Special Rapporteur, assisted in furthering the Commission's consideration of the topic; the second in 2005, chaired by Mr. Enrique Candioti, reviewed and revised the 25 draft articles on the law of transboundary aquifers proposed by the Special Rapporteur in his third report taking into account the debate in the Commission; and the third in 2006, also chaired by Mr. Enrique Candioti, completed the review and revision of the draft articles submitted by the Special Rapporteur in his third report.

157. At its fifty-eighth session (2006), the Commission, following its consideration of the report of the Working Group containing 19 draft articles[297] and the report of the Drafting Committee, adopted on first reading the draft articles on the law of transboundary aquifers consisting of 19 draft articles,[298] together with commentaries thereto,[299] and decided, in accordance with articles 16 to 21 of its Statute, to transmit the draft articles, through the Secretary-General, to Governments for comments and

observations, with the request that such comments and observations be submitted to the Secretary-General by 1 January 2008.[300]

B. Consideration of the topic at the present session

158. At the present session, the Commission had before it the fourth report of the Special Rapporteur (A/CN.4/580), which was introduced by the Special Rapporteur at the 2921st meeting of the Commission, on 18 May 2007. On the same day, the Special Rapporteur gave an informal briefing intended particularly for new members of the Commission on the draft articles on the law of transboundary aquifers. The Commission considered the fourth report at its 2930th and 2931st meetings, on 4 and 5 June 2007, respectively.

159. At its 2920th meeting, on 16 May 2007, the Commission established a Working Group on shared natural resources, under the chairpersonship of Mr. Enrique Candioti, to assist the Special Rapporteur in considering a future work programme, taking into account the views expressed in the Commission. The Working Group held four meetings on 18 May, 4 and 5 June and 17 July 2007. At its 2947th meeting, on 3 August 2007, the Commission took note of the report of the Working Group (see section C, below). The Secretariat was also requested to circulate to Governments the questionnaire seeking information on State practice regarding oil and gas.

1. INTRODUCTION BY THE SPECIAL RAPPORTEUR OF HIS FOURTH REPORT

160. The Special Rapporteur recalled that the Commission at its session in 2006 completed, on first reading, the draft articles on the law of transboundary aquifers. Since written comments and observations of Governments were expected by 1 January 2008, the second reading of the draft articles would have to be deferred until the sixtieth session of the Commission in 2008. The fourth report therefore only addressed one particular aspect concerning the relationship between the work on transboundary aquifers and any future work on oil and gas. The Special Rapporteur proposed that the Commission should proceed with the second reading of the draft articles on the law of transboundary aquifers in 2008 and treat that subject independently of any future work by the Commission on oil and gas. The looming prospect of a water crisis that would affect hundreds of millions of people, particularly in the developing world, required an urgent formulation of an international legal framework for reasonable and equitable management of water resources, international cooperation, as well as settlement of disputes.

---

[293] *Yearbook ... 2002*, vol. II (Part Two), p. 100, paras. 518–519. The General Assembly, in paragraph 2 of resolution 57/21 of 19 November 2002, took note of the Commission's decision to include the topic "Shared natural resources" in its programme of work. See also General Assembly resolution 55/152 of 12 December 2000.

[294] *Yearbook ... 2000*, vol. II (Part Two), Annex, p. 149.

[295] *Yearbook ... 2002*, vol. II (Part Two), pp. 101–102, para. 520.

[296] First report: *Yearbook ... 2003*, vol. II (Part One), document A/CN.4/533 and Add.1; second report: *Yearbook ... 2004*, vol. II (Part One), document A/CN.4/539 and Add.1; and third report: *Yearbook ... 2005*, vol. II (Part One), document A/CN.4/551 and Add.1.

[297] At the 2878th and 2879th meetings, on 18 and 19 May 2006. At the 2879th meeting, the Commission decided to refer the 19 draft articles to the Drafting Committee.

[298] At the 2885th meeting, on 9 June 2006.

[299] At the 2903rd, 2905th and 2906th meetings on 2, 3 and 4 August 2006, respectively. See the draft articles with the commentary thereto adopted by the Commission on first reading in *Yearbook ... 2006*, vol. II (Part Two), chap. VI, sect. C, pp. 91 *et seq.*

[300] See the 2885th and 2903rd meetings.

(a) Relationship between the work on groundwaters and that on oil and gas

161. The Special Rapporteur prefaced the discussion by addressing the similarities and dissimilarities between oil and gas on the one hand and aquifers on the other, from scientific and technical perspectives, as well as in the light of the political, economic and environmental aspects, noting that in the main, there existed a close similarity between the physical features of a non-recharging aquifer and the reservoir rock of oil and gas. On the whole, however, the differences pointed to the need for separate treatment. The Special Rapporteur highlighted the fact that freshwater was a life-supporting resource vital for the human being for which there existed no alternative resource. Freshwater was also (*a*) a vital resource for hygienic living of the human being; (*b*) indispensable for food production; and (*c*) an essential ingredient of natural ecosystems and organic life of the planet. These considerations necessitated a management policy of groundwaters that was to be different from that of oil and gas.

(b) Oil and gas

162. The Special Rapporteur reached the above conclusions by offering an overview of the opposing theories relating to the origin of oil and gas, their formation, the history of the modern oil industry and the impact of exploitation on the environment, primarily noting that the organic material source theory, in particular the *kerogen* origin theory, now prevailed over the earlier inorganic source theory. According to the *kerogen* theory, living organisms (animal and plant) that accumulated at the bottom of oceans and lakes, together with sediment, fossilized and formed material called "*kerogen*". With the combined effect of bacteria, geothermal heat and underground pressure, *kerogen* turns into petroleum and residual water. This process of formation and accumulation of hydrocarbons occurred over long periods stretching over hundreds of millions of years. Although such processes were continuing, any current recharge of hydrocarbons in existing oil fields was negligible for practical purposes. Accordingly, oil and natural gas should be considered a non-renewable resource.

163. Underground pressure forced the petroleum and water to move upward through rock formations until such petroleum and water were stored in pores of reservoir rock. The reservoir rock was a geological formation, which usually consisted of sand, sandstone or various kinds of limestone. The reservoir rock was usually of marine origin and the water was brine.[301] Petroleum and water were distributed within the reservoir rock vertically in the order of their densities: natural gas, in the upper zone, oil in the lower zone where both oil and natural gas existed, and water at the very bottom. The gas zone was not sharply separated from the oil zone. However, there was a transition zone between the oil and water zones, or between the gas and water zones, in the absence of oil. A cap rock overlaying the reservoir rock functioned as a seal that prevented further

upward movement of oil and natural gas and it only shot up when a well was drilled through the cap rock. As oil and natural gas often coexisted in the same reservoir rock, although they also existed singly, they should be treated as one resource for the purpose of any work of the Commission.

164. As for the history of the modern oil industry, it was not until 1859 that E. L. Drake successfully drilled the first oil well in Pennsylvania. Over the year, production had increased exponentially in almost every continent and on continental shelves.[302] It was now taking place within the jurisdiction of more than 70 States and reached millions of barrels per day.

165. In general, States or their political subdivisions retained the right to lease oil fields under their jurisdiction. In exceptional cases, oil and gas were treated as private property of the owner of the land above the reservoir rock. Petroleum was explored, produced and traded[303] by private oil companies or State enterprises. Activities of State enterprises in this context would be deemed to be of a commercial nature under current international law. As oil and natural gas were fluid, exploitation by one party may affect other parties in another jurisdiction sharing an oil field. However, information on this aspect was not readily available and extensive research would be required in the future.

166. As regards pollution affecting oil and natural gas stored in the reservoir rock itself, it seemed to be minimal. On the other hand, the exploitation of an oil field and transportation of petroleum had a risk of causing significant harm to the environment. Uses of petroleum as an energy source emitting large amounts of greenhouse effect gases were also a major contributing factor to global warming. Similarly, waste disposal of petrochemical products was a source of environmental concern.

(c) The draft articles on the law on transboundary aquifers adopted on first reading

167. The Special Rapporteur also informed the Commission that UNESCO, whose experts had assisted the Commission in the development of the draft articles on the law of transboundary aquifers, was organizing regional seminars, in association with regional organizations, to brief and sensitize Governments on the draft articles adopted on first reading with a view also to encouraging them to submit their comments on the text. Such meetings were planned for European States in Paris in May 2007, and for North American, Latin American and Caribbean States in Montreal, Canada, in September 2007. UNESCO was also seeking regional cooperating partners to organize sessions for Asian and African States. Arrangements were also made with the Asian–African Legal Consultative Organization for the Special Rapporteur to brief its session in Cape Town, South Africa, in July 2007 on the draft articles.

---

[301] It is worth noting in respect of groundwaters that submarine aquifers also exist.

[302] The survey and extraction of groundwaters is predominantly land-based.

[303] Compared to groundwaters, there are differences in ways in which oil and gas are internationally traded.

2. SUMMARY OF THE DEBATE

(a) *Relationship between the work on groundwaters and that on oil and gas*

168. In their comments, members of the Commission focused their particular attention on the relationship between the work on groundwaters and that on oil and gas. Members welcomed the report of the Special Rapporteur, which succinctly and starkly made a good case for the separate treatment of the law on transboundary groundwaters and issues concerning oil and gas and, on the whole, they agreed with the Special Rapporteur's overview of the similarities and dissimilarities and his recommendation that the Commission should proceed with and complete the second reading of the law of transboundary aquifers independently of any future work on oil and natural gas.

169. However, members expressed different views regarding whether and how the Commission should deal with oil and gas. Some members viewed it essential that the Commission take up the matter only once it had completed the second reading of the law of transboundary groundwaters, including deciding whether or not oil and gas should be considered at all. It was noted that the debate in the Sixth Committee on the matter during the sixty-first session (2006) appeared to be inconclusive as to the direction that the Commission should take and, bearing in mind the complexity of the subject, these members advocated a more cautious approach. In this connection, it was suggested that some additional preliminary research work, preferably with the assistance of the Secretariat, be carried out, on State practice, including on treaty practice, before taking a definitive position on whether the progressive development and codification of the law in the area was merited. It was pointed out in this regard that the Secretariat had already done some work in this field while preparing the *Handbook on the Delimitation of Maritime Boundaries*, which could be updated and tailored to assist the Commission in its work.[304]

170. Some other members recalled that the topic as originally conceived in the 2000 syllabus[305] already included the study of oil and gas, and that a step-by-step approach, beginning with groundwaters, was proposed by the Special Rapporteur. Some members stated that the General Assembly resolution had given a mandate to the Commission to deal with oil and gas, which was one part of the topic. As such, there was no further need to consider whether or not the Commission should take up the remaining part of the topic, irrespective of the final outcome of such an exercise. In this context, it was necessary that the Commission establish a clear timetable that would lead to the commencement of work on oil and gas as a matter of priority. While acknowledging that some delegations in

---

[304] *Handbook on the Delimitation of Maritime Boundaries* (United Nations publication, Sales No. E.01.V.2). See also *The Law of the Sea: Maritime Boundary Agreements, 1970–1984* (United Nations publication, Sales No. E.87.V.12); *1942–1969* (Sales No. E.91.V.11); and *1985–1991* (Sales No. E.92.V.2); and *The Law of the Sea: Current Developments in State Practice*, No. I (United Nations publication, Sales No. E.87.V.3); No. II (Sales No. E.89.V.7); No. III (Sales No. E.92.V.13); and No. IV (Sales No. E.95.V.10).

[305] *Yearbook ... 2000*, vol. II (Part Two), Annex, p. 149 (see footnote 294 above).

the Sixth Committee had expressed concern regarding the complexity of taking up oil and gas, the point was made that it was precisely because such resources would have a transboundary component, and *a fortiori* parts thereof would fall under the jurisdiction of another State, that guidelines would be useful to provide adequate protection of the resource in question and promote cooperation in inter-State relations. The sharing of the resource did not at all imply any qualification of the sovereignty of the State over the resources within its territory. Similarly, it was pointed out that the shared character of the resource was the essential criterion in the Commission's choice to deal with a particular resource within the context of the topic. Although oil and gas might not be vital to human life as were groundwaters, such resources were of strategic importance to States, and the search for energy resources was one of the pressing issues of contemporary times. An elaboration of a regime for their exploitation would provide legal clarity, and would help to foster peace and stability among States. There was State practice on which to proceed. Indeed, there were more agreements in this field than on groundwaters.

171. Yet some other members observed that while it may not be necessary to complete the consideration of groundwaters first before the Commission begins work on oil and gas, including through the conduct of background research work, it would still be necessary to bear in mind the possible impact that the two subjects may have on each other and such a relationship should not be rejected *a priori*.

172. While indeed the two subjects would be treated independently of each other some members noted that there were already certain aspects in the law relating to transboundary aquifers which may be relevant in respect of oil and gas, and that this was the case with regard to provisions on general principles, in particular concerning sovereignty, equitable and reasonable utilization, and the obligation not to cause significant harm, as well as the general obligation to cooperate, even though in some instances the content of the rule or obligation may not be same.

173. Some other members stressed the differences in the characteristics between groundwaters and oil and gas, noting in particular that States deal with oil and gas as an economic and industrial necessity. Accordingly, a different approach was called for; in particular, the principle of unitization for joint development was essential in developing the regime on oil and gas.

(b) *The draft articles on the law on transboundary aquifers adopted on first reading*

174. Members in general welcomed the completion by the Commission of the draft articles on the law of transboundary aquifers adopted on first reading, acknowledging also that the briefing by the Special Rapporteur during the current session helped to highlight the significance of the topic and its relevance in relations among States. They also looked forward to embarking on a second reading of the text once comments and observations from Governments were received. The work undertaken thus far was based on well-founded principles of international law and

had preserved a crucial balance that revolved around the permanent sovereignty of States over natural resources, their reasonable and equitable utilization, their preservation and protection, and the obligation not to cause significant harm. The work would also help in fostering cooperation among States.

175. Regarding the final form, some members favoured model principles, including in the form of a model convention for use bilaterally or regionally, taking into account specific needs of the States concerned, while some other members expressed preference for a framework convention. It was also pointed out that the two possibilities should not be considered to be exclusive of each other. Yet some members felt that it was premature to decide on the final form.

176. Some members also welcomed the initiative by UNESCO to organize regional meetings to sensitize Governments on the draft articles and expressed the hope that all regions will be able to benefit from such meetings. Despite the accomplishment of the Commission there was still much that needed to be done in terms of disseminating knowledge regarding the importance of groundwaters and their regulation.

3. Special Rapporteur's concluding remarks

177. The Special Rapporteur expressed his appreciation to members for their positive reaction to the recommendation that the Commission proceed with the second reading of the law of transboundary aquifers independently of issues concerning oil and gas. Although different views had been expressed on whether or not a decision had been made that oil and gas were part of the topic, the Special Rapporteur felt that there was a general recognition of the need to conduct preliminary studies on oil and gas, including a compilation of State practice.

C. Report of the Working Group

178. The Working Group decided to deal with three issues, namely (*a*) the substance of the draft articles on the law of transboundary aquifers adopted on first reading; (*b*) the final form that the draft articles should take; and (*c*) issues involved in the consideration of oil and gas.

179. The Working Group had before it informal papers circulated by the Special Rapporteur containing excerpts from the summary records of the debate on the topic "Shared national resources" in the Sixth Committee during the sixty-first session of the General Assembly, and excerpts of the topical summary on the topic "Shared natural resources" (A/CN.4/577 and Add.1–2, sect. A), as well as a preliminary bibliography on oil and gas prepared with the assistance of the Chairperson of the Working Group. The Working Group held four meetings, on 18 May, 4 and 5 June and 17 July 2007.

180. The Working Group was mindful of the fact that the draft articles on the law of transboundary aquifers adopted on first reading had already been submitted to Governments for their comments and observations, including on the final form. Accordingly, the comments made in the Working Group were informal in character

and only intended to facilitate the Special Rapporteur's work in the preparation of his fifth report, as part of a brainstorming exercise, and did not prejudge or prejudice any further analysis and discussion to be made during the second reading of the draft articles, taking into account the comments and observations of Governments. Some members indicated the importance of maintaining the balance achieved in the first reading text, in particular with respect to draft articles 1 (Scope) and 14 (Planned activities). Some other members made comments or sought specific clarifications regarding the draft articles, in particular with respect to draft articles 1 (Scope), 2 (Use of terms), 3 (Sovereignty of aquifer States), 4 (Equitable and reasonable utilization), 5 (Factors relevant to equitable and reasonable utilization), 7 (General obligation to cooperate), 8 (Regular exchange of data and information), 11 (Prevention, reduction and control of pollution), 14 (Planned activities) and 19 (Bilateral and regional agreements and arrangements). Still other members preferred to make their comments at the appropriate time during the consideration of the second reading of the draft articles. The Special Rapporteur responded to the questions posed and took note of the comments made.

181. It was recalled that the Commission makes a recommendation on the final form to the General Assembly at the conclusion of a second reading. Since the final form would have a bearing on the substance of the text, including on issues relating to the relationship between any future binding instrument and existing bilateral agreements or arrangements, as well as concerning dispute settlement, it was noted that an early exchange of views on the matter would assist the Special Rapporteur in the preparation of his fifth report. While members expressed views on the different possibilities, including preference for either a non-binding instrument in the form of a declaration of principles or a binding format by way of a framework convention, the Working Group refrained from taking any definitive position on the final form. Some members also stressed the importance of the normative formulation of the draft articles adopted on first reading.

182. Regarding issues involved in the consideration of transboundary oil and gas resources, a suggestion was made that the Secretariat prepare a survey of State practice on oil and gas. Such a survey would assist the Commission in sketching out the future treatment of that part of the topic. Following a discussion on the various options, the Working Group agreed as a first step to prepare a questionnaire on State practice for circulation to Governments. Such a questionnaire would, *inter alia*, seek to determine whether there were any agreements, arrangements or practice regarding the exploration and exploitation of transboundary oil and gas resources or for any other cooperation for such oil or gas, including, as appropriate, maritime boundary delimitation agreements as well as unitization and joint development agreements or other arrangements; the content of such agreements or arrangements or a description of the practice; as well as any further comments or information, including legislation, judicial decisions, which Governments may consider to be relevant or useful to the Commission in the consideration of issues regarding oil and gas.

183.　Some members were of the view that the assistance of the Secretariat would subsequently be necessary for analysis of the State practice. It was also suggested that the Secretariat assist in the identification of expertise within the United Nations system to provide, at the appropriate time, the scientific and technical background information in the elaboration of the subject, as was done with the draft articles on law of transboundary aquifers.

Chapter VI

EXPULSION OF ALIENS

A. Introduction

184. The Commission at its fiftieth session (1998) took note of the report of the Planning Group identifying, *inter alia*, the topic of "Expulsion of aliens" for possible inclusion in the Commission's long-term programme of work,[306] which was subsequently done at the fifty-second session (2000).[307] A brief syllabus describing the possible overall structure of and approach to the topic was annexed to the report of the Commission to the General Assembly on the work of that session.[308] In paragraph 8 of resolution 55/152 of 12 December 2000, the General Assembly took note of the topic's inclusion in the long-term programme of work.

185. At its fifty-sixth session, the Commission decided, at its 2830th meeting, on 6 August 2004, to include the topic "Expulsion of aliens" in its current programme of work, and to appoint Mr. Maurice Kamto as Special Rapporteur for the topic.[309] The General Assembly, in paragraph 5 of its resolution 59/41 of 2 December 2004, endorsed the decision of the Commission to include the topic in its agenda.

186. At its fifty-seventh session (2005), the Commission considered, at its 2849th to 2852nd meetings,[310] the preliminary report of the Special Rapporteur.[311]

187. At its fifty-eighth session (2006), the Commission had before it the second report of the Special Rapporteur[312] and a study prepared by the Secretariat.[313] At that session, the Commission decided to consider the second report at its next session, in 2007.[314]

B. Consideration of the topic at the present session

188. At the present session, the Commission had before it the second and third reports of the Special Rapporteur (A/CN.4/581), which it considered at its 2923rd to 2926th meetings, from 23 to 29 May 2007, and at its 2941st to 2944th meetings, from 24 to 27 July 2007, respectively. At its 2926th meeting, held on 29 May 2007, the Commission decided to refer to the Drafting Committee draft articles 1 and 2, as revised by the Special Rapporteur at that

meeting.[315] At its 2944th meeting, held on 27 July 2007, the Commission decided to refer to the Drafting Committee draft articles 3 to 7.

1. INTRODUCTION BY THE SPECIAL RAPPORTEUR OF HIS SECOND AND THIRD REPORTS

189. The Special Rapporteur recalled that the Commission had endorsed most of the Special Rapporteur's choices and, broadly speaking, the draft work plan contained in Annex I to the preliminary report.[316] The States that had spoken at the 2005 session of the Sixth Committee of the General Assembly had expressed support for the general approach proposed by the Special Rapporteur, emphasizing the interest, urgency and complexity of the topic.

190. The topic indisputably lent itself to codification, given the existence of a body of customary rules, numerous treaties, long-standing doctrine and well-established, albeit relatively recent, international and regional jurisprudence. The study of the topic by the Commission was all the more urgent in the light of the increasing tendency among States to carry out expulsions without observing fundamental human rights norms, notably in the context of efforts to combat terrorism and in the face of the rising phenomenon of illegal immigration and refugee flows.

191. The second report,[317] which embarked on a study of the general rules on expulsion of aliens, addressed the scope of the topic and the definition of its constituent elements, and proposed two draft articles (draft articles 1 and 2).

192. There had appeared to be a consensus, both in the Commission and in the Sixth Committee, that the topic should cover persons residing in the territory of a State of which they did not have nationality, with a distinction being made between persons in a regular situation and those in an irregular situation, including those who had been residing for a long time in the expelling State. Refugees, asylum seekers, stateless persons and migrant workers should also be included. On the other hand, some members and delegations had expressed doubt as to whether the topic should include denial of admission with regard to illegal immigrants, the situation of persons who had changed nationality following a change in the status of the territory where they were resident in the context of decolonization, and the situation of nationals of a State in a situation of armed conflict. In the opinion of the Special

---

[306] *Yearbook ... 1998*, vol. II (Part Two), pp. 110–111, para. 554.

[307] *Yearbook ... 2000*, vol. II (Part Two), p. 131, para. 729.

[308] *Ibid.*, Annex, p. 142.

[309] *Yearbook ... 2004*, vol. II (Part Two), p. 120, para. 364.

[310] *Yearbook ... 2005*, vol. II (Part Two), pp. 54–58, paras. 242–274.

[311] *Yearbook ... 2005*, vol. II (Part One), document A/CN.4/554.

[312] *Yearbook ... 2006*, vol. II (Part One), document A/CN.4/573.

[313] A/CN.4/565 and Corr.1 (mimeographed; available on the Commission's website).

[314] *Yearbook ... 2006*, vol. II (Part Two), p. 185, para. 252.

[315] See footnotes 326 and 327 below.

[316] See footnote 311 above.

[317] See footnote 312 above.

Rapporteur, denial of admission and the situation of aliens entitled to privileges and immunities under international law should be excluded from the topic. According to draft article 1,[318] the topic should include aliens with regular or irregular status, refugees, asylum seekers, stateless persons, migrant workers, nationals of an enemy State and nationals of the expelling State who had lost their nationality or been deprived of it.

193. With regard to the definition of the terms used, which was dealt with in draft article 2,[319] the Special Rapporteur proposed that the concept of "alien" should be defined in opposition to that of "*ressortissant*", rather than that of "national". Despite the variable senses in which the term "*ressortissant*" was used, it could be assigned a broader meaning than that of "national" in order also to cover persons subject to the authority of a State as the result of a particular legal connection, such as refugees, asylum-seekers, stateless persons or persons affiliated with territories under a mandate or protectorate. If necessary, draft article 2, paragraph 2 (*d*), could be reformulated to make nationality the main legal bond in this context.[320]

194. In the preliminary report, the term "expulsion" denoted a unilateral act by which a State compelled an alien to leave its territory. Nevertheless, taking into account the comments made by certain members as well as recent international case law, the Special Rapporteur had come to the conclusion that "expulsion" also covered cases where a State, by its conduct, compelled an individual to leave its territory.

195. Since expulsion involved leaving the territory of a State by crossing a frontier, draft article 2 also proposed a definition of the terms "frontier" and "territory".

---

[318] Draft article 1 reads as follows:

"*Scope*

"1. The present draft articles shall apply to any person who is present in a State of which he or she is not a national (*ressortissant*).

"2. They shall apply, in particular, to aliens who are present in the host country, lawfully or with irregular status, to refugees, asylum seekers, stateless persons, migrant workers, nationals (*ressortissants*) of an enemy State and nationals (*ressortissants*) of the expelling State who have lost their nationality or been deprived of it."

[319] Draft article 2 reads as follows:

"*Definitions*

"For the purposes of the draft articles:

"1. The expulsion of an alien means the act or conduct by which an expelling State compels a *ressortissant* of another State to leave its territory.

"2. (*a*) An alien means a *ressortissant* of a State other than the territorial or expelling State:

(*b*) Expulsion means an act or conduct by which the expelling State compels an alien to leave its territory;

(*c*) Frontier means the zone at the limits of the territory of an expelling State in which the alien no longer enjoys resident status and beyond which the national expulsion procedure is completed;

(*d*) *Ressortissant* means any person who, by any legal bond including nationality, comes under [the jurisdiction] [the personal jurisdiction] of a State;

(*e*) Territory means the domain in which the State exercises all the powers deriving from its sovereignty.

[320] The Special Rapporteur proposed the following alternative formulation: "Any person who has the nationality of a State or who, by any other legal bond, comes under [the personal jurisdiction] [the jurisdiction] of a State."

196. The third report initiated consideration of the general principles relating to the expulsion of aliens, proposing five draft articles (draft articles 3 to 7). A State's right to expel aliens was presented as a right inherent in State sovereignty, deriving from the territorial competence of each State, rather than a customary right conferred on a State by an "external" rule. However, this right was subject to limits, among which a distinction should be drawn between limits inherent in the international legal order (covered by draft article 3)[321] which exist independently of other constraints relating to special areas of international law, and limits deriving from international human rights law. Draft articles 4 to 7 related to the limits *ratione personae* of the right of expulsion.

197. A first limit, which was set out in draft article 4,[322] was the prohibition of expulsion by a State of its own nationals. However, this prohibition, which is well established in contemporary general international law, was subject to certain exceptions or derogations, which were confirmed by practice. Yet the expulsion by a State of one of its nationals was always subject to the requirement of consent by a receiving State; it was nevertheless without prejudice to the right of the person expelled to return to his or her country at the request of the receiving State.

198. Draft articles 5[323] and 6[324] related to the situation of refugees and stateless persons respectively. They were designed to complement the rules set out in the

---

[321] Draft article 3 reads as follows:

"*Right of expulsion*

"1. A State has the right to expel an alien from its territory.

"2. However, expulsion must be carried out in compliance with the fundamental principles of international law. In particular, the State must act in good faith and in compliance with its international obligations."

[322] Draft article 4 reads as follows:

"*Non-expulsion by a State of its nationals*

"1. A State may not expel its own nationals.

"2. However, if, for exceptional reasons, it must take such action, it may do so only with the consent of a receiving State.

"3. A national expelled from his or her own country shall have the right to return to it at any time at the request of the receiving State."

[323] Draft article 5 reads as follows:

"*Non-expulsion of refugees*

"1. A State may not expel a refugee lawfully in its territory save on grounds of national security or public order [or terrorism], or if the person, having been convicted by a final judgement of a particularly serious crime or offence, constitutes a danger to the community of that State.

"2. The provisions of paragraph 1 of this article shall also apply to any person who, being in an unlawful situation in the territory of the receiving State, has applied for refugee status, unless the sole manifest purpose of such application is to thwart an expulsion order likely to be handed down against him or her [against such person]."

[324] Draft article 6 reads as follows:

"*Non-expulsion of stateless persons*

"1. A State may not expel a stateless person [lawfully] in its territory save on grounds of national security or public order [or terrorism], or if the person, having been convicted by a final judgment of a particularly serious crime or offence, constitutes a danger to the community of that State.

"2. A State which expels a stateless person under the conditions set forth in these draft articles shall allow such person a reasonable period within which to seek legal admission into another country. [However, if after this period it appears that the stateless person has not been able to obtain admission into a host country, the State may [, in agreement with the person,] expel the person to any State which agrees to host him or her]."

relevant provisions of the 1951 Convention relating to the Status of Refugees and the 1954 Convention relating to the Status of Stateless Persons. In the light of recent developments in efforts to combat terrorism, and also Security Council resolution 1373 (2001) of 28 September 2001, it was possible to explicitly refer to terrorist activities (as well as behaviour intended to facilitate such activities) among the grounds which could justify the expulsion of a refugee or stateless person, even if such activities could be covered by the general ground of expulsion based on "national security". Where stateless persons were concerned, it was perhaps desirable, in view of their special status, not to make the extent of their protection conditional on whether they were in a regular or irregular situation in the expelling State. Under the heading of progressive development, it was also possible to consider stipulating that the expelling State could be involved in the search for a receiving State in the event that the stateless person had not found one within a reasonable period of time.

199. Draft article 7[325] set out the principle of the prohibition of the collective expulsion of aliens, and for that purpose distinguished between collective expulsions in peacetime and those occurring in wartime.

200. The prohibition of collective expulsions in peacetime was absolute in nature and was confirmed by a variety of legal instruments, as well as the case law of regional human rights institutions. However, the expulsion of a group of persons whose cases had each been examined individually did not fall under this ban. In this regard, the first paragraph of draft article 7, which referred to the criterion of "reasonable and objective examination" of the particular case of each of the aliens concerned, drew on the relevant case law of the European Court of Human Rights.

201. The collective expulsion of the nationals (*ressortissants*) of an enemy State in wartime was not governed by either the international law of armed conflict or by international humanitarian law. Practice in this area was variable, and did not give rise either to a general obligation for States to keep the nationals of an enemy State on their territory, or to an obligation to expel them. However, practice and doctrine tended to show that the collective expulsion of the nationals of an enemy State should be confined to aliens who were hostile to the receiving State; in contrast, it would seem that the expulsion of nationals of an enemy State who were behaving peacefully should be prohibited, as the ordinary rules relating to expulsion in peacetime remained applicable to them.

---

[325] Draft article 7 reads as follows:

"*Prohibition of collective expulsion*

"1. The collective expulsion of aliens, including migrant workers and members of their family, is prohibited. However, a State may expel concomitantly the members of a group of aliens, provided that the expulsion measure is taken after and on the basis of a reasonable and objective examination of the particular case of each individual alien of the group.

"2. Collective expulsion means an act or behaviour by which a State compels a group of aliens to leave its territory.

"3. Foreign nationals of a State engaged in armed conflict shall not be subject to measures of collective expulsion unless, taken together as a group, they have demonstrated hostility towards the receiving State."

2. SUMMARY OF THE DEBATE

(a) *General comments and methodology*

202. The Special Rapporteur was commended on the quality and depth of his second and third reports. Great appreciation was also expressed for the analytical study prepared by the Secretariat, which constituted a very valuable tool for the Commission in addressing the topic.

203. Several members emphasized the importance, urgency and complexity of the topic, taking into account, in particular, the upsurge in the phenomenon of migration, including irregular migration, and the challenges posed by the fight against terrorism.

204. The view was expressed that expulsion of aliens was a topic more suited to political negotiation than to codification by an expert body. However, several members were of the opinion that the topic lent itself to codification, and it was asserted that codification could take the form of draft articles with a view to the adoption of an international convention.

205. Some members were of the view that all the existing rules in different areas, including treaty rules, should be examined in an effort to develop a general regime that would nevertheless preserve the special rules established by certain specific regimes. Others considered that it was not advisable to attempt to elaborate general rules on the issue and that the Commission should instead focus on defining the rules applicable to the various categories of aliens.

206. Several members expressed support for the general approach taken by the Special Rapporteur, emphasizing in particular the need to reconcile the right of a State to expel aliens with the relevant rules of international law, including those relating to the protection of human rights and to the minimum standards for the treatment of aliens. It was also asserted that the Commission should focus on the rights and obligations of States, and not only on the relationship between the expelling State and the expelled individual.

207. It was observed that the issue of expulsion of aliens was mainly governed by national laws, with States having an indisputable right to expel, subject to respect for the relevant rules of international law. Special attention must be given to national jurisprudence, which contributed to the development of certain criteria designed to prevent the arbitrary use of the right to expel. However, several members emphasized the role of the rules of customary international law in the establishment of limits to the right to expel.

(b) *Specific comments*

Article 1. Scope

208. Several members emphasized the need clearly to define the scope of the topic, which was not limited to the *ratione personae* aspect. The debate was concerned with removal measures and with the situations and persons to be covered. Some members suggested simplifying

draft article 1, paragraph 1, as proposed by the Special Rapporteur, by stating that the draft articles applied to the expulsion of aliens. A proposal was made to delete draft article 1, since draft article 2, which dealt with definitions, might suffice to delineate the parameters of the topic.

(i) *Removal measures and situations covered by the topic*

209. While several members supported excluding non-admission of aliens from the scope of the topic, certain members expressed a preference for its inclusion, *inter alia*, to take into account the interests of the situation of the numerous illegal immigrants who were detained for long periods. The view was expressed that the real problem that the Commission should address was not confined to expulsion but concerned more generally the means—including refusal of admission—by which States could control the presence of aliens in their territory. It was also suggested that the topic should include aliens applying for admission to a State while already in the international zone of that State. Furthermore, in some cases, refusal of admission could be incompatible with the principle of *non-refoulement*.

210. A number of members agreed that extradition should be excluded from the scope of the topic. However, it was suggested that the scenario of an expulsion constituting disguised extradition should be addressed. In addition, certain members objected to the Special Rapporteur's proposal to exclude from the scope of the topic extraordinary or extrajudicial transfer (or rendition), which raised serious problems in international law.

211. Conflicting opinions were expressed concerning the possible inclusion in the scope of the topic of expulsions carried out in situations of armed conflict. While some members were of the view that the Commission should deal with this issue, others considered that the Commission should exclude from the draft articles, if necessary by means of an explicit provision, an issue covered by well-established rules of the law of armed conflict, notably concerning expulsions in the context of military occupation. It was also proposed that a "without prejudice" clause should be included in respect of the rules of international humanitarian law.

212. It was suggested that the Commission should study the issue of ethnic cleansing aimed at aliens, as well as deprivation of nationality followed by expulsion, as its conformity with international law was questionable. It was considered necessary for the topic to cover the situation of persons who became aliens following the creation of a new State.

(ii) *Categories of persons covered by the topic*

213. Several members considered that the draft articles should apply to aliens physically present in the territory of the expelling State, whether legally or illegally. However, a legal regime governing expulsion must take account of the distinction between these two categories of aliens. It was also proposed that it should be specified that the draft articles applied only to natural persons, not to legal persons.

214. While some members emphasized the usefulness of draft article 1, paragraph 2, which contained a list of categories of aliens to be covered, others considered that this paragraph was unnecessary and that the examples cited should at the very most be included in the commentary. It was also suggested that paragraphs 1 and 2 of the draft article should be combined, deleting the words "in particular" in paragraph 2. Another view was that the current scope of the draft articles was too broad and that the Commission should limit its work to certain categories of aliens, which should be defined.

215. While certain members clearly supported excluding individuals entitled to privileges and immunities under international law from the scope of the topic, conflicting opinions were expressed concerning the possible inclusion of migrant workers. Some members suggested excluding refugees and stateless persons, since their status with regard to expulsion was well established and covered by a body of existing rules, including treaty rules. On the other hand, other members considered that refugees and stateless persons should be covered by the draft articles, at least insofar as there remained gaps or shortcomings in the rules applicable to these categories of persons. In this regard, it was suggested that the Commission should take into account the recommendations of the Executive Committee of the Programme of the United Nations High Commissioner for Refugees. It was also suggested that a "without prejudice" clause should be included in the draft articles in respect of the rules relating to refugees.

Article 2. Definitions

216. While certain members emphasized the importance of clarifying the key concepts of the topic at this stage and ensuring consistent use of the terms (including "expelling State", "receiving State" or "territorial State") in the draft articles, others were of the view that the Commission should advance with its work before deciding on definitions.

(i) *The concept of "alien"*

217. Several members questioned the Special Rapporteur's approach, which consisted in defining the concept of "alien" in opposition to that of "*ressortissant*", rather than that of "national". In particular, it was pointed out that the definition of "*ressortissant*" proposed by the Special Rapporteur was too broad and created confusion, and that the term in question could not be translated, for example, into English and Spanish; accordingly, the criterion of nationality alone should be used. Likewise, certain members proposed amending the language of draft article 2, paragraph 2 (*a*), by defining "alien" as a person who was not a national of the expelling State, without making any reference to the ties the individual concerned might have with another State. It was also suggested that the Commission should look into the issue of dual nationality in the light of the rule whereby expulsion of nationals ought to be prohibited; in addition, it should be specified that the definition of "aliens" included stateless persons.

218. It was observed that certain categories of aliens, such as "refugees", "asylum seekers" and "migrant workers", needed to be defined. It was suggested that a broad definition should be retained for the term "refugee", taking into account recent developments that had affected this concept.

(ii) *The concept of "expulsion"*

219. Several members agreed with the Special Rapporteur's broad definition of the concept of "expulsion", contained in draft article 2, paragraph 2 (*b*), which was based on the element of "compulsion", exercised by means of a legal act or conduct by the expelling State. However, it was considered necessary to indicate that this definition did not cover extradition (with the possible exception of an expulsion constituting a disguised form of extradition). In addition, the need to elaborate criteria for determining whether the conduct of a State should be qualified as expulsion was emphasized. In this vein, it was suggested that the draft articles should specify that the said conduct must involve compulsion that left the alien no option but to leave the territory of the State. Another view was that expulsion should be defined as an "act", "conduct" by the State being relevant mainly in the context of responsibility for an internationally wrongful act. The view was also expressed that a definition should be devised covering the entire process of effecting the expulsion of an alien.

(iii) *The concepts of "territory" and "frontier"*

220. Certain reservations were expressed concerning the definitions contained in draft article 2, paragraphs 2 (*c*) and 2 (*e*). In addition, it was asserted that the Commission should consider the legal implications of the presence of an alien in the territorial sea, internal waters or archipelagic waters of a State.

221. Doubts were expressed as to the relevance of the concept of "residence", alluded to in draft article 2, paragraph 2 (*c*), in defining State frontiers. It was emphasized that, in airport zones, States must respect all their international obligations, including the right to consular assistance. In addition, certain members were of the view that a proper definition of the concept of "territory" would make it unnecessary to define the term "frontier".

Article 3. Right of expulsion

222. A number of members considered that draft article 3 established a fair balance between the right of the State to expel aliens and the guarantees which should be granted to expellees. Others considered that draft article 3 suffered from the defect of omitting any direct reference to the rights of the expellee and reflected a questionable approach whereby only the rules considered by the Special Rapporteur as inherent in the international legal order because they derived from sovereignty placed limits on the right of expulsion, as opposed to other rules—such as those relating to human rights—which limited only its exercise. A preference was also expressed for recognition that the right of expulsion was not "inherent", in the words of the Special Rapporteur, but customary in nature.

223. Several members endorsed draft article 3, paragraph 1, which set out the right of a State to expel an alien. However, some members suggested combining paragraphs 1 and 2, adding to the present paragraph 1 a reference to the limits imposed by international law on the right of expulsion, including those stemming from the international protection of human rights.

224. It was pointed out that in its present form, paragraph 2 of draft article 3 was either unnecessary or incomplete. One view was that it was preferable to stipulate that the right to expel aliens was subject to the provisions of the present draft articles and to the special obligations arising from the treaties by which the expelling State was bound, while other members were of the view that a reference to the obligation to respect international law could suffice. Some members considered that the reference to the "fundamental principles of international law" was too narrow. It was also suggested that a reference should be included to *jus cogens* as well as to certain rules specific to expulsion, such as those set out in article 13 of the International Covenant on Civil and Political Rights.

225. Conflicting views were expressed on the need for an explicit reference to the principle of good faith. It was also stated that deciding on the content of paragraph 2, and in particular whether a reference to the provisions of the present draft articles could suffice, would depend on how exhaustive the articles were to be.

Article 4. Non-expulsion by a State of its nationals

226. A large number of members approved the inclusion in the draft articles of a provision relating to expulsion of nationals. However, it was suggested that draft article 4 should be deleted and the problem of expulsion of nationals addressed in the commentary on draft article 3. Others considered that only deprivation of nationality as a possible preliminary to expulsion fell within the framework of the present topic.

227. It was observed that the issue of the expulsion of persons having two or more nationalities should be studied in more detail and resolved within draft article 4, or in a separate draft article. In particular, it was necessary to consider whether the criterion of effectiveness ought to play a role. Others considered that it was not appropriate to address this topic in this context, especially if the Commission's intention was to help strengthen the rule prohibiting the expulsion of nationals. It was also observed that the issue of deprivation of nationality, which was sometimes used as a preliminary to expulsion, deserved thorough study. In that regard, it was suggested that steps of that kind should be prohibited. It was also suggested that a reference to "banning" should be included in draft article 4.

228. Several members supported the prohibition on the expulsion of nationals as set out in draft article 4, paragraph 1. It was also suggested that such protection should be extended to individuals deprived of their nationality and to certain categories of aliens who had particularly close ties with the expelling State.

229. Some members underlined the unconditional and absolute nature of the prohibition on the expulsion of nationals, in the light of various international instruments. In that context, it was suggested that paragraph 2 of draft article 4, which recognized the possibility of exceptions to the principle of non-expulsion, should be deleted. In particular, it was held that certain examples which the Special Rapporteur had cited in support of such exceptions were of purely historical interest, or involved cases of extradition rather than expulsion. Expulsion of nationals

could at best be justified, in extreme cases, in terms of a state of necessity. Another proposal was that paragraphs 2 and 3 should be modified so as to highlight the fact that extradition or exile imposed by a judicial authority as an alternative to prison were the only lawful measures by means of which nationals could be removed.

230.   It was suggested that the wording of the exceptions in paragraph 2 of draft article 4 should be tightened up and that the concept of "exceptional reasons" which could be used to justify the expulsion of a national should be clarified. The question was also raised of whether such reasons should not in any case be set out in the law.

231.   It was suggested that draft article 4 should include a reference to the procedural safeguards that should be granted to expelled individuals. Emphasis was also placed on the importance of acknowledging that expelled nationals had the right to return to their own country when the reasons which had led to their expulsion had ceased to exist, or when, as a result of the emergence of new elements, the expulsion was no longer justified.

232.   It was asked whether the issue of collective expulsion of nationals was covered in draft article 4. Moreover, it was necessary to clarify that that provision was without prejudice to the extradition of nationals, which was authorized under international law.

Article 5.   Non-expulsion of stateless persons

Article 6.   Non-expulsion of refugees

233.   While some members expressed opposition to draft articles on refugees and stateless persons which went beyond a reference to the 1951 Convention relating to the Status of Refugees and the 1954 Convention relating to the Status of Stateless Persons, other members were in favour, provided that the content of such draft articles did not give rise to contradictions with the treaty regimes currently in force. A briefing session by an expert from the Office of the United Nations High Commissioner for Refugees was also suggested.

234.   Several members were against the inclusion of an express reference to "terrorism" among the grounds for the expulsion of a refugee or stateless person. In that regard, it was stated that there was no universal definition of terrorism, that "national security" grounds already covered measures of expulsion on grounds of terrorism and that the problem was not one specific to refugees and stateless persons. Furthermore, expulsion on grounds of terrorism could give rise to problems in terms of the application of the principle of *aut dedere aut judicare*. Some Commission members, however, favoured a reference to terrorism as a ground for expulsion of refugees and stateless persons. In particular, it was suggested that terrorism should be included by linking it to the concept of "national security", or that of "*ordre public*", and that the commentary should note recent trends in State practice aimed at combating abuse of refugee status by terrorists. As an alternative, it was suggested that reference should be made to specific offences, such as those defined in widely accepted multilateral instruments intended to combat terrorism.

235.   With specific reference to refugees, the grounds for expulsion set out in draft article 5, paragraph 1, were said to be too broad; on this point, article 33 of the 1951 Convention relating to the Status of Refugees, which set forth the principle of *non-refoulement*, was more restrictive. Criticism was also voiced of the fact that only part of the rules contained in the Convention had been taken up, and of the Special Rapporteur's attempt to combine articles 32 and 33 of that Convention. Lastly, it was suggested that a reference should be included to the principle of *non-refoulement*, as well as to the situation of persons who were waiting to be granted refugee status or who had been denied such status, who should enjoy a degree of protection.

236.   Where stateless persons were concerned, some members opposed the Special Rapporteur's suggestion for a draft article which, in contrast to article 31 of the 1954 Convention relating to the Status of Stateless Persons, would protect both stateless persons who were in a regular situation and those who were in an irregular situation, so as to avoid creating potentially contradictory legal regimes. Others, on the other hand, said that even stateless persons in an irregular situation should be granted protection.

237.   Paragraph 2 of draft article 6, and in particular the reference to intervention by the host State in the search for a receiving State, was described as an important contribution to progressive development which was designed to fill a gap in the law.

Article 7.   Prohibition of collective expulsion

238.   Several members expressed support for the inclusion in the draft articles of a provision on collective expulsion. Others considered that the concept of "collective expulsion" was unclear and that it was therefore preferable to focus on the issue of discriminatory expulsions. It was also stated that the issue of collective expulsions in time of armed conflict should not be addressed in the present draft articles, since it fell under international humanitarian law.

239.   Several members expressed support for paragraph 1 of draft article 7, considering that the collective expulsion of aliens was prohibited by contemporary international law, at least in peacetime. Others considered that there was no universal rule prohibiting the collective expulsion of aliens, but only an emerging principle, based on regional practice, which recognized a prohibition subject to exceptions; in addition, the non-arbitrary expulsion of a group of persons was not unlawful as long as all the persons concerned enjoyed procedural safeguards.

240.   A number of members expressed agreement with the definition of "collective expulsion" set out in paragraph 2 of draft article 7. Some members considered, however, that the definition should be refined and that a number of issues remained open, such as the criteria underlying the definition of a "group" and the question of the number of persons expelled. On the latter point, it was stated that the key element was not quantitative but qualitative; in particular, it was important to know whether the expulsion was based on discriminatory grounds or whether each of the persons concerned had benefited from procedural safeguards.

241. One view was that it was not appropriate to draw a distinction between collective expulsions in peacetime and those carried out in wartime, as both were prohibited by the principal international legal instruments. In that context, it was suggested that paragraph 3 of draft article 7 should be deleted, or that it should set forth the right of each person, even in time of armed conflict, to have his or her case examined individually. Another view was that the proposed provision ran counter to the practice and present state of international law, which recognized the lawfulness of collective expulsions of enemy nationals in time of armed conflict.

242. It was contended that international humanitarian law did not contain a rule which prohibited expulsions of the nationals (*ressortissants*) of an enemy State in time of armed conflict. It was suggested that it should be made clear that paragraph 3 of draft article 7 applied solely to individuals who were nationals of a State engaged in an armed conflict with the expelling State. Moreover, the terminology used in paragraph 3 was too vague; in particular, the right of collective expulsion of enemy nationals should be limited to situations in which the latter demonstrated "serious" or "grave" hostility towards the expelling State, or to cases of persons who had "clearly acted" in a hostile manner. Provision could also be made for an exception based on extreme considerations of national security. In addition, it was suggested that it should be made clear that a State retained the right to expel the nationals of an enemy State if that was necessary to protect them from a revenge-seeking local population. In that context, measures taken in order to protect aliens from a hostile environment should, it was suggested, be described as "temporary removal" rather than "expulsion".

243. Some members suggested adding a separate article on migrant workers having regard to their particular vulnerability, but other members were opposed.

(c) *Comments on other issues*

244. It was maintained that article 13 of the International Covenant on Civil and Political Rights reflected universally accepted principles that could constitute an appropriate basis for the Commission's work. Provisions of certain regional human rights instruments were also mentioned, including Protocols Nos. 4 and 7 to the Convention for the Protection of Human Rights and Fundamental Freedoms, the American Convention on Human Rights: "Pact of San José, Costa Rica", the African Charter on Human and Peoples' Rights, and the Arab Charter on Human Rights (new version of 2004).

245. It was suggested that the draft articles should contain a provision on migrant workers and members of their families, taking as a basis article 22 of the 1990 International Convention on the Protection of the Rights of All Migrant Workers and Members of their Families, and also a provision on the beneficiaries of treaties on friendship, commerce and navigation.

246. It was suggested that the Commission consider the possible grounds for the illegality of an expulsion, as well as looking into the lawfulness of the expropriation or confiscation measures that sometimes accompanied the expulsion of an alien. However, it was pointed out that a detailed analysis of the regulations relating to expropriation was not within the Commission's purview.

247. The question of whether and to what extent the expelling State must give the expelled alien the possibility of choosing the State of destination was mentioned. In this context, it was particularly important to determine nationality since, in principle, only the national State had the obligation to accept an expelled person.

248. In addition, it was maintained that the prohibition of *refoulement* was a rule of *jus cogens*.

3. Special Rapporteur's concluding remarks

249. The Special Rapporteur thanked the Commission members for their comments and observations, to which he had listened very closely. Certain comments, however, concerned aspects which had already been debated by the Commission and on which the Commission had already given the Special Rapporteur guidance approved by the General Assembly. The Special Rapporteur remained of the view that the topic lent itself to codification by an expert body, it being understood that States could subsequently initiate political negotiation on the fruits of the Commission's work.

250. In response to certain comments on methodology, the Special Rapporteur reiterated his preference—endorsed by the Commission—for a study of the general rules on the issue, to be followed by a consideration of the rules applicable to specific categories of aliens. The legal consequences of an expulsion, as well as its potential effects on an alien's property, would not be overlooked in subsequent reports; there was no need, however, to refer to those issues in draft article 1, which dealt with the scope of the topic.

251. The Special Rapporteur supported the proposal to specify, in the commentary to draft article 1, that the draft articles applied only to natural persons. Responding to members who had expressed support for the exclusion of refugees and stateless persons from the scope of the topic, the Special Rapporteur pointed out that the existing legal instruments did not establish a comprehensive regime for the expulsion of these categories of persons. The Commission should therefore examine the rules applicable to these persons—including *non-refoulement* of refugees—keeping in mind contemporary law and practice. The same comment applied to the expulsion of enemy aliens, which was not governed by international humanitarian law instruments.

252. In the Special Rapporteur's opinion, the enumeration of the various categories of aliens in draft article 1, paragraph 2, was necessary. Deleting this paragraph, as had been proposed by certain members, would unduly expand the *ratione personae* scope of the draft articles to any category of aliens, including, for example, those entitled to privileges and immunities under international law.

253. The Commission and almost all the States that had spoken in the Sixth Committee had expressed a preference for excluding non-admission from the scope of the

topic. The Special Rapporteur continued to share this view, since an alien could not be expelled before being admitted and the right to admit was inherent to the sovereignty of each State. Nevertheless, in international zones, States must respect all the relevant rules of international law, including those relating to the fundamental rights of the human being.

254. The issue of extradition disguised as expulsion would be addressed in a subsequent report. On the other hand, the Special Rapporteur did not support the proposal to include in the topic the issue of transfers of criminals, which came under international criminal law. Making such transfers subject to the rules on expulsion of aliens would risk compromising efficient cooperation between States in the fight against crime, including terrorism.

255. The Special Rapporteur took note of the reservations expressed by several Commission members concerning the use of the term "*ressortissant*". It would be used henceforth as a synonym for "national". However, the concepts of "non-national" and "alien" were not always equivalent, since certain categories of "non-nationals" were not considered aliens for the purposes of expulsion under the law of certain States. The problem of dual nationality would be discussed in subsequent reports.

256. The Special Rapporteur agreed that it was necessary to define the compulsion that the conduct of a State must involve in order for it to be qualified as "expulsion".

257. With regard to the concepts of "territory" and "frontier", the Special Rapporteur insisted on keeping the proposed definitions. The definition of "territory" corresponded to the unanimously accepted one, which included, in particular, internal waters and the territorial sea. A specific definition should be given for the concept of "frontier" in the context of the present topic. For the purposes of immigration, the frontier was a zone (for example, a port, airport or customs zone), rather than a line.

258. In the light of these considerations, the Special Rapporteur submitted to the Commission a revised version of draft articles 1[326] and 2.[327]

---

[326] Draft article 1 as revised reads as follows:

"*Scope*

"1. The present draft articles shall apply to the expulsion of aliens, as enumerated in paragraph 2 of this article, who are present in the territory of the expelling State."

or:

"1. The present draft articles shall apply to the expulsion by a State of those aliens enumerated in paragraph 2 of this article who are present in its territory.

"2. They shall apply to aliens who are lawfully or unlawfully present in the expelling State, refugees, asylum seekers, stateless persons, migrant workers, nationals of an enemy State and nationals of the expelling State who have lost their nationality or been deprived of it."

[327] Draft article 2 as revised reads as follows:

"*Definitions*

"For the purposes of the draft articles:

"(*a*) *expulsion* means a legal act or a conduct by which a State compels an alien to leave its territory;

"(*b*) *alien* means a person who does not have the nationality of the State in whose territory he or she is present, except where the legislation of that State provides otherwise;

259. Concerning the five draft articles proposed in the third report, the members had made conflicting observations which were sometimes based on personal preferences, losing sight of current practice and the applicable law.

260. The Special Rapporteur was not opposed to the suggestion that paragraphs 1 and 2 of draft article 3 should be combined. Bearing in mind the proposals made and the various views expressed, it might be stipulated that expulsion should take place "in a context of respect for the relevant rules of international law, in particular the fundamental rights of the human person, and the present draft articles".

261. The Special Rapporteur continued to believe that draft article 4 should be retained, if only to emphasize the prohibition on expulsion of nationals. Possible exceptions to the prohibition had been observed in practice, and the examples mentioned in the third report were indeed cases of expulsion and not cases of extradition. The Special Rapporteur supported the proposal that the "exceptional circumstances" which might justify the expulsion of a national should be clarified. It was not desirable to deal with the issue of dual nationals in connection with draft article 4, as protection from expulsion should be provided in respect of any State of which a person was a national. That issue could, however, have an impact in the context of the exercise of diplomatic protection in cases of unlawful expulsion. In order to respond to the questions posed by several members, the Special Rapporteur planned to analyse further the issue of expulsion of dual nationals in a forthcoming report; he also planned to study, with the help of the Secretariat, the question of deprivation of nationality as a prelude to expulsion. On the other hand, it was not necessary to introduce a reference to "banning", which was already covered by the concept of "expulsion" as adopted.

262. Concerning draft articles 5 and 6, the Special Rapporteur continued to believe that efforts should be made to improve the protection granted to refugees and stateless persons under existing international conventions. It was not so much a question of modifying the current rules as of complementing them by setting forth the prohibition of expulsion and dealing in particular with the temporary protection and the residual rights of *de facto* refugees or persons who had been denied refugee status. Moreover, any incompatibility which might arise between different rules would not be insurmountable, since international law offered the tools needed to resolve such cases. Considering the divergent views which had been expressed on that issue, it was important for the Commission to provide the Special Rapporteur with clear indications as to how to address the issue of refugees and stateless persons. Since almost all the members were opposed to including an explicit reference to terrorism as a ground for expelling a refugee or stateless person, it was desirable to specify in

---

"(*c*) *conduct* means any act by the authorities of the expelling State against which the alien has no remedy and which leaves him or her no choice but to leave the territory of that State;

"(*d*) *territory* means the domain in which the State exercises all the powers deriving from its sovereignty;

"(*e*) *frontier* means the zone at the limits of the territory of an expelling State in which the alien does not enjoy resident status and beyond which the expulsion procedure is completed."

the commentary that terrorism could constitute a justification for expulsion on grounds of "national security".

263. Concerning draft article 7 on the prohibition of collective expulsions, the Special Rapporteur did not believe it was necessary to insert a specific provision relating to migrant workers, since they were covered by the prohibition on collective expulsion of aliens in general.

264. Concerning the expulsion of nationals of an enemy State in time of armed conflict, the Special Rapporteur reiterated his view that the issue was not clearly regulated in international humanitarian law. Whereas the individual expulsion of a national of an enemy State should fall under the ordinary regime of expulsion of aliens, practice as regards collective expulsion in time of armed conflict varied, with a tendency to be tolerant towards individuals who did not display a hostile attitude. Taking into account the proposals made by a number of members concerning the scope and wording of draft article 7, paragraph 3, the Special Rapporteur suggested the following wording: "Foreign nationals of a State engaged in armed conflict with the receiving State shall not be subject to measures of collective expulsion unless, taken collectively as a group, they are victims of hostile acts or are engaged in activities hostile to the receiving State."

265. Lastly, the Special Rapporteur indicated that other matters raised during the discussions, such as the principle of *non-refoulement* or the problem of discriminatory expulsions, would be dealt with during the consideration of the limits *ratione materiae* of the right of expulsion.

Chapter VII

EFFECTS OF ARMED CONFLICTS ON TREATIES

A. Introduction

266. The Commission, at its fifty-second session (2000), identified the topic "Effects of armed conflicts on treaties" for inclusion in its long-term programme of work.[328] A brief syllabus describing the possible overall structure and approach to the topic was annexed to the report of the Commission to the General Assembly on the work of that session.[329] In paragraph 8 of its resolution 55/152 of 12 December 2000, the General Assembly took note of the topic's inclusion.

267. During its fifty-sixth session (2004), the Commission decided, at its 2830th meeting, on 6 August 2004, to include the topic "Effects of armed conflicts on treaties" in its current programme of work, and to appoint Mr. Ian Brownlie as Special Rapporteur for the topic.[330] The General Assembly, in paragraph 5 of its resolution 59/41 of 2 December 2004, endorsed the decision of the Commission to include the topic in its agenda.

268. At its fifty-seventh (2005) and fifty-eighth (2006) sessions, the Commission had before it the first[331] and second[332] reports of the Special Rapporteur, as well as a memorandum prepared by the Secretariat entitled "The effects of armed conflict on treaties: an examination of practice and doctrine".[333] At its 2866th meeting, on 5 August 2005, the Commission endorsed the Special Rapporteur's suggestion that the Secretariat be requested to circulate a note to Governments requesting information about their practice with regard to this topic, in particular the more contemporary practice, as well as any other relevant information.[334]

B. Consideration of the topic at the present session

269. At the present session, the Commission had before it the third report of the Special Rapporteur (A/CN.4/578). The Commission considered the Special Rapporteur's report at its 2926th to 2929th meetings, from 29 May to 1 June 2007.

270. At the 2928th meeting, on 31 May 2007, the Commission decided to establish a working group, under the chairpersonship of Mr. Lucius Caflisch, to provide further guidance regarding several issues which had been identified in the Commission's consideration of the Special Rapporteur's third report. At its 2946th meeting, on 2 August 2007, the Commission adopted the report of the Working Group (see section C below).

271. Also at the 2946th meeting, the Commission decided to refer to the Drafting Committee draft articles 1 to 3, 5, 5 *bis*, 7, 10 and 11, as proposed by the Special Rapporteur in his third report, together with the guidance in subparagraph (1) (*a*) to (1) (*d*) of paragraph 324 below containing the recommendations of the Working Group (see section C below), as well as draft article 4, as proposed by the Working Group.

272. The Commission also approved the recommendation of the Working Group that the Secretariat circulate a note to international organizations requesting information about their practice with regard to the effect of armed conflict on treaties involving them.

1. GENERAL REMARKS ON THE TOPIC

(a) *Introduction by the Special Rapporteur*

273. The Special Rapporteur briefly recapitulated the circumstances of the consideration of his first and second reports.[335] It was pointed out that the first report continued to be the foundation for the subsequent reports, and that all three reports had to be read together. He recalled that he had proposed an entire set of draft articles as a package so as to present a comprehensive scheme. However, there was no intention to produce a definitive and dogmatic set of solutions. Moreover, a portion of the articles was deliberately expository in character.

274. The Special Rapporteur recalled that the overall goals of his reports were to: (*a*) clarify the legal position; (*b*) promote the security of legal relations between States, through the assertion in draft article 3 that the outbreak of an armed conflict does not as such involve the termination or suspension of a treaty; and (*c*) possibly stimulate the appearance of evidence concerning State practice.

275. The Special Rapporteur referred to the problem of sources, particularly the problem of the significance of State practice. Having surveyed the available legal sources, there were two different situations: (*a*) treaties creating permanent regimes which did have a firm base in State practice; and (*b*) legal positions which had a firm basis in the jurisprudence of municipal courts and executive advice to courts but were not supported by State practice in the conventional mode. In the view of the

---

[328] *Yearbook ... 2000*, vol. II (Part Two), p. 131, para. 729.

[329] *Ibid.*, Annex, p. 135.

[330] *Yearbook ... 2004*, vol. II (Part Two), p. 120, para. 364.

[331] *Yearbook ... 2005*, vol. II (Part One), document A/CN.4/552.

[332] *Yearbook ... 2006*, vol. II (Part One), document A/CN.4/570.

[333] Document A/CN.4/550 and Corr.1–2 (mimeographed; available on the Commission's website, documents of fifty-seventh session).

[334] *Yearbook ... 2005*, vol. II (Part Two), p. 27, para. 112.

[335] See footnotes 331 and 332 above.

Special Rapporteur, it seemed inappropriate to insist that the categories of treaties listed in the second paragraph of draft article 7 should all constitute a part of existing general international law. Furthermore, as regards the question of the evidence of State practice, it was noted that the likelihood of a substantial flow of information from States was low,[336] and that the identification of relevant State practice was unusually difficult. It often was the case that some of the modern State practice which was sometimes cited referred for the most part to the different questions of the effects of a fundamental change of circumstances or to that of the supervening impossibility of performance of the treaty and was accordingly irrelevant. Furthermore, the Special Rapporteur reiterated his position that, in view of the uncertainty as to sources, it was more than usually pertinent to refer to considerations of policy.

276. In terms of the Commission's working methods, the Special Rapporteur proposed the establishment of a working group in order to consider a number of key issues on which the taking of a collective view was necessary.

(b) *Summary of the debate*

277. Some members identified several issues regarding the general approach taken in the draft articles for further consideration. These included: the continued reliance on the criterion of intention throughout the draft articles; the proposed reliance on a list of categories of treaties presumed to continue in operation during armed conflict, without a clear indication of the criteria applied in drawing up the list; the need for further consideration of all aspects of the effects that the prohibition of the threat or use of force would have on treaties; the idea that the topic is primarily a matter of the law of treaties; and the exclusion of non-international armed conflicts. It was further suggested that several distinctions be drawn, for example, between parties to an armed conflict and third States, including neutral States; between States parties to a treaty and signatories; between treaties in force and those which have been ratified by an insufficient number of parties; between treaties concluded between the States themselves or between those States and international organizations that the States parties to a conflict are members of; between the effects on specific provisions of a treaty as opposed to the entire treaty; between situations of suspension and situations of termination of treaties; between the effects concerning international conflicts and internal conflicts, between the effects on treaties of large-scale conflicts as opposed to those of small-scale conflicts; and between the effects on bilateral treaties as opposed to multilateral treaties, especially those multilateral treaties which were widely ratified.

278. The Secretariat was again commended for the memorandum on the topic it submitted to the Commission in 2005.[337]

2. COMMENTS ON DRAFT ARTICLES

Article 1. Scope[338]

(a) *Introduction by the Special Rapporteur*

279. The Special Rapporteur recalled that draft article 1 had not caused much difficulty in the Sixth Committee. He was of the view that such suggestions to expand the scope of the topic to include treaties entered into by international organizations failed to consider the difficulties inherent in what was a qualitatively different subject matter.

(b) *Summary of the debate*

280. Support was expressed for the inclusion of international organizations within the scope of the topic. Issue was taken with the Special Rapporteur's position that the inclusion of international organizations would amount to an expansion of the topic, since the subject did not automatically imply that it was restricted to treaties between States. Nor was it considered as necessarily being too complex a matter to take on in the context of the Commission's consideration of the topic. It was noted that, given the increased numbers of treaties to which international organizations were parties, it was conceivable that such organizations could be affected by the termination or suspension of a treaty to which they were a party as a result of the use of force.

281. Other members agreed with the Special Rapporteur's reluctance to include international organizations within the scope of the topic, for the practical reasons he mentioned. It was noted that separate conventions had been developed for the law of treaties, and that the Commission was following that exact pattern with regard to the topic of responsibility of international organizations. In terms of a further suggestion, any decision on such expansion of the scope of the topic could be postponed until the work on the topic had been developed further.

282. As regards the position of third States, it was suggested that if any special rule existed with regard to the termination or suspension of a treaty in case of outbreak of hostilities, such rule would likely affect only the relation of a State which is a party to an armed conflict with another State which is also a party to that conflict. As a matter of treaty law, an armed conflict which a State party to a treaty may have with a third State would only produce the consequences generally provided by the 1969 Vienna Convention, in particular fundamental change of circumstances and the supervening impossibility of performance.

283. As to the suggestion that the draft articles cover treaties being provisionally applied between parties, some members expressed doubts about the Special Rapporteur's view that the matter could be resolved through the application of article 25 of the 1969 Vienna Convention.

---

[336] No response had been received to a note from the Secretariat, circulated to Governments in 2005 upon the request of the Commission, seeking information about their practice, particularly contemporary practice, on the topic. See footnote 334 above.

[337] See footnote 333 above.

---

[338] Draft article 1 reads as follows:

"*Scope*

"The present draft articles apply to the effects of an armed conflict in respect of treaties between States."

Article 2.   Use of terms [339]

(a) Introduction by the Special Rapporteur

284.   In introducing draft article 2, the Special Rapporteur emphasized the fact that the definitions contained therein were, under the express terms of the provision, "for the purposes of the present draft articles". Subparagraph (a) contained a definition of the term "treaty", based on that found in the 1969 Vienna Convention. The provision had not given rise to any difficulties. On the contrary, the definition of "armed conflict" in subparagraph (b) had been the subject of much debate. There had been an almost equal division of opinion both in the Commission and in the Sixth Committee on, for example, the inclusion of internal armed conflict. In addition, he noted that part of the difficulty was that the policy considerations pointed in different directions. For example, it was unrealistic to segregate internal armed conflict strictly speaking from other types of internal armed conflict which in fact had foreign connections and causes. At the same time, such an approach could undermine the integrity of treaty relations by expanding the possible factual bases for alleging that an armed conflict existed for the purposes of the draft articles and with the consequence of the suspension or termination of treaty relations.

(b)   Summary of the debate

285.   General support existed for the definition of "treaty" in subparagraph (a).

286.   As regards the definition of "armed conflict" in subparagraph (b), views continued to be divided. Support existed among several members for the express inclusion of non-international armed conflicts. It was noted that their frequency and intensity in modern times, and the fact that they may have effects on the operation of treaties between States, militated in favour of their inclusion. Including such conflicts would enhance the practical value of the draft articles. It was noted that such an approach would be commensurate with recent trends in international humanitarian law which tended to de-emphasize the distinction between international and non-international armed conflicts. Support was expressed for a definition of "armed conflict" which encompassed military occupations. A definition, based on the formulation in the Tadić case[340] as

---

[339] Draft article 2 reads as follows:

"Use of terms

"For the purposes of the present draft articles:

"(a) 'treaty' means an international agreement concluded between States in written form and governed by international law, whether embodied in a single instrument or in two or more related instruments, and whatever its particular designation;

"(b) 'armed conflict' means a state of war or a conflict which involves armed operations which by their nature or extent are likely to affect the operation of treaties between States parties to the armed conflict or between States parties to the armed conflict and third States, regardless of a formal declaration of war or other declaration by any or all of the parties to the armed conflict."

[340] Prosecutor v. Duško Tadić, Case No. IT-94-1-A, Judgement of 15 July 1999, Appeals Chamber, International Tribunal for the Former Yugoslavia, para. 84:

"It is indisputable that an armed conflict is international if it takes place between two or more States. In addition, in case of an internal armed conflict breaking out on the territory of a State, it may become international (or, depending upon the circumstances, be international in character alongside an internal armed conflict) if (i) another State intervenes in that conflict through its troops, or alternatively if (ii) some

---

well as the 1954 Convention for the Protection of Cultural Property in the Event of Armed Conflict, was preferred.

287.   Other members preferred to confine the definition exclusively to international or interstate conflicts. It was noted that such an approach would maintain consistency with how the phrase was used in draft article 1. It was suggested that the guiding criteria was whether internal conflicts by their nature were likely to affect the operation of treaties between a State party in which the conflict took place and another State party or a third State, as opposed to the frequency of internal conflicts. While it was conceded that some examples of such an impact might exist, it was doubted whether those constituted significant State practice or established doctrine. The view was also expressed that there existed a qualitative difference between international armed conflicts and non-international armed conflicts. It was also noted that it was not feasible to deal with all conflicts, international and internal, in the same manner. Instead, the focus could be on considering the relationship between the application of treaties involving States in which internal conflicts take place and other obligations that States might have, in particular the obligation of neutrality towards States involved in conflicts.[341] One should also consider the relationship between obligations created under a treaty and other obligations.

288.   It was further suggested that a possible compromise could be found in a provision similar to that contained in article 3 of the 1969 Vienna Convention, dealing with international agreements not within the scope of that Convention. It was also noted that the phrase "state of war" was outmoded, and could be replaced with "state of belligerency". Another suggestion was that the definition should not cover "police enforcement" activity.

Article 3.   Non-automatic termination or suspension [342]

(a)   Introduction by the Special Rapporteur

289.   The Special Rapporteur pointed out that two alterations to the text had been made in the third report: (1) the title had been changed; and (2) the phrase "ipso facto" had been replaced by "necessarily". It was recalled that the provision remained central to the entire set of draft articles, and that it was based on the resolution adopted by the Institute of International Law in 1985.[343] It was noted that the majority of the delegations in the Sixth Committee had not found draft article 3 to be problematical.

(b)   Summary of the debate

290.   There was general recognition among members of the importance of the doctrine of continuity in draft

---

of the participants in the internal armed conflict act on behalf of that other State" (Judicial Supplement No. 6, June/July 1999. See also ILM, vol. 38 (1999), p. 1518).

[341] See the case of the SS "Wimbledon" (footnote 148 above).

[342] Draft article 3 reads as follows:

"Non-automatic termination or suspension

"The outbreak of an armed conflict does not necessarily terminate or suspend the operation of treaties as:

"(a) between the parties to the armed conflict;

"(b) between one or more parties to the armed conflict and a third State."

[343] See Institute of International Law, Yearbook, vol. 61 (1986), Session of Helsinki (1985), Part II, pp. 278–283.

article 3 to the entire scheme of the draft articles. It was suggested that draft article 3 be presented more affirmatively by, for example, reformulating the provision as follows: "[i]n general, the outbreak of an armed conflict does not lead to the termination or suspension of the operation of treaties". In terms of a further suggestion the following additional clause could be added to the new formulation: "save in exceptional circumstances where armed conflict is lawful or justified under international law". It was also noted that the survival of treaties was not exclusively dependent on the outbreak of armed conflict, but also on the likelihood of the compatibility of such armed conflict not only with the object and purpose of the treaty, but with the Charter of the United Nations.

291. While support was expressed for the new terminology employed by the Special Rapporteur, reference was also made by a member to the inconsistency between the use of the phrases "Non-automatic" in the title, and "not necessarily" in the provision itself. A preference was expressed for using "non-automatic" in the text. Other members also took issue with the view that "*ipso facto*" and "necessarily" were synonymous.

Article 4. The indicia of susceptibility to termination or suspension of treaties in case of an armed conflict [344]

(a) Introduction by the Special Rapporteur

292. The Special Rapporteur recalled that opinion in the Sixth Committee on the inclusion of the criterion of intention had been almost equally divided (as had been the case in the Commission itself). He noted that the opposition to the reliance upon intention was normally based upon the problems of ascertaining the intention of the parties, but this was true of many legal rules, including legislation and constitutional provisions. Furthermore, the difference between the two points of view expressed in the Sixth Committee was probably not, in practical terms, substantial. The existence and interpretation of a treaty was not a matter of intention as an abstraction, but the intention of the parties as expressed in the words used by them and in the light of the surrounding circumstances.

(b) Summary of the debate

293. The Commission's consideration of draft article 4 focused on the appropriateness of maintaining the criterion of the intention of the parties at the time the treaty was concluded as the predominant criteria for determining the susceptibility to termination or suspension of a treaty because of an armed conflict between States parties. Such an approach was again criticized by several members who reiterated their view that the resort to the presumed intention

of the parties remained one of the key difficulties underlying the entire draft articles. It was maintained that while the intention of parties to treaties could be one possible criterion for the fate of a treaty in the case of armed conflict, it could not be the exclusive or the predominant criterion. Nor was it feasible to anticipate that the States parties to the treaty would at the time of concluding the treaty anticipate its fate should an armed conflict arise between them. Nor was the reference to articles 31 and 32 of the 1969 Vienna Convention deemed sufficient; the incorporation by reference, *inter alia*, to the criteria of the object and purpose (a criterion also referred to in draft article 7) as a means of determining the intention of the parties to a treaty was too complicated or too uncertain and risked mixing several criteria, some subjective and others objective. Furthermore, those provisions of the 1969 Vienna Convention dealt with the interpretation of the provisions of a treaty; however, in most cases, there would be no specific reference in the treaty to the consequence of the outbreak of armed conflict between the States parties.

294. It was proposed that more suitable criteria be adopted, such as the viability of the continuation of the operation of certain provisions of the treaty in armed conflicts. This could be assisted through the inclusion (in draft article 7, or equivalent thereto) of a list of factors that could be taken as indicative of whether the treaty continued to operate in a situation of armed conflict, including: the nature of the treaty, i.e. its subject matter; the object of the treaty, i.e. whether continuation is viable; the existence of an express provision in the treaty to armed conflict; the nature and extent of the conflict; the number of the parties to the treaty; the importance of the continuation of the treaty even in situations of war; and the compatibility of the performance under the treaty with the exercise of individual or collective self-defence under the Charter of the United Nations.

295. Other members pointed out that the differences in position were not as broad as it seemed: resort to the criterion of intention, even if presumed intention, was a common practice in the interpretation of domestic legislation. The possible source of confusion, therefore, was the inclusion of the phrase "at the time the treaty was concluded". It was proposed that this phrase be removed. Furthermore, it was suggested that draft article 7 could be included under draft article 4, as a new paragraph 3.

Article 5. Express provisions on the operation of treaties [345]

Article 5 bis. The conclusion of treaties during armed conflict [346]

---

[344] Draft article 4 reads as follows:

"*The indicia of susceptibility to termination or suspension of treaties in case of an armed conflict*

"1. The susceptibility to termination or suspension of treaties in case of an armed conflict is determined in accordance with the intention of the parties at the time the treaty was concluded.

"2. The intention of the parties to a treaty relating to its susceptibility to termination or suspension shall be determined in accordance:

"(*a*) with the provisions of articles 31 and 32 of the Vienna Convention on the Law of Treaties; and

"(*b*) the nature and extent of the armed conflict in question."

[345] Draft article 5 reads as follows:

"*Express provisions on the operation of treaties*

"Treaties applicable to situations of armed conflict in accordance with their express provisions are operative in case of an armed conflict, without prejudice to the conclusion of lawful agreements between the parties to the armed conflict involving suspension or waiver of the relevant treaties."

[346] Draft article 5 *bis* reads as follows:

"*The conclusion of treaties during armed conflict*

"The outbreak of an armed conflict does not affect the capacity of the parties to the armed conflict to conclude treaties in accordance with the Vienna Convention on the Law of Treaties."

(a) *Introduction by the Special Rapporteur*

296.   The Special Rapporteur recalled that, on a strict view of drafting, draft article 5 was redundant, but it was generally accepted that such a provision should be included for the sake of clarity.

297.   It was noted that draft article 5 *bis* had previously been included as paragraph 2 of draft article 5, but was now presented as a separate draft article following suggestions that the provision was to be distinguished from that in draft article 5. The term "competence" had been deleted and replaced by "capacity". The draft article was intended to reflect the experience of belligerents in an armed conflict concluding agreements between themselves during the conflict.

(b) *Summary of the debate*

298.   No opposition to draft article 5 was expressed during the debate. General support was expressed for draft article 5 *bis*, and for its placement as a separate provision. As regards replacing the term "competence" by "capacity", it was pointed out that during an armed conflict the parties maintained their treaty-making power. So what was at stake was less the capacity or competence but the freedom to conclude a treaty.

Article 6 bis.[347]   *The law applicable in armed conflict*[348]

(a) *Introduction by the Special Rapporteur*

299.   Draft article 6 *bis* was a new provision. It had been included in response to a number of suggestions made both in the Sixth Committee and the Commission that a provision be included to reflect the principle, stated by the ICJ in the *Legality of the Threat or Use of Nuclear Weapons* advisory opinion[349] relating to the relation, in the context of armed conflict, between human rights and the applicable *lex specialis*, the law applicable in armed conflict which is designed to regulate the conduct of hostilities. The Special Rapporteur noted that while the principle was, strictly speaking, redundant, the draft article provide a useful clarification in an expository manner.

(b) *Summary of the debate*

300.   While several members agreed with the inclusion of draft article 6 *bis*, it was suggested that consideration also had to be given to the formulation adopted by the ICJ in the advisory opinion on the *Legal Consequences of the Construction of a Wall in the Occupied Palestinian Territory*,[350]

---

[347] Draft article 6 was withdrawn by the Special Rapporteur. See *Yearbook … 2006*, vol. II (Part Two), p. 170, paras. 207–208, and the third report of the Special Rapporteur, para. 29.

[348] Draft article 6 *bis* reads as follows:

"*The law applicable in armed conflict*

"The application of standard-setting treaties, including treaties concerning human rights and environmental protection, continues in time of armed conflict, but their application is determined by reference to the applicable *lex specialis*, namely, the law applicable in armed conflict."

[349] *Legality of the Threat or Use of Nuclear Weapons, Advisory Opinion, I.C.J. Reports 1996*, p. 226, at p. 240, para. 25.

[350] *Legal Consequences of the Construction of a Wall in the Occupied Palestinian Territory* (see footnote 99 above), p. 178, para. 106.

so as to clarify that human rights treaties were not to be excluded as a result of the operation of the *lex specialis* which consists of international humanitarian law. Another suggestion was to reformulate the provision in more general terms without restricting it to standard-setting treaties. A further view was that it was unnecessary to make specific reference to the humanitarian law of armed conflict as *lex specialis* since the operation of the *lex specialis* principle would occur in any case if the specific situation so warranted. Some other members were of the view that the draft article should be deleted because the application of human rights law, environmental law or international humanitarian law depended on specific circumstances which could not be subsumed under a general article.

Article 7.   The operation of treaties on the basis of necessary implication from their object and purpose[351]

(a) *Introduction by the Special Rapporteur*

301.   The Special Rapporteur emphasized the importance of draft article 7 to the entire scheme of the draft articles. The key issue had related to the inclusion of an indicative list of categories of treaties the object and purpose of which involved the necessary implication that they continued in operation during an armed conflict. He recalled the different views expressed on the matter in the Sixth Committee and the Commission, and reiterated his own preference to retain such a list in one form or another, including possibly as an annex to the draft articles. He further noted that, given the complexity of the topic, room had to be found in the list for those categories which were based on State practice as well as those which were not, but which enjoyed support in legal practice of a reputable character.

(b) *Summary of the debate*

302.   Support was expressed for the principle enunciated in draft article 7 as well as the list of categories contained therein, so as to counterbalance the criterion of intention

---

[351] Draft article 7 reads as follows:

"*The operation of treaties on the basis of necessary implication from their object and purpose*

"1. In the case of treaties the object and purpose of which involve the necessary implication that they continue in operation during an armed conflict, the incidence of an armed conflict will not as such inhibit their operation.

"2. Treaties of this character include the following:

"(*a*) treaties expressly applicable in case of an armed conflict;

"(*b*) treaties declaring, creating, or regulating permanent rights or a permanent regime or status;

"(*c*) treaties of friendship, commerce and navigation and analogous agreements concerning private rights;

"(*d*) treaties for the protection of human rights;

"(*e*) treaties relating to the protection of the environment;

"(*f*) treaties relating to international watercourses and related installations and facilities;

"(*g*) multilateral law-making treaties;

"(*h*) treaties relating to the settlement of disputes between States by peaceful means, including resort to conciliation, mediation, arbitration and the International Court of Justice;

"(*i*) obligations arising under multilateral conventions relating to commercial arbitration and the enforcement of awards;

"(*j*) treaties relating to diplomatic relations;

"(*k*) treaties relating to consular relations."

in draft article 4. It was suggested that further categories could be added to the list. Other members pointed out that any illustrative list of categories of treaties had to be based on a set of agreed upon criteria, which, in turn, had to be rooted in State practice. It was also noted that the list approach was limited by the fact that while some treaties might, as a whole, continue in the event of armed conflict, in other cases it may be more a matter of particular treaty provisions that are susceptible to continuation rather than the treaty as a whole. Another suggestion was to take a different approach whereby, instead of a list of categories of treaties, the provision would list relevant factors or general criteria which could be taken into account when ascertaining whether their object and purpose implied that they continued in operation during an armed conflict.[352] Furthermore, a distinction could be made between categories of treaties which in no circumstances could be terminated by an armed conflict, and those which could be considered as suspended or terminated during an armed conflict, depending on the circumstances.

303. Disagreement was expressed with the Special Rapporteur's preference not to include treaties codifying rules of *jus cogens*. It was also suggested that the list include treaties or agreements delineating land and maritime boundaries which by their nature also belong to the category of permanent regimes. Another view was that the discussion on the particular provisions or types of provisions in treaties which would continue in the event of armed conflict was best dealt with in the commentaries. It was further proposed that draft article 7 could be included in draft article 4.

Article 8. Mode of suspension or termination[353]

(a) Introduction by the Special Rapporteur

304. The Special Rapporteur noted that, as was the case with a number of the provisions in the second half of the draft articles, draft article 8 was, strictly speaking, superfluous because of its expository nature. To his mind, it would not be necessary to attempt to define suspension or termination.

(b) Summary of the debate

305. It was observed in the Commission that the expository nature of the provision did not preclude the possibility of in-depth discussion of the consequences of the application of articles 42 to 45 of the 1969 Vienna Convention, and that such further reflection might reveal the fact that those provisions would not all necessarily be applicable to the context of treaties suspended or terminated in the event of an armed conflict. Some members also stated that the procedures foreseen in articles 65 *et seq.* of the 1969 Vienna Convention might not be applicable to situations of armed conflicts for which the procedure should be simpler.

[352] See above the discussion on draft article 4.

[353] Draft article 8 reads as follows:

"*Mode of suspension or termination*

"In case of an armed conflict the mode of suspension or termination shall be the same as in those forms of suspension or termination included in the provisions of articles 42 to 45 of the Vienna Convention on the Law of Treaties."

Article 9. The resumption of suspended treaties[354]

(a) Introduction by the Special Rapporteur

306. The Special Rapporteur recalled that draft article 9 was also not strictly necessary, but constituted a useful further development of the principles in draft articles 3 and 4.

(b) Summary of the debate

307. It was noted that the same concerns as to the general rule of intention as the foundation for determining whether a treaty is terminated or suspended in the event of armed conflict, raised in the context of draft article 4, applied to draft article 9. It was also observed that, in accordance with the principle of continuity in draft article 3, if the effect of the armed conflict were to be the suspension of the application of the treaty, then it should be presumed that once the armed conflict ceased, the resumption of the treaty should be automatic unless there was a contrary intention.

Article 10. Effect of the exercise of the right to individual or collective self-defence on a treaty[355]

(a) Introduction by the Special Rapporteur

308. The Special Rapporteur pointed out that it was not true that he had not dealt with the question of illegality. In his first report[356] he had proposed a provision which was compatible with draft article 3, and had also set out the relevant parts of the resolution of the Institute of International Law in 1985,[357] which took a different approach. He maintained further that his initial proposal, namely, that the illegality of a use of force did not affect the question whether an armed conflict had an automatic or necessary outcome of suspension or termination, had been analytically correct for the reason that at the moment of the outbreak of an armed conflict it was not always immediately clear who was the aggressor. However, in response to the opposition to his initial proposal, the Special Rapporteur

[354] Draft article 9 reads as follows:

"*The resumption of suspended treaties*

"1. The operation of a treaty suspended as a consequence of an armed conflict shall be resumed provided that this is determined in accordance with the intention of the parties at the time the treaty was concluded.

"2. The intention of the parties to a treaty, the operation of which has been suspended as a consequence of an armed conflict, concerning the susceptibility of the treaty to resumption of operation shall be determined in accordance:

"(*a*) with the provisions of articles 31 and 32 of the Vienna Convention on the Law of Treaties; and

"(*b*) with the nature and extent of the armed conflict in question."

[355] Draft article 10 reads as follows:

"*Effect of the exercise of the right to individual or collective self-defence on a treaty*

"A State exercising its right of individual or collective self-defence in accordance with the Charter of the United Nations is entitled to suspend in whole or in part the operation of a treaty incompatible with the exercise of that right, subject to any consequences resulting from a later determination by the Security Council of that State as an aggressor."

[356] *Yearbook ... 2005*, vol. II (Part One), document A/CN.4/552 (see footnote 331 above).

[357] *Institute of International Law, Yearbook,* vol. 61 (1986), Session of Helsinki (1985), Part II, pp. 278–283 (see footnote 343 above).

had included a new draft article 10 as an attempt to meet the criticism that his earlier formulation appeared to ignore the question of the illegality of certain forms of the use or threat of force. The provision was based on article 7 of the resolution of the Institute of International Law adopted in 1985.

(b)   *Summary of the debate*

309.   While the inclusion of draft article 10 was welcomed as a step in the right direction, it was suggested that provision also be made for the position of the State complying with a Security Council resolution adopted under Chapter VII of the Charter of the United Nations, as well as that of the State committing aggression, which were covered in articles 8 and 9 of the resolution of the Institute of International Law. It was further suggested that the illegality of the use of force and its linkage to the subject required a more in-depth consideration, particularly as regards the position of the aggressor State and the determination of the existence of an act of aggression, so as to draw more detailed conclusions on the fate of treaties which are already in force in the relationship between the parties to the conflict, and between those parties and third parties. It was also suggested that it was worth considering the situation of bilateral treaties between the aggressor and the self-defending State and the possibility of having a speedier procedure for the self-defending State to terminate or suspend a treaty. This was especially the case given the reference, in draft article 8, to the applicability of the procedure in articles 42 to 45 of the 1969 Vienna Convention for the suspension or termination of treaties, which established procedures which did not accord with the reality of an armed conflict.

Article 11.   Decisions of the Security Council[358]

Article 12.   Status of third States as neutrals[359]

Article 13.   Cases of termination or suspension[360]

Article 14.   The revival of terminated or suspended treaties[361]

---

[358] Draft article 11 reads as follows:

"*Decisions of the Security Council*

"These articles are without prejudice to the legal effects of decisions of the Security Council in accordance with the provisions of Chapter VII of the Charter of the United Nations."

[359] Draft article 12 reads as follows:

"*Status of third States as neutrals*

"The present draft articles are without prejudice to the status of third States as neutrals in relation to an armed conflict."

[360] Draft article 13 reads as follows:

"*Cases of termination or suspension*

"The present draft articles are without prejudice to the termination or suspension of treaties as a consequence of:

"(*a*)   the agreement of the parties; or

"(*b*)   a material breach; or

"(*c*)   supervening impossibility of performance; or

"(*d*)   a fundamental change of circumstances."

[361] Draft article 14 reads as follows:

"*The revival of terminated or suspended treaties*

"The present draft articles are without prejudice to the competence of parties to an armed conflict to regulate the question of the maintenance in force or revival of treaties, suspended or terminated as a result of the armed conflict, on the basis of agreement."

(a)   *Introduction by the Special Rapporteur*

310.   The Special Rapporteur observed that draft articles 11 to 14 were primarily expository in character. As regards article 12, the Special Rapporteur explained that he had attempted to make a reference to the issue without embarking on an excursus on neutrality under contemporary international law, which was a complex subject. The point was that the issue of neutrality had not been ignored; it was just that the draft articles were to be without prejudice to it. He noted that it was useful to retain draft article 13 given the amount of confusion there existed between cases of termination or suspension as a consequence of the outbreak of armed conflict as opposed to the situations listed in the draft article.

(b)   *Summary of the debate*

311.   Regarding draft article 11, the concern was expressed that the issue of the application of Chapter VII of the Charter of the United Nations, which related to threats to the peace, breaches of the peace, and acts of aggression, was too central to the topic at hand to be relegated to a "without prejudice" clause modelled on article 75 of the 1969 Vienna Convention. While that solution was understandable in the context of the Vienna Convention, it was considered insufficient specifically in terms of the effects of armed conflicts on treaties. It was proposed that the provision be replaced by articles 8 and 9 of the resolution adopted by the Institute of International Law in 1985.

312.   Difficulties were expressed with the use of the word "neutral" in draft article 12: would it apply to those States which declared themselves neutral or those which enjoyed permanent neutrality status? The situation had evolved since the establishment of the United Nations, and in some cases, neutrality was no longer possible, for example, in the context of decisions taken under Chapter VII of the Charter of the United Nations. Reference was further made to the existence of examples of States which were non-belligerents but not neutrals. That distinction was important for the debate on the impact on third States: third States were not automatically neutral, and neutral States were not automatically third States. It was further proposed that the reference to neutrality be deleted from the provision entirely.

313.   With regard to draft article 14, it was suggested that the word "competence" be replaced by "capacity", in line with the text of draft article 5 *bis*.

3.   SPECIAL RAPPORTEUR'S CONCLUDING REMARKS

314.   The Special Rapporteur referred to the areas of convergence in the debate, such as on the inclusion of internal armed conflicts. He noted that he had approached the topic from three overlapping perspectives. First, he had delved into the literature of the subject, with the assistance of the Secretariat. His three reports were largely based on State practice and what knowledge could be gleaned from learned authors. Secondly, the draft articles constituted a clear but careful reflection of the fact that he adopted the principle of stability, or continuity, as a policy datum. However, in his view, the principle of continuity

was qualified by the need to reflect the evidence in State practice that, to some extent, armed conflict did indeed result in the suspension or termination of treaties. Thirdly, he had consciously attempted to protect the project by carefully segregating other controversial areas, such as the law relating to the use of force by States, that lay outside the scope of the topic as approved by the General Assembly.

315. With regard to draft article 1 (Scope), the Special Rapporteur confirmed that he had no strong position on the issue of the provisional application of treaties. The question of international organizations was also one of the issues of principle to be considered. Some members seemed to have not distinguished between whether the effects of armed conflict on treaties of international organizations was a viable subject—which it probably was—and the very different question of whether it could be grafted on to the topic that the General Assembly had requested the Commission to study.

316. As for draft article 2 (Use of terms), the Special Rapporteur noted that the definition of "armed conflict" was central to the Commission's project, yet it also came close to the borderline with other areas of international law. The debate had revolved around the question of whether internal armed conflict was or was not to be included, but the article was not drafted in those terms. He noted that the issue of the intensity of the armed conflict was covered by the use of the phrase "nature or extent". To his mind, armed conflict should not be defined in quantitative terms. Everything depended on the nature not only of the conflict but also of the treaty provision concerned.

317. The Special Rapporteur acknowledged that draft article 3 (Non-automatic termination or suspension) was problematical, and recalled that he had said as much in his first report. There were three related aspects of the provision. First, it was deliberately chronological: it simply asserted that the outbreak of armed conflict did not, as such, terminate or suspend the operation of a treaty. At a later stage, when the legality of the situation came to be assessed on the basis of the facts, the question of the applicable law would arise. The second aspect was that of continuity, and he noted the suggestion that the draft article should be reformulated to state the principle of continuity more forcefully. The third aspect of draft article 3 was that it represented a major historical advance at the doctorinal level that a significant majority of members of the Institute of International Law from different nationalities and backgrounds had been willing to move to that position.

318. The Special Rapporteur remarked that, in draft article 4 (The indicia of susceptibility to termination or suspension of treaties in case of an armed conflict), he had carefully avoided using the term "intention" in the abstract. The issue was one of interpretation, in accordance with articles 31 and 32 of the Vienna Convention. Moreover, draft article 4 also referred to the nature and extent of the armed conflict. In response to the suggestion that a more direct reference was needed to specific criteria of compatibility, he maintained that those criteria were already covered. Furthermore, he recalled that in judicial

practice, when discussing other topics of the law of treaties, intention was constantly referred to. It also featured in standard legal dictionaries. Accordingly, intention could not be simply dismissed out of hand. Furthermore, if intention were to be set aside, what would happen when there was direct evidence of it? While it was correct to say that intention was often constructed and accordingly fictitious, there was no particular difficulty with that. The real difficulty was proving intention.

319. With regard to draft article 6 *bis* (The law applicable in armed conflict) the Special Rapporteur noted that the provision had attracted a good deal of valid criticism and would need further work. His instructions had been to take into account what the ICJ had said in its advisory opinion in the case concerning the *Legality of the Threat or Use of Nuclear Weapons*, yet he now conceded that the text should also refer to the 2004 advisory opinion on the *Legal Consequences of the Construction of a Wall in the Occupied Palestinian Territory*.

320. The Special Rapporteur observed that draft article 7 (The operation of treaties on the basis of necessary implication from their object and purpose), which he hoped would be retained in one form or another, played an important function. While State practice was not as plentiful as might be desired in certain categories, it was fairly abundant. Draft article 7 was the vehicle for expressing that State practice in an orderly way. The Commission had to decide whether to include in the list in paragraph 2 treaties codifying *jus cogens* rules. The Secretariat memorandum had suggested that such treaties be included, but that raised the problem of borderlines with other subjects. He was not sure that it was even technically correct to include such treaties, and if they were to be included, yet another "without prejudice" clause would be necessary.

321. With regard to draft article 10 (Effect of the exercise of the right to individual or collective self-defence on a treaty), the Special Rapporteur noted the general view in the Commission that references to the law relating to the use of force should be strengthened. However, he noted that the redrafted version of the draft article was a careful compromise, and to go any further might be to venture into uncharted juridical seas.

322. The Special Rapporteur pointed out that, in connection with draft article 12 (Status of third States as neutrals), there had arisen the question of the extent to which the draft articles should refer to other fields of international law such as neutrality or permanent neutrality. In his view, the Commission had to be careful: armed conflict was self-evidently a core part of the topic, but other areas like neutrality were genuine borderline cases. It was recalled that draft article 13 (Cases of termination or suspension) simply made the obvious point that the draft was without prejudice to the provisions set forth in the 1969 Vienna Convention. As in the law of tort, there might be several overlapping causes of action. Thus, the effect of war on treaties might be paralleled by other types of fundamental change of circumstances. Furthermore, separability had not been overlooked, but deliberately left aside.

C. Report of the Working Group

1. INTRODUCTION

323. The work programme of the Working Group was organized into three clusters of issues: (*a*) matters related to the scope of the draft articles; (*b*) questions concerning draft articles 3, 4 and 7, as proposed by the Special Rapporteur in his third report; and (*c*) other matters raised during the debate in the plenary. The Working Group completed its consideration of the first two clusters, but was unable to complete its work on the third cluster. The Working Group held eight meetings from 10 to 24 July 2007.

2. RECOMMENDATIONS OF THE WORKING GROUP

324. The Working Group recommended that:

(1) Draft articles 1 to 3, 5, 5 *bis*, 7, 10 and 11, as proposed by the Special Rapporteur in his third report, be referred to the Drafting Committee, with the following guidance:

(*a*) As regards draft article 1:

(i) the draft articles should apply to all treaties between States where at least one of which is a party to an armed conflict;

(ii) in principle, the consideration of treaties involving international intergovernmental organizations should be left in abeyance until a later stage of the Commission's work on the overall topic, at which point issues of the definition of international organizations and which types of treaties (namely whether treaties between States and international organizations or also those between international organizations *inter se*) would be considered;

(iii) the Secretariat should be asked to circulate a note to international organizations requesting information about their practice with regard to the effect of armed conflict on treaties involving them.

(*b*) With regard to the definition of "armed conflict" reflected in article 2, paragraph (*b*), for purposes of the draft articles:

(i) in principle, the definition of armed conflict should cover internal armed conflicts with the proviso that States should only be able to invoke the existence of internal armed conflicts in order to suspend or terminate treaties when the conflict has reached a certain level of intensity;

(ii) occupation in the course of an armed conflict should not be excluded from the definition of "armed conflict".

(*c*) Concerning draft article 7:

(i) the phrase "object and purpose" in paragraph 1 should be replaced by "subject matter" to be in line with the formulation proposed for draft article 4 (see below); and the provision be placed closer to draft article 4;

(ii) paragraph 2 should be deleted and the list contained therein be included in an appendix to the draft articles with the indication that:[362]

  – the list is non-exhaustive;

  – the various types of treaties on the list may be subject to termination or suspension either in whole or in part;

  – the list is based on practice and, accordingly, its contents may change over time.

(*d*) As regards draft articles 10 and 11, the Drafting Committee should proceed along the lines of articles 7, 8 and 9 of the resolution of the Institute of International Law adopted in 1985.

(2) The following revised formulation for draft article 4 should be referred to the Drafting Committee:

"In order to ascertain whether a treaty is susceptible to termination or suspension in the event of an armed conflict, resort shall be had to:

(*a*) articles 31 and 32 of the Vienna Convention on the Law of Treaties; and

(*b*) the nature and extent of the armed conflict, the effect of the armed conflict on the treaty, the subject matter of the treaty and the number of parties to the treaty."

(3) Draft article 6 *bis* should be deleted and its subject matter reflected in the commentaries, possibly to draft article 7.

(4) The Working Group should be re-established at the sixtieth session of the Commission, in 2008, to complete its work on remaining issues relating to draft articles 8, 9, and 12 to 14.

---

[362] The Drafting Committee should reconsider the list taking into account the views expressed in the plenary debate.

Chapter VIII

RESPONSIBILITY OF INTERNATIONAL ORGANIZATIONS

A. Introduction

325.   At its fifty-second session (2000), the Commission decided to include the topic "Responsibility of international organizations" in its long-term programme of work.[363] The General Assembly, in paragraph 8 of its resolution 55/152 of 12 December 2000, took note of the Commission's decision with regard to the long-term programme of work, and of the syllabus for the new topic annexed to the report of the Commission to the General Assembly on the work of that session. The General Assembly, in paragraph 8 of its resolution 56/82 of 12 December 2001, requested the Commission to begin its work on the topic "Responsibility of international organizations".

326.   At its fifty-fourth session, the Commission decided, at its 2717th meeting, held on 8 May 2002, to include the topic in its programme of work and appointed Mr. Giorgio Gaja as Special Rapporteur for the topic.[364] At the same session, the Commission established a Working Group on the topic.[365] The Working Group in its report[366] briefly considered the scope of the topic, the relations between the new project and the draft articles on "Responsibility of States for internationally wrongful acts" adopted by the Commission at its fifty-third session,[367] questions of attribution, issues relating to the responsibility of member States for conduct that is attributed to an international organization, and questions relating to the content of international responsibility, implementation of responsibility and settlement of disputes. At the end of its fifty-fourth session, the Commission adopted the report of the Working Group.[368]

327.   From its fifty-fifth (2003) to its fifty-eighth (2006) sessions, the Commission had received and considered four reports from the Special Rapporteur,[369] and provisionally adopted draft articles 1 to 30.[370]

B. Consideration of the topic at the present session

328.   At the present session, the Commission had before it the fifth report of the Special Rapporteur (A/CN.4/583), as well as written comments received so far from international organizations.[371]

329.   The fifth report of the Special Rapporteur, dealing with the content of the international responsibility of an international organization, followed, like the previous reports, the general pattern of the articles on responsibility of States for internationally wrongful acts.

330.   In introducing its fifth report, the Special Rapporteur addressed some comments made on the draft articles provisionally adopted by the Commission. As to the view that the current draft did not take sufficiently into account the great variety of international organizations, he indicated that the draft articles had a level of generality which made them appropriate for most, if not all, international organizations; this did not exclude, if the particular features of certain organizations so warranted, the application of special rules.

331.   The Special Rapporteur also referred to the insufficient availability of practice in respect of the responsibility of international organizations. While calling for more information on relevant instances being provided to the Commission, he emphasized the usefulness of the draft articles as an analytical framework, which should assist States and international organizations in focusing on the main legal issues raised by the topic.

332.   In introducing the draft articles contained in his fifth report, the Special Rapporteur indicated that the work undertaken by the Commission did not consist in merely reiterating the articles on responsibility of States for internationally wrongful acts. Whether or not the legal issues addressed were covered by these articles, they were considered on their own merits with regard to international organizations. Given the level of generality of the draft however, he deemed it reasonable to adopt a similar wording to that used in the articles on State responsibility

---

[363] *Yearbook ... 2000*, vol. II (Part Two), p. 131, para. 729.

[364] *Yearbook ... 2002*, vol. II (Part Two), p. 93, paras. 461 and 463.

[365] *Ibid.*, p. 93, para. 462.

[366] *Ibid.*, pp. 93–96, paras. 465–488.

[367] *Yearbook ... 2001*, vol. II (Part Two) and corrigendum, pp. 26–30, para. 76.

[368] *Yearbook ... 2002*, vol. II (Part Two), para. 464.

[369] First report: *Yearbook ... 2003*, vol. II (Part One), document A/CN.4/532; second report: *Yearbook ... 2004*, vol. II (Part One), document A/CN.4/541; third report: *Yearbook ... 2005*, vol. II (Part One), document A/CN.4/553; and fourth report: *Yearbook ... 2006*, vol. II (Part One), document A/CN.4/564 and Add.1–2.

[370] Draft articles 1 to 3 were adopted at the fifty-fifth session (*Yearbook ... 2003*, vol. II (Part Two), p. 18, para. 49); draft articles 4 to 7 at the fifty-sixth session (*Yearbook ... 2004*, vol. II (Part Two), p. 46, para. 69); draft articles 8 to 16 [15] at the fifty-seventh session (*Yearbook ... 2005*, vol. II (Part Two), p. 40, para. 203); and draft articles 17 to 30 at the fifty-eighth session (*Yearbook ... 2006*, vol. II (Part Two), p. 118, para. 88).

[371] Following the recommendations of the Commission (*Yearbook ... 2002*, vol. II (Part Two), p. 93, para. 464 and p. 96, para. 488 and *Yearbook ... 2003*, vol. II (Part Two), p. 18, para. 52.), the Secretariat, on an annual basis, has been circulating the relevant chapter of the report of the Commission to international organizations asking for their comments and for any relevant materials which they could provide to the Commission. For comments from Governments and international organizations, see *Yearbook ... 2004*, vol. II (Part One), documents A/CN.4/545; *Yearbook ... 2005*, vol. II (Part One), document A/CN.4/547 and A/CN.4/556; and *Yearbook ... 2006*, vol. II (Part One), document A/CN.4/568 and Add.1. See also document A/CN.4/582 (reproduced in *Yearbook ... 2007*, vol. II (Part One)).

in the many instances where the provisions could equally apply to States and to international organizations. This was actually the case for most of the draft articles proposed in his fifth report.

333. The fifth report contained 14 draft articles, corresponding to Part Two of the articles on State responsibility. Draft articles 31 to 36 dealt with general principles of the content of international responsibility of an international organization; draft articles 37 to 42 related to reparation for injury and draft articles 43 and 44 addressed the issue of serious breaches of obligations under peremptory norms of general international law.

334. The Special Rapporteur presented the six draft articles embodying general principles, namely: draft article 31 (Legal consequences of an internationally wrongful act),[372] draft article 32 (Continued duty of performance),[373] draft article 33 (Cessation and non-repetition),[374] draft article 34 (Reparation),[375] draft article 35 (Irrelevance of the rules of the organization),[376] and draft article 36 (Scope of international obligations set out in this Part).[377]

335. Draft articles 31 to 34 and 36 followed closely the wording of the corresponding provisions on responsibility

---

[372] Draft article 31 reads as follows:

"Legal consequences of an internationally wrongful act

"The international responsibility of an international organization which is entailed by an internationally wrongful act in accordance with the provisions of Part One involves legal consequences as set out in this Part."

[373] Draft article 32 reads as follows:

"Continued duty of performance

"The legal consequences of an internationally wrongful act under this Part do not affect the continued duty of the responsible international organization to perform the obligation breached."

[374] Draft article 33 reads as follows:

"Cessation and non-repetition

"The international organization responsible for the internationally wrongful act is under an obligation:

"(*a*) to cease that act, if it is continuing;

"(*b*) to offer appropriate assurances and guarantees of non-repetition, if circumstances so require."

[375] Draft article 34 reads as follows:

"Reparation

"1. The responsible international organization is under an obligation to make full reparation for the injury caused by the internationally wrongful act.

"2. Injury includes any damage, whether material or moral, caused by the internationally wrongful act of an international organization."

[376] Draft article 35 reads as follows:

"Irrelevance of the rules of the organization

"Unless the rules of the organization otherwise provide for the relations between an international organization and its member States and organizations, the responsible organization may not rely on the provisions of its pertinent rules as justification for failure to comply with the obligations under this Part."

[377] Draft article 36 reads as follows:

"Scope of international obligations set out in this Part

"1. The obligations of the responsible international organization set out in this Part may be owed to one or more other organizations, to one or more States, or to the international community as a whole, depending in particular on the character and content of the international obligation and on the circumstances of the breach.

"2. This Part is without prejudice to any right, arising from the international responsibility of an international organization, which may accrue directly to a person or entity other than a State or an international organization."

of States for internationally wrongful acts. In the view of the Special Rapporteur, the principles contained in these articles were equally applicable to international organizations. The situation was somewhat different in respect of draft article 35: whereas a State could not rely on the provisions of its internal law as justification for failure to comply with the obligations entailed by its responsibility, an international organization might be entitled to rely on its internal rules as a justification for not giving reparation towards its members. The proviso in draft article 35 was designed to deal with this particular assumption.

336. The Special Rapporteur also introduced six draft articles in respect of reparation for injury, namely: draft article 37 (Forms of reparation),[378] draft article 38 (Restitution),[379] draft article 39 (Compensation),[380] draft article 40 (Satisfaction),[381] draft article 41 (Interest),[382] and draft article 42 (Contribution to the injury).[383]

337. Despite the paucity of relevant practice as far as international organizations were concerned, the few

---

[378] Draft article 37 reads as follows:

"Forms of reparation

"Full reparation for the injury caused by the internationally wrongful act shall take the form of restitution, compensation and satisfaction, either singly or in combination, in accordance with the provisions of this chapter."

[379] Draft article 38 reads as follows:

"Restitution

"An international organization responsible for an internationally wrongful act is under an obligation to make restitution, that is, to re-establish the situation which existed before the wrongful act was committed, provided and to the extent that restitution:

"(*a*) is not materially impossible;

"(*b*) does not involve a burden out of all proportion to the benefit deriving from restitution instead of compensation."

[380] Draft article 39 reads as follows:

"Compensation

"1. The international organization responsible for an internationally wrongful act is under an obligation to compensate for the damage caused thereby, insofar as such damage is not made good by restitution.

"2. The compensation shall cover any financially assessable damage including loss of profits insofar as it is established."

[381] Draft article 40 reads as follows:

"Satisfaction

"1. The international organization responsible for an internationally wrongful act is under an obligation to give satisfaction for the injury caused by that act insofar as it cannot be made good by restitution or compensation.

"2. Satisfaction may consist in an acknowledgement of the breach, an expression of regret, a formal apology or another appropriate modality.

"3. Satisfaction shall not be out of proportion to the injury and may not take a form humiliating to the responsible international organization."

[382] Draft article 41 reads as follows:

"Interest

"1. Interest on any principal sum payable under this chapter shall be payable when necessary in order to ensure full reparation. The interest rate and mode of calculation shall be set so as to achieve that result.

"2. Interest runs from the date when the principal sum should have been paid until the date the obligation to pay is fulfilled."

[383] Draft article 42 reads as follows:

"Contribution to the injury

"In the determination of reparation, account shall be taken of the contribution to the injury by wilful or negligent action or omission of the injured State or international organization or of any person or entity in relation to whom reparation is sought."

instances that could be found confirmed the applicability to them of the rules on reparation adopted in respect of States. There was thus no reason for departing from the text of the articles on State responsibility in that regard.

338. The Special Rapporteur then presented two draft articles dealing with serious breaches of obligations under peremptory norms of general international law, namely: draft article 43 (Application of this chapter),[384] and draft article 44 (Particular consequences of a serious breach of an obligation under this chapter).[385]

339. Regarding serious breaches of obligations under peremptory norms of general international law, the Special Rapporteur recalled the comments made by States and international organizations in response to questions addressed by the Commission in its previous report.[386] He deemed it reasonable to consider that both States and international organizations had the obligation to co-operate to bring the breach to an end, not to recognize the situation as lawful and not to render aid or assistance in maintaining it. This did not imply that the organization should act beyond its powers under its constitutive instrument or other pertinent rules.

340. The Commission considered the fifth report of the Special Rapporteur at its 2932nd to 2935th and 2938th meetings from 9 to 12 July 2007 and on 18 July 2007. At its 2935th meeting, on 12 July 2007, the Commission referred draft articles 31 to 44 to the Drafting Committee. At the same meeting, a supplementary draft article was proposed by a member of the Commission.[387] The Special Rapporteur proposed a different supplementary article on the same issue. At the 2938th meeting, on 18 July 2007, the Commission referred the draft article proposed by the Special Rapporteur to the Drafting Committee.[388]

---

[384] Draft article 43 reads as follows:

"*Application of this chapter*

"1. This chapter applies to the international responsibility which is entailed by a serious breach by an international organization of an obligation arising under a peremptory norm of general international law.

"2. Breach of such an obligation is serious if it involves a gross or systematic failure by the responsible international organization to fulfil the obligation."

[385] Draft article 44 reads as follows:

"*Particular consequences of a serious breach of an obligation under this chapter*

"1. States and international organizations shall cooperate to bring to an end through lawful means any serious breach within the meaning of article 43.

"2. No State or international organization shall recognize as lawful a situation created by a serious breach within the meaning of article 43, nor render aid or assistance in maintaining that situation.

"3. This article is without prejudice to the other consequences referred to in this Part and to such further consequences that a breach to which this chapter applies may entail under international law."

[386] *Yearbook ... 2006*, vol. II (Part Two), p. 21, para. 28.

[387] The supplementary draft article reads as follows:

"The member States of the responsible international organization shall provide the organization with the means to effectively carry out its obligations arising under the present part."

[388] In its amended version, the supplementary draft article reads as follows:

"In accordance with the rules of the responsible international organization, its members are required to take all appropriate measures in

341. The Commission considered and adopted the report of the Drafting Committee on draft articles 31 to 44 [45] at its 2945th meeting, on 31 July 2007 (sect. C.1 below).

342. At its 2949th to 2954th meetings, on 6, 7 and 8 August 2007, the Commission adopted the commentaries to the aforementioned draft articles (sect. C.2 below).

C. Text of the draft articles on responsibility of international organizations provisionally adopted so far by the Commission

1. TEXT OF THE DRAFT ARTICLES

343. The text of the draft articles provisionally adopted so far by the Commission is reproduced below.

RESPONSIBILITY OF INTERNATIONAL ORGANIZATIONS

PART ONE

THE INTERNATIONALLY WRONGFUL ACT OF AN INTERNATIONAL ORGANIZATION

CHAPTER I

INTRODUCTION

Article 1.[389]   *Scope of the present draft articles*

1.   **The present draft articles apply to the international responsibility of an international organization for an act that is wrongful under international law.**

2.   **The present draft articles also apply to the international responsibility of a State for the internationally wrongful act of an international organization.**

Article 2.[390]   *Use of terms*

For the purposes of the present draft articles, the term "international organization" refers to an organization established by a treaty or other instrument governed by international law and possessing its own international legal personality. International organizations may include as members, in addition to States, other entities.

Article 3.[391]   *General principles*

1.   **Every internationally wrongful act of an international organization entails the international responsibility of the international organization.**

2.   **There is an internationally wrongful act of an international organization when conduct consisting of an action or omission:**

(*a*)   **is attributable to the international organization under international law; and**

(*b*)   **constitutes a breach of an international obligation of that international organization.**

---

order to provide the organization with the means for effectively fulfilling its obligations under the present chapter."

[389] For the commentary to this article, see *Yearbook ... 2003*, vol. II (Part Two), chapter IV, section C.2, pp. 18–19, paragraph 54.

[390] *Idem.*

[391] *Idem.*

CHAPTER II[392]

ATTRIBUTION OF CONDUCT TO AN INTERNATIONAL ORGANIZATION

Article 4.[393]   *General rule on attribution of conduct to an international organization*

1.   The conduct of an organ or agent of an international organization in the performance of functions of that organ or agent shall be considered as an act of that organization under international law whatever position the organ or agent holds in respect of the organization.

2.   For the purposes of paragraph 1, the term "agent" includes officials and other persons or entities through whom the organization acts.[394]

3.   Rules of the organization shall apply to the determination of the functions of its organs and agents.

4.   For the purpose of the present draft article, "rules of the organization" means, in particular: the constituent instruments; decisions, resolutions and other acts taken by the organization in accordance with those instruments; and established practice of the organization.[395]

Article 5.[396]   *Conduct of organs or agents placed at the disposal of an international organization by a State or another international organization*

The conduct of an organ of a State or an organ or agent of an international organization that is placed at the disposal of another international organization shall be considered under international law an act of the latter organization if the organization exercises effective control over that conduct.

Article 6.[397]   *Excess of authority or contravention of instructions*

The conduct of an organ or an agent of an international organization shall be considered an act of that organization under international law if the organ or agent acts in that capacity, even though the conduct exceeds the authority of that organ or agent or contravenes instructions.

Article 7.[398]   *Conduct acknowledged and adopted by an international organization as its own*

Conduct which is not attributable to an international organization under the preceding draft articles shall nevertheless be considered an act of that international organization under international law if and to the extent that the organization acknowledges and adopts the conduct in question as its own.

CHAPTER III[399]

BREACH OF AN INTERNATIONAL OBLIGATION

Article 8.[400]   *Existence of a breach of an international obligation*

1.   There is a breach of an international obligation by an international organization when an act of that international organization is not in conformity with what is required of it by that obligation, regardless of its origin and character.

2.   Paragraph 1 also applies to the breach of an obligation under international law established by a rule of the international organization.

Article 9.[401]   *International obligation in force for an international organization*

An act of an international organization does not constitute a breach of an international obligation unless the international organization is bound by the obligation in question at the time the act occurs.

Article 10.[402]   *Extension in time of the breach of an international obligation*

1.   The breach of an international obligation by an act of an international organization not having a continuing character occurs at the moment when the act is performed, even if its effects continue.

2.   The breach of an international obligation by an act of an international organization having a continuing character extends over the entire period during which the act continues and remains not in conformity with the international obligation.

3.   The breach of an international obligation requiring an international organization to prevent a given event occurs when the event occurs and extends over the entire period during which the event continues and remains not in conformity with that obligation.

Article 11.[403]   *Breach consisting of a composite act*

1.   The breach of an international obligation by an international organization through a series of actions and omissions defined in aggregate as wrongful, occurs when the action or omission occurs which, taken with the other actions or omissions, is sufficient to constitute the wrongful act.

2.   In such a case, the breach extends over the entire period starting with the first of the actions or omissions of the series and lasts for as long as these actions or omissions are repeated and remain not in conformity with the international obligation.

CHAPTER IV[404]

RESPONSIBILITY OF AN INTERNATIONAL ORGANIZATION IN CONNECTION WITH THE ACT OF A STATE OR ANOTHER INTERNATIONAL ORGANIZATION

Article 12.[405]   *Aid or assistance in the commission of an internationally wrongful act*

An international organization which aids or assists a State or another international organization in the commission of an internationally wrongful act by the State or the latter organization is internationally responsible for doing so if:

(*a*)   that organization does so with knowledge of the circumstances of the internationally wrongful act; and

(*b*)   the act would be internationally wrongful if committed by that organization.

Article 13.[406]   *Direction and control exercised over the commission of an internationally wrongful act*

An international organization which directs and controls a State or another international organization in the commission of an internationally wrongful act by the State or the latter organization is internationally responsible for that act if:

(*a*)   that organization does so with knowledge of the circumstances of the internationally wrongful act; and

---

[392] For the commentary to this chapter, see *Yearbook ... 2004*, vol. II (Part Two), chapter V, section C.2, p. 47, paragraph 72.

[393] For the commentary to this article, see *idem*, pp. 48–50.

[394] The location of paragraph 2 may be reconsidered at a later stage with a view to eventually placing all definitions of terms in article 2.

[395] The location of paragraph 4 may be reconsidered at a later stage with a view to eventually placing all definitions of terms in article 2.

[396] For the commentary to this article, see *Yearbook ... 2004*, vol. II (Part Two), chapter V, section C.2, paragraph 72, pp. 50–52.

[397] *Idem*, pp. 52–53.

[398] *Idem*, pp. 53–54.

[399] For the commentary to this chapter, see *Yearbook ... 2005*, vol. II (Part Two), chapter VI, section C.2, paragraph 206, p. 42.

[400] For the commentary to this article, see *idem*, pp. 42–43.

[401] *Idem*, pp. 43–44.

[402] *Idem*, p. 44.

[403] *Idem*, p. 44.

[404] For the commentary to this chapter, see *idem*, pp. 44–45.

[405] For the commentary to this article, see *idem*, p. 45.

[406] *Idem*, p. 46.

(b)   the act would be internationally wrongful if committed by that organization.

Article 14.[407]   Coercion of a State or another international organization

An international organization which coerces a State or another international organization to commit an act is internationally responsible for that act if:

(a)   the act would, but for the coercion, be an internationally wrongful act of the coerced State or international organization; and

(b)   the coercing international organization does so with knowledge of the circumstances of the act.

Article 15 [16].[408]   Decisions, recommendations and authorizations addressed to member States and international organizations

1.   An international organization incurs international responsibility if it adopts a decision binding a member State or international organization to commit an act that would be internationally wrongful if committed by the former organization and would circumvent an international obligation of the former organization.

2.   An international organization incurs international responsibility if:

(a)   it authorizes a member State or international organization to commit an act that would be internationally wrongful if committed by the former organization and would circumvent an international obligation of the former organization, or recommends that a member State or international organization commit such an act; and

(b)   that State or international organization commits the act in question in reliance on that authorization or recommendation.

3.   Paragraphs 1 and 2 apply whether or not the act in question is internationally wrongful for the member State or international organization to which the decision, authorization or recommendation is directed.

Article 16 [15].[409]   Effect of this chapter

This chapter is without prejudice to the international responsibility of the State or international organization which commits the act in question, or of any other State or international organization.

CHAPTER V[410]

CIRCUMSTANCES PRECLUDING WRONGFULNESS

Article 17.[411]   Consent

Valid consent by a State or an international organization to the commission of a given act by another international organization precludes the wrongfulness of that act in relation to that State or the former organization to the extent that the act remains within the limits of that consent.

Article 18.[412]   Self-defence

The wrongfulness of an act of an international organization is precluded if the act constitutes a lawful measure of self-defence taken in conformity with the principles of international law embodied in the Charter of the United Nations.

Article 19.[413]   Countermeasures

...[414]

Article 20.[415]   Force majeure

1.   The wrongfulness of an act of an international organization not in conformity with an international obligation of that organization is precluded if the act is due to force majeure, that is, the occurrence of an irresistible force or of an unforeseen event, beyond the control of the organization, making it materially impossible in the circumstances to perform the obligation.

2.   Paragraph 1 does not apply if:

(a)   the situation of force majeure is due, either alone or in combination with other factors, to the conduct of the organization invoking it; or

(b)   the organization has assumed the risk of that situation occurring.

Article 21.[416]   Distress

1.   The wrongfulness of an act of an international organization not in conformity with an international obligation of that organization is precluded if the author of the act in question has no other reasonable way, in a situation of distress, of saving the author's life or the lives of other persons entrusted to the author's care.

2.   Paragraph 1 does not apply if:

(a)   the situation of distress is due, either alone or in combination with other factors, to the conduct of the organization invoking it; or

(b)   the act in question is likely to create a comparable or greater peril.

Article 22.[417]   Necessity

1.   Necessity may not be invoked by an international organization as a ground for precluding the wrongfulness of an act not in conformity with an international obligation of that organization unless the act:

(a)   is the only means for the organization to safeguard against a grave and imminent peril an essential interest of the international community as a whole when the organization has, in accordance with international law, the function to protect that interest; and

(b)   does not seriously impair an essential interest of the State or States towards which the obligation exists, or of the international community as a whole.

2.   In any case, necessity may not be invoked by an international organization as a ground for precluding wrongfulness if:

(a)   the international obligation in question excludes the possibility of invoking necessity; or

(b)   the organization has contributed to the situation of necessity.

Article 23.[418]   Compliance with peremptory norms

Nothing in this chapter precludes the wrongfulness of any act of an international organization which is not in conformity with an obligation arising under a peremptory norm of general international law.

---

[407] Idem, pp. 46–47.

[408] Idem, pp. 47–48. The square bracket refers to the corresponding article in the third report of the Special Rapporteur, Yearbook ... 2005, vol. II (Part One), document A/CN.4/553.

[409] For the commentary to this article, see Yearbook ... 2005, vol. II (Part Two), chapter VI, section C.2, paragraph 206, p. 48.

[410] For the commentary to this chapter, see Yearbook ... 2006, vol. II (Part Two), chapter VII, section C.2, paragraph 91, p. 121.

[411] For the commentary to this article, see ibid., pp. 121–122.

[412] Idem, pp. 122–123.

[413] Idem.

[414] Draft article 19 concerns countermeasures by an international organization in respect of an internationally wrongful act of another international organization or a State as circumstances precluding wrongfulness. The text of this draft article will be drafted at a later stage, when the issues relating to countermeasures by an international organization will be examined in the context of the implementation of the responsibility of an international organization.

[415] For the commentary to this article, see Yearbook ... 2006, vol. II (Part Two), chapter VII, section C.2, paragraph 91, p. 123.

[416] For the commentary to this article, see ibid., p. 124.

[417] Idem, pp. 124–125.

[418] Idem, p. 125.

Article 24.[419]   *Consequences of invoking a*
circumstance precluding wrongfulness

The invocation of a circumstance precluding wrongfulness in accordance with this chapter is without prejudice to:

(*a*)   compliance with the obligation in question, if and to the extent that the circumstance precluding wrongfulness no longer exists;

(*b*)   the question of compensation for any material loss caused by the act in question.

CHAPTER (X)[420]

RESPONSIBILITY OF A STATE IN CONNECTION WITH THE ACT OF AN INTERNATIONAL ORGANIZATION

Article 25.[421]   *Aid or assistance by a State in the commission of an internationally wrongful act by an international organization*

A State which aids or assists an international organization in the commission of an internationally wrongful act by the latter is internationally responsible for doing so if:

(*a*)   that State does so with knowledge of the circumstances of the internationally wrongful act; and

(*b*)   the act would be internationally wrongful if committed by that State.

Article 26.[422]   *Direction and control exercised by a State over the commission of an internationally wrongful act by an international organization*

A State which directs and controls an international organization in the commission of an internationally wrongful act by the latter is internationally responsible for that act if:

(*a*)   that State does so with knowledge of the circumstances of the internationally wrongful act; and

(*b*)   the act would be internationally wrongful if committed by that State.

Article 27.[423]   *Coercion of an international organization by a State*

A State which coerces an international organization to commit an act is internationally responsible for that act if:

(*a*)   the act would, but for the coercion, be an internationally wrongful act of that international organization; and

(*b*)   that State does so with knowledge of the circumstances of the act.

Article 28.[424]   *International responsibility in case of provision of competence to an international organization*

1.   A State member of an international organization incurs international responsibility if it circumvents one of its international obligations by providing the organization with competence in relation to that obligation, and the organization commits an act that, if committed by that State, would have constituted a breach of that obligation.

2.   Paragraph 1 applies whether or not the act in question is internationally wrongful for the international organization.

Article 29.[425]   *Responsibility of a State member of an international organization for the internationally wrongful act of that organization*

1.   Without prejudice to draft articles 25 to 28, a State member of an international organization is responsible for an internationally wrongful act of that organization if:

(*a*)   it has accepted responsibility for that act; or

(*b*)   it has led the injured party to rely on its responsibility.

2.   The international responsibility of a State which is entailed in accordance with paragraph 1 is presumed to be subsidiary.

Article 30.[426]   *Effect of this chapter*

This chapter is without prejudice to the international responsibility, under other provisions of these draft articles, of the international organization which commits the act in question, or of any other international organization.

PART TWO[427]

CONTENT OF THE INTERNATIONAL RESPONSIBILITY OF AN INTERNATIONAL ORGANIZATION

CHAPTER I

GENERAL PRINCIPLES

Article 31.[428]   *Legal consequences of an internationally wrongful act*

The international responsibility of an international organization which is entailed by an internationally wrongful act in accordance with the provisions of Part One involves legal consequences as set out in this Part.

Article 32.[429]   *Continued duty of performance*

The legal consequences of an internationally wrongful act under this Part do not affect the continued duty of the responsible international organization to perform the obligation breached.

Article 33.[430]   *Cessation and non-repetition*

The international organization responsible for the internationally wrongful act is under an obligation:

(*a*)   to cease that act, if it is continuing;

(*b*)   to offer appropriate assurances and guarantees of non-repetition, if circumstances so require.

Article 34.[431]   *Reparation*

1.   The responsible international organization is under an obligation to make full reparation for the injury caused by the internationally wrongful act.

2.   Injury includes any damage, whether material or moral, caused by the internationally wrongful act of an international organization.

Article 35.[432] *Irrelevance of the rules of the organization*

1.   The responsible international organization may not rely on its rules as justification for failure to comply with its obligations under this Part.

2.   Paragraph 1 is without prejudice to the applicability of the rules of an international organization in respect of the responsibility of the organization towards its member States and organizations.

---

[419] *Idem*, at p. 126.

[420] The location of this chapter will be determined at a later stage. For the commentary to this chapter, see *ibid.*

[421] For the commentary to this article, see *ibid.*

[422] *Idem*, at p. 135.

[423] *Idem*, at pp. 135–136.

[424] *Idem*, at pp. 136–137.

[425] *Idem*, at pp. 137–139.

[426] *Idem*, at p. 139.

[427] The commentary to this Part is in section C.2 below, at p. 77.

[428] The commentary to this article is in section C.2 below, at p. 78.

[429] *Idem*, at p. 78.

[430] *Idem*, at pp. 78–79.

[431] *Idem*, at p. 79.

[432] *Idem*, at pp. 79–80.

Article 36.[433] *Scope of international obligations set out in this Part*

1.   The obligations of the responsible international organization set out in this Part may be owed to one or more other organizations, to one or more States, or to the international community as a whole, depending in particular on the character and content of the international obligation and on the circumstances of the breach.

2.   This Part is without prejudice to any right, arising from the international responsibility of an international organization, which may accrue directly to any person or entity other than a State or an international organization.

CHAPTER II

REPARATION FOR INJURY

Article 37.[434] *Forms of reparation*

Full reparation for the injury caused by the internationally wrongful act shall take the form of restitution, compensation and satisfaction, either singly or in combination, in accordance with the provisions of this chapter.

Article 38.[435] *Restitution*

An international organization responsible for an internationally wrongful act is under an obligation to make restitution, that is, to re-establish the situation which existed before the wrongful act was committed, provided and to the extent that restitution:

(*a*)   is not materially impossible;

(*b*)   does not involve a burden out of all proportion to the benefit deriving from restitution instead of compensation.

Article 39.[436] *Compensation*

1.   The international organization responsible for an internationally wrongful act is under an obligation to compensate for the damage caused thereby, insofar as such damage is not made good by restitution.

2.   The compensation shall cover any financially assessable damage including loss of profits insofar as it is established.

Article 40.[437] *Satisfaction*

1.   The international organization responsible for an internationally wrongful act is under an obligation to give satisfaction for the injury caused by that act insofar as it cannot be made good by restitution or compensation.

2.   Satisfaction may consist in an acknowledgement of the breach, an expression of regret, a formal apology or another appropriate modality.

3.   Satisfaction shall not be out of proportion to the injury and may not take a form humiliating to the responsible international organization.

Article 41.[438] *Interest*

1.   Interest on any principal sum due under this chapter shall be payable when necessary in order to ensure full reparation. The interest rate and mode of calculation shall be set so as to achieve that result.

2.   Interest runs from the date when the principal sum should have been paid until the date the obligation to pay is fulfilled.

Article 42.[439] *Contribution to the injury*

In the determination of reparation, account shall be taken of the contribution to the injury by wilful or negligent action or omission of the injured State or international organization or of any person or entity in relation to whom reparation is sought.

Article 43.[440] [441] *Ensuring the effective performance of the obligation of reparation*

The members of a responsible international organization are required to take, in accordance with the rules of the organization, all appropriate measures in order to provide the organization with the means for effectively fulfilling its obligations under this chapter.

CHAPTER III

SERIOUS BREACHES OF OBLIGATIONS UNDER PEREMPTORY NORMS OF GENERAL INTERNATIONAL LAW

Article 44 [43].[442]   *Application of this chapter*

1.   This chapter applies to the international responsibility which is entailed by a serious breach by an international organization of an obligation arising under a peremptory norm of general international law.

2.   A breach of such an obligation is serious if it involves a gross or systematic failure by the responsible international organization to fulfil the obligation.

Article 45 [44].[443]   *Particular consequences of a serious breach of an obligation under this chapter*

1.   States and international organizations shall cooperate to bring to an end through lawful means any serious breach within the meaning of article 44 [43].

2.   No State or international organization shall recognize as lawful a situation created by a serious breach within the meaning of article 44 [43], nor render aid or assistance in maintaining that situation.

3.   This article is without prejudice to the other consequences referred to in this Part and to such further consequences that a breach to which this chapter applies may entail under international law.

2.   TEXT OF THE DRAFT ARTICLES WITH COMMENTARIES THERETO ADOPTED BY THE COMMISSION AT ITS FIFTY-NINTH SESSION

344.   The text of draft articles together with commentaries thereto provisionally adopted by the Commission at its fifty-ninth session is reproduced below.

PART TWO

CONTENT OF THE INTERNATIONAL RESPONSIBILITY OF AN INTERNATIONAL ORGANIZATION

(1)   Part Two of the present draft defines the legal consequences of internationally wrongful acts of international organizations. This Part is organized in three chapters, which follow the general pattern of the draft articles

---

[433] *Idem*, at p. 80.

[434] *Idem*, at p. 81.

[435] *Idem*, at p. 81.

[436] *Idem*, at pp. 81–82.

[437] *Idem*, at p. 82.

[438] *Idem*, at p. 82.

[439] *Idem*, at p. 83.

[440] *Idem*, at pp. 83–84.

[441] The following text was proposed, discussed and supported by some members: "The responsible international organization shall take all appropriate measures in accordance with its rules in order to ensure that its members provide the organization with the means for effectively fulfilling its obligations under this chapter."

[442] For the commentary, see section C.2 below, at p. 84. The square bracket refers to the corresponding article in the fifth report of the Special Rapporteur (A/CN.4/583).

[443] *Idem*, at pp. 84–85.

on responsibility of States for internationally wrongful acts.[444]

(2) Chapter I (arts. 31 to 36) lays down certain general principles and sets out the scope of Part Two. Chapter II (arts. 37 to 43) specifies the obligation of reparation in its various forms. Chapter III (arts. 44 [43] and 45 [44]) considers the additional consequences that are attached to internationally wrongful acts consisting of serious breaches of obligations under peremptory norms of general international law.

CHAPTER I

GENERAL PRINCIPLES

Article 31. Legal consequences of an internationally wrongful act

The international responsibility of an international organization which is entailed by an internationally wrongful act in accordance with the provisions of Part One involves legal consequences as set out in this Part.

Commentary

This provision has an introductory character. It corresponds to article 28 of the draft articles on responsibility of States for internationally wrongful acts,[445] with the only difference that the term "international organization" replaces the term "State". There would be no justification for using a different wording in the present draft.

Article 32. Continued duty of performance

The legal consequences of an internationally wrongful act under this Part do not affect the continued duty of the responsible international organization to perform the obligation breached.

Commentary

(1) This provision states the principle that the breach of an obligation under international law by an international organization does not *per se* affect the existence of that obligation. This is not intended to exclude that the obligation may terminate in connection with the breach: for instance, because the obligation arises under a treaty and the injured State or organization avails itself of the right to suspend or terminate the treaty in accordance with article 60 of the 1986 Vienna Convention.

(2) The principle that an obligation is not *per se* affected by a breach does not imply that performance of the obligation will still be possible after the breach occurs. This will depend on the character of the obligation concerned and of the breach. Should, for instance, an international organization be under the obligation to transfer some persons or property to a certain State, that obligation could no longer be performed once those persons or that property have been transferred to another State in breach of the obligation.

(3) The conditions under which an obligation may be suspended or terminated are governed by the primary rules concerning the obligation. The same applies with regard to the possibility of performing the obligation after the breach. These rules need not be examined in the context of the law of responsibility of international organizations.

(4) With regard to the statement of the continued duty of performance after a breach, there is no reason for distinguishing between the situation of States and that of international organizations. Thus the present article uses the same wording as article 29 of the draft articles on responsibility of States for internationally wrongful acts,[446] with the only difference that the term "State" is replaced with the term "international organization".

Article 33. Cessation and non-repetition

The international organization responsible for the internationally wrongful act is under an obligation:

(*a*) to cease that act, if it is continuing;

(*b*) to offer appropriate assurances and guarantees of non-repetition, if circumstances so require.

Commentary

(1) The principle that the breach of an obligation under international law does not *per se* affect the existence of that obligation, as stated in article 32, has the corollary that, if the wrongful act is continuing, the obligation has still to be complied with. Thus, the wrongful act is required to cease by the primary rule providing for the obligation.

(2) When the breach of an obligation occurs and the wrongful act continues, the main object pursued by the injured State or international organization will often be cessation of the wrongful conduct. Although a claim would refer to the breach, what would actually be sought is compliance with the obligation under the primary rule. This is not a new obligation that arises as a consequence of the wrongful act.

(3) The existence of an obligation to offer assurances and guarantees of non-repetition will depend on the circumstances of the case. For this obligation to arise, it is not necessary for the breach to be continuing. The obligation seems justified especially when the conduct of the responsible entity shows a pattern of breaches.

(4) Examples of assurances and guarantees of non-repetition given by international organizations are hard to find. However, there may be situations in which these assurances and guarantees are as appropriate as in the case of States. For instance, should an international organization be found in the persistent breach of a certain obligation—such as that of preventing sexual abuses by its officials or by members of its forces—guarantees of non-repetition would hardly be out of place.

---

[444] *Yearbook ... 2001*, vol. II (Part Two) and corrigendum, pp. 26 *et seq.*, para. 76.

[445] *Ibid.*, pp. 87–88.

[446] *Ibid.*, pp. 87–89.

(5) Assurances and guarantees of non-repetition are considered in the same context as cessation because they all concern compliance with the obligation set out in the primary rule. However, unlike the obligation to cease a continuing wrongful act, the obligation to offer assurances and guarantees of non-repetition may be regarded as a new obligation that arises as a consequence of the wrongful act, which signals the risk of future violations.

(6) Given the similarity of the situation of States and that of international organizations in respect of cessation and assurances and guarantees of non-repetition, the present article follows the same wording as article 30 of the draft articles on responsibility of States for internationally wrongful acts,[447] with the replacement of the word "State" with "international organization".

Article 34. Reparation

1. The responsible international organization is under an obligation to make full reparation for the injury caused by the internationally wrongful act.

2. Injury includes any damage, whether material or moral, caused by the internationally wrongful act of an international organization.

Commentary

(1) The present article sets out the principle that the responsible international organization is required to make full reparation for the injury caused. This principle seeks to protect the injured party from being adversely affected by the internationally wrongful act.

(2) With regard to international organizations as with regard to States, the principle of full reparation is often applied in practice in a flexible manner. The injured party may be mainly interested in the cessation of a continuing wrongful act or in the non-repetition of the wrongful act. The ensuing claim to reparation may therefore be limited. This especially occurs when the injured State or organization puts forward a claim for its own benefit and not for that of individuals or entities whom it seeks to protect. However, the restraint on the part of the injured State or organization in the exercise of its rights does not generally imply that the same party would not regard itself as entitled to full reparation. Thus the principle of full reparation is not put in question.

(3) It may be difficult for an international organization to have all the necessary means for making the required reparation. This fact is linked to the inadequacy of the financial resources that are generally given to international organizations for meeting this type of expense. However, that inadequacy cannot exempt a responsible organization from the legal consequences resulting from its responsibility under international law.

(4) The fact that international organizations sometimes grant compensation *ex gratia* is not due to abundance of resources, but rather to a reluctance, which

organizations share with States, to admit their own international responsibility.

(5) In setting out the principle of full reparation, the present article mainly refers to the more frequent case in which an international organization is solely responsible for an internationally wrongful act. The assertion of a duty of full reparation for the organization does not necessarily imply that the same principle applies when the organization is held responsible for a certain act together with one or more States or one or more other organizations: for instance, when the organization aids or assists a State in the commission of the wrongful act.[448]

(6) The present article reproduces article 31 of the draft articles on responsibility of States for internationally wrongful acts,[449] with the replacement in both paragraphs of the term "State" with "international organization".

Article 35. Irrelevance of the rules of the organization

1. The responsible international organization may not rely on its rules as justification for failure to comply with its obligations under this Part.

2. Paragraph 1 is without prejudice to the applicability of the rules of an international organization in respect of the responsibility of the organization towards its member States and organizations.

Commentary

(1) Paragraph 1 states the principle that an international organization cannot invoke its rules in order to justify non-compliance with its obligations under international law entailed by the commission of an internationally wrongful act. This principle finds a parallel in the principle that a State may not rely on its internal law as a justification for failure to comply its obligations under Part Two of the articles on responsibility of States for internationally wrongful acts. The text of paragraph 1 replicates article 32 on State responsibility,[450] with two changes: the term "international organization" replaces "State" and the reference to the rules of the organization replaces that to the internal law of the State.

(2) A similar approach was taken by article 27, paragraph 2, of the 1986 Vienna Convention, which parallels the corresponding provision of the 1969 Vienna Convention by saying that "[a]n international organization party to a treaty may not invoke the rules of the organization as justification for its failure to perform the treaty".

(3) In the relations between an international organization and a non-member State or organization, it seems clear that the rules of the former organization cannot *per se* affect the obligations that arise as a consequence of an internationally wrongful act. The same principle does

---

[447] *Ibid.*, pp. 88–91.

[448] See draft article 12 of the present draft articles, adopted by the Commission at its fifty-seventh session, in 2005, *Yearbook ... 2005*, vol. II (Part Two), Chapter VI, section C.2, p.45, para. 206.

[449] *Yearbook ... 2001*, vol. II (Part Two) and corrigendum, pp. 91–94.

[450] *Ibid.*, p. 94.

not necessarily apply to the relations between an organization and its members. Rules of the organization could affect the application of the principles and rules set out in this Part. They may, for instance, modify the rules on the forms of reparation that a responsible organization may have to make towards its members.

(4)   Rules of the organization may also affect the application of the principles and rules set out in Part One in the relations between an international organization and its members, for instance in the matter of attribution. They would be regarded as special rules and need not be made the object of a special reference. On the contrary, in Part Two a "without prejudice" provision concerning the application of the rules of the organization in respect of members seems useful in view of the implications that may otherwise be inferred from the principle of irrelevance of the rules of the organization. The presence of such a "without prejudice" provision would alert the reader to the fact that the general statement in paragraph 1 may admit of exceptions in the relations between an international organization and its member States and organizations.

(5)   The provision in question, which is set out in paragraph 2, only applies insofar as the obligations in Part Two relate to the international responsibility that an international organization may have towards its member States and organizations. It cannot affect in any manner the legal consequences entailed by an internationally wrongful act towards a non-member State or organization. Nor can it affect the consequences relating to breaches of obligations under peremptory norms, as these breaches would affect the international community as a whole.

Article 36.   Scope of international obligations set out in this Part

1.   The obligations of the responsible international organization set out in this Part may be owed to one or more other organizations, to one or more States, or to the international community as a whole, depending in particular on the character and content of the international obligation and on the circumstances of the breach.

2.   This Part is without prejudice to any right, arising from the international responsibility of an international organization, which may accrue directly to any person or entity other than a State or an international organization.

Commentary

(1)   In the articles on responsibility of States for internationally wrongful acts, Part One considers any breach of an obligation under international law that may be attributed to a State, irrespective of the nature of the entity or person to whom the obligation is owed. The scope of Part Two of those articles is limited to obligations that arise for a State towards another State. This seems due to the difficulty of considering the consequences of an internationally wrongful act and thereafter the implementation of responsibility in respect of an injured party whose

breaches of international obligations are not covered in Part One. The reference to responsibility existing towards the international community as a whole does not raise a similar problem, since it is hardly conceivable that the international community as a whole incur international responsibility.

(2)   Should one take a similar approach with regard to international organizations in the present draft, one would have to limit the scope of Part Two to obligations arising for international organizations towards other international organizations or towards the international community as a whole. However, it seems logical also to include obligations that organizations have towards States, given the existence of the articles on State responsibility. As a result, Part Two of the draft will encompass obligations that an international organization may have towards one or more other organizations, one or more States, or the international community as a whole.

(3)   With the change in the reference to the responsible entity and with the explained addition, paragraph 1 follows the wording of article 33, paragraph 1, of the draft articles on State responsibility.[451]

(4)   While the scope of Part Two is limited according to the definition in paragraph 1, this does not mean that obligations entailed by an internationally wrongful act do not arise towards persons or entities other than States and international organizations. Like article 33, paragraph 2, on State responsibility, paragraph 2 sets out that Part Two is without prejudice to any right that arises out of international responsibility and may accrue directly to those persons and entities.

(5)   With regard to international responsibility of international organizations, one significant area in which rights accrue to persons other than States or organizations is that of breaches by international organizations of their obligations under rules of international law concerning employment. Another area is that of breaches committed by peacekeeping forces and affecting individuals.[452] While the consequences of these breaches, as stated in paragraph 1, are not covered by the draft, certain issues of international responsibility arising in the context of employment are arguably similar to those that are examined in the draft.

CHAPTER II

REPARATION FOR INJURY

Article 37.   Forms of reparation

Full reparation for the injury caused by the internationally wrongful act shall take the form of restitution, compensation and satisfaction, either singly or in combination, in accordance with the provisions of this chapter.

---

[451] *Ibid.*, p. 94.

[452] See, for instance, resolution 52/247 of the General Assembly, of 26 June 1998, on "Third-party liability: temporal and financial limitations".

Commentary

(1) The above provision is identical to article 34 on responsibility of States for internationally wrongful acts.[453] This seems justified since the forms of reparation consisting of restitution, compensation and satisfaction are applied in practice to international organizations as well as to States. Certain examples relating to international organizations are given in the commentaries to the following articles, which specifically address the various forms of reparation.

(2) A note by the Director General of the International Atomic Energy Agency provides an instance in which the three forms of reparation are considered to apply to a responsible international organization. Concerning the "international responsibility of the Agency in relation to safeguards", he wrote on 24 June 1970:

Although there may be circumstances when the giving of satisfaction by the Agency may be appropriate, it is proposed to give consideration only to reparation properly so called. Generally speaking, reparation properly so called may be either restitution in kind or payment of compensation.[454]

It has to be noted that, according to the prevailing use, which is reflected in article 34 on State responsibility and the article above, reparation is considered to include satisfaction.

Article 38. Restitution

An international organization responsible for an internationally wrongful act is under an obligation to make restitution, that is, to re-establish the situation which existed before the wrongful act was committed, provided and to the extent that restitution:

(*a*) is not materially impossible;

(*b*) does not involve a burden out of all proportion to the benefit deriving from restitution instead of compensation.

Commentary

The concept of restitution and the related conditions, as defined in article 35 on responsibility of States for internationally wrongful acts,[455] appear to be applicable also to international organizations. There is no reason that would suggest a different approach with regard to the latter. The text above therefore reproduces article 35 of the draft articles on State responsibility, with the only difference that the term "State" is replaced by "international organization".

Article 39. Compensation

1. The international organization responsible for an internationally wrongful act is under an obligation to compensate for the damage caused thereby, insofar as such damage is not made good by restitution.

2. The compensation shall cover any financially assessable damage including loss of profits insofar as it is established.

Commentary

(1) Compensation is the form of reparation most frequently made by international organizations. The best-known instance of practice concerns the settlement of claims arising from the United Nations operation in the Congo. Compensation to nationals of Belgium, Greece, Italy, Luxembourg and Switzerland was granted through exchanges of letters between the Secretary-General and the Permanent Missions of the respective States in keeping with the United Nations Declaration contained in these letters according to which the United Nations:

stated that it would not evade responsibility where it was established that United Nations agents had in fact caused unjustifiable damage to innocent parties.[456]

With regard to the same operation, further settlements were made with France, Zambia, the United States of America, the United Kingdom,[457] and also with the International Committee of the Red Cross.[458]

(2) The fact that such compensation was given as reparation for breaches of obligations under international law may be gathered not only from some of the claims but also from a letter, dated 6 August 1965, addressed by the Secretary-General to the Acting Permanent Representative of the Union of Soviet Socialist Republics. In this letter, the Secretary-General said:

It has always been the policy of the United Nations, acting through the Secretary-General, to compensate individuals who have suffered damages for which the Organization was legally liable. This policy is in keeping with generally recognized legal principles and with the Convention on Privileges and Immunities of the United Nations. In addition, in regard to the United Nations activities in the Congo, it is reinforced by the principles set forth in the international conventions concerning the protection of the life and property of civilian population during hostilities as well as by considerations of equity and humanity which the United Nations cannot ignore.[459]

---

[453] *Ibid.*, pp. 95–96.

[454] GOV/COM.22/27, para. 27. See *Yearbook ... 2004*, vol. II (Part One), document A/CN.4/545, annex. The note is on file with the Codification Division of the Office of Legal Affairs.

[455] *Yearbook ... 2001*, vol. II (Part Two) and corrigendum, pp. 96–98.

[456] Exchange of letters constituting an agreement relating to the settlement of claims filed against the United Nations in the Congo by Belgian nationals (New York, 20 February 1965), United Nations, *Treaty Series*, vol. 535, No. 7780, p. 197; Exchange of letters (with annex) constituting an agreement relating to the settlement of claims filed against the United Nations in the Congo by Swiss nationals (New York, 3 June 1966), *ibid.*, vol. 564, p. 193; Exchange of letters constituting an agreement relating to the settlement of claims filed against the United Nations in the Congo by Greek nationals (New York, 20 June 1966), *ibid.*, vol. 565, No. 8230, p. 3; Exchange of letters constituting an agreement relating to the settlement of claims filed against the United Nations in the Congo by Luxembourg nationals (New York, 28 December 1966), *ibid.*, vol. 585, No. 8487, p. 147; and Exchange of letters constituting an agreement relating to the settlement of claims filed against the United Nations in the Congo by Italian nationals (New York, 18 January 1967), *ibid.*, vol. 588, No. 8525, p. 197.

[457] See K. Schmalenbach, *Die Haftung Internationaler Organisationen im Rahmen von Militäreinsätzen und Territorialverwaltungen*, Frankfurt am Main. Peter Lang, 2004, at pp. 314–321.

[458] The text of the agreement was reproduced by K. Ginther, *Die völkerrechtliche Verantwortlichkeit internationaler Organisationen gegenüber Drittstaaten*, Vienna/New York, Springer, 1969) pp. 166–167.

[459] United Nations, *Juridical Yearbook 1965* (Sales No. 67.V.3), p. 41, note 26 (document S/6597). The view that the United Nations placed its responsibility at the international level was maintained by J. J. A. Salmon, "Les accords Spaak–U Thant du 20 février 1965", *Annuaire français de droit international*, vol. 11 (1965), p. 468, at pp. 483 and 487.

(3)   A reference to the obligation on the United Nations to pay compensation was also made by the ICJ in its advisory opinion on *Difference Relating to Immunity from Legal Process of a Special Rapporteur of the Commission on Human Rights*.[460]

(4)   With regard to compensation there would not be any reason for departing from the text of article 36 of the draft articles on responsibility of States for internationally wrongful acts,[461] apart from replacing the term "State" with "international organization".

Article 40.   Satisfaction

1.   The international organization responsible for an internationally wrongful act is under an obligation to give satisfaction for the injury caused by that act insofar as it cannot be made good by restitution or compensation.

2.   Satisfaction may consist in an acknowledgement of the breach, an expression of regret, a formal apology or another appropriate modality.

3.   Satisfaction shall not be out of proportion to the injury and may not take a form humiliating to the responsible international organization.

Commentary

(1)   Practice offers some examples of satisfaction on the part of international organizations, generally in the form of an apology or an expression of regret. Although the examples that follow do not expressly refer to the existence of a breach of an obligation under international law, they at least imply that an apology or an expression of regret by an international organization would be one of the appropriate legal consequences for such a breach.

(2)   With regard to the fall of Srebrenica, the United Nations Secretary-General said:

The United Nations experience in Bosnia was one of the most difficult and painful in our history. It is with the deepest regret and remorse that we have reviewed our own actions and decisions in the face of the assault on Srebrenica.[462]

(3)   On 16 December 1999, upon receiving the report of the Independent Inquiry into the actions of the United Nations during the 1994 genocide in Rwanda, the Secretary-General stated:

All of us must bitterly regret that we did not do more to prevent it. There was a United Nations force in the country at the time, but it was neither mandated nor equipped for the kind of forceful action which would have been needed to prevent or halt the genocide. On behalf of the United Nations, I acknowledge this failure and express my deep remorse.[463]

(4)   Shortly after the NATO bombing of the Chinese embassy in Belgrade, a NATO spokesman, Jamie Shea, said in a press conference:

I think we have done what anybody would do in these circumstances, first of all we have acknowledged responsibility clearly, unambiguously, quickly; we have expressed our regrets to the Chinese authorities.[464]

A further apology was addressed on 12 May 1999 by German Chancellor Gerhard Schröder on behalf of Germany, NATO and NATO Secretary-General Javier Solana to Foreign Minister Tang Jiaxuan and Premier Zhu Rongji.[465]

(5)   The modalities and conditions of satisfaction that concern States are applicable also to international organizations. A form of satisfaction intended to humiliate the responsible international organization may be unlikely, but is not unimaginable. A theoretical example would be that of the request of a formal apology in terms that would be demeaning to the organization or one of its organs. The request could also refer to the conduct taken by one or more member States or organizations within the framework of the responsible organization. Although the request for satisfaction might then specifically target one or more members, the responsible organization would have to give it and would necessarily be affected.

(6)   Thus, the paragraphs of article 37 of the draft articles on responsibility of States for internationally wrongful acts[466] may be transposed, with the replacement of the term "State" with "international organization" in paragraphs 1 and 3.

Article 41.   Interest

1.   Interest on any principal sum due under this chapter shall be payable when necessary in order to ensure full reparation. The interest rate and mode of calculation shall be set so as to achieve that result.

2.   Interest runs from the date when the principal sum should have been paid until the date the obligation to pay is fulfilled.

Commentary

The rules contained in article 38 of the draft articles on responsibility of States for internationally wrongful acts[467] with regard to interest are intended to ensure application of the principle of full reparation. Similar considerations in this regard apply to international organizations. Therefore, both paragraphs of article 38 of the draft articles on State responsibility are here reproduced without change.

[460] *Difference Relating to Immunity from Legal Process of a Special Rapporteur of the Commission on Human Rights, Advisory Opinion, I.C.J. Reports 1999*, pp. 88–89, para. 66.

[461] *Yearbook ... 2001*, vol. II (Part Two) and corrigendum, pp. 98–105.

[462] Report of the Secretary-General pursuant to General Assembly resolution 53/35: the fall of Srebrenica (A/54/549), para. 503.

[463] www.un.org/News/Press/docs/1999/19991216.sgsm7263.doc.html (last accessed 25 October 2013). See the report of the Independent

Inquiry into the actions of the United Nations during the 1994 genocide in Rwanda in S/1999/1257, enclosure.

[464] www.ess.uwe.ac.uk/Kosovo/Kosovo-Mistakes2.htm (accessed 19 March 2013).

[465] "NATO apologises to Beijing", http://news.bbc.co.uk/2/hi/asia-pacific/341533.stm (accessed 12 March 2013).

[466] *Yearbook ... 2001*, vol. II (Part Two) and corrigendum, pp. 105–107.

[467] *Ibid.*, pp. 107–109.

Article 42. Contribution to the injury

In the determination of reparation, account shall be taken of the contribution to the injury by wilful or negligent action or omission of the injured State or international organization or of any person or entity in relation to whom reparation is sought.

Commentary

(1) No apparent reason would preclude extending to international organizations the provision set out in article 39 of the draft articles on responsibility of States for internationally wrongful acts.[468] Such an extension is made in two directions: first, international organizations are also entitled to invoke contribution to the injury in order to diminish their responsibility; second, the entities that may have contributed to the injury include international organizations. The latter extension would require the addition of the words "or international organization" after "State" in the corresponding article on State responsibility.

(2) One instance of relevant practice in which contribution to the injury was invoked concerns the shooting of a civilian vehicle in the Congo. In this case, compensation by the United Nations was reduced because of the contributory negligence by the driver of the vehicle.[469]

(3) This article is without prejudice to any obligation to mitigate the injury that the injured party may have under international law. The existence of such an obligation would arise under a primary rule. Thus, it does not need to be discussed here.

(4) The reference to "any person or entity in relation to whom reparation is sought" has to be read in conjunction with the definition given in article 36 of the scope of the international obligations set out in Part Two. This scope is limited to obligations arising for a responsible international organization towards States, other international organizations or the international community as a whole. The above reference seems appropriately worded in this context. The existence of rights that directly accrue to other persons or entities is thereby not prejudiced.

Article 43. Ensuring the effective performance of the obligation of reparation

The members of a responsible international organization are required to take, in accordance with the rules of the organization, all appropriate measures in order to provide the organization with the means for effectively fulfilling its obligations under this chapter.

Commentary

(1) International organizations that are considered to have a separate international legal personality are in principle the only subjects whose internationally wrongful acts may entail legal consequences. When an international organization is responsible for an internationally wrongful act, States and other organizations incur responsibility because of their membership in a responsible organization according to the conditions stated in articles 28 and 29. The present article does not envisage any further instance in which States and international organizations would be held internationally responsible for the act of the organization of which they are members.

(2) Consistent with the views expressed by several States that responded to a question raised by the Commission in its 2006 report to the General Assembly,[470] no subsidiary obligation of members towards the injured party is considered to arise when the responsible organization is not in a position to make reparation.[471] The same opinion was expressed in statements by the International Monetary Fund and the Organization for the Prohibition of Chemical Weapons.[472] This approach appears to conform to practice, which does not show any support for the existence of the obligation in question under international law.

(3) Thus, the injured party would have to rely only on the fulfilment by the responsible international organization of its obligations. It is expected that in order to comply with its obligation to make reparation, the responsible organization would use all available means that exist under its rules. In most cases this would involve requesting contributions by the members of the organization concerned.

(4) A proposal was made to state expressly that "[t]he responsible international organization shall take all appropriate measures in accordance with its rules in order to ensure that its members provide the organization with the means for effectively fulfilling its obligations under this chapter". This proposal received some support. However, the majority of the Commission considered that such a provision was not necessary, because the stated obligation would already be implied in the obligation to make reparation.

---

[468] *Ibid.*, pp. 109–110.

[469] See P. Klein, *La responsabilité des organisations internationales dans les ordres juridiques internes et en droit des gens*, Brussels, Bruylant/Editions de l'Université de Bruxelles, 1998, at p. 606.

[470] *Yearbook ... 2006*, vol. II (Part Two), p. 21, para. 28 (see footnote 386 above).

[471] The delegation of the Netherlands noted that there would be "no basis for such an obligation" (*Official Records of the General Assembly, Sixty-first Session, Sixth Committee, 14th meeting*, A/C.6/61/SR.14, para. 23). Similar views were expressed by Denmark, on behalf of the Nordic countries (Denmark, Finland, Iceland, Norway and Sweden) (*ibid.*, 13th meeting, A/C.6/61/SR.13, para. 32); Belgium (*ibid.*, 14th meeting, A/C.6/61/SR.14, paras. 41–42); Spain (*ibid.*, paras. 52–53); France (*ibid.*, para. 63); Italy (*ibid.*, para. 66); United States (*ibid.*, para. 83); Belarus (*ibid.*, para. 100); Switzerland (*ibid.*, 15th meeting, A/C.6/61/SR.15, para. 5); Cuba (*ibid.*, 16th meeting, A/C.6/61/SR.16, para. 13); Romania (*ibid.*, 19th meeting, A/C.6/61/SR.19, para. 60). The delegation of Belarus, however, suggested that a "scheme of subsidiary responsibility for compensation could be established as a special rule, for example in cases where the work of the organization was connected with the exploitation of dangerous resources" (*ibid.*, 14th meeting, A/C.6/61/SR.14, para. 100). Although sharing the prevailing view, the delegation of Argentina (*ibid.*, 13th meeting, A/C.6/61/SR.13, para. 49) requested the Commission to "analyse whether the special characteristics and rules of each organization, as well as considerations of justice and equity, called for exceptions to the basic rule, depending on the circumstances of each case".

[472] A/CN.4/582, sect. II. U.1 (reproduced in *Yearbook ... 2007*, vol. II (Part One)).

(5)   The majority of the Commission was in favour of including the present article, which had not been proposed in the Special Rapporteur's report. This article is essentially of an expository character. It intends to remind members of a responsible international organization that they are required to take, in accordance with the rules of the organization, all appropriate measures in order to provide the organization with the means for effectively fulfilling its obligation to make reparation.

(6)   The reference to the rules of the organization is meant to define the basis of the requirement in question.[473] While the rules of the organization may not necessarily consider the matter in an express manner, an obligation for members to finance the organization as part of the general duty to cooperate with the organization may be taken as generally implied under the relevant rules. As was noted by Judge Sir Gerald Fitzmaurice in his separate opinion relating to the advisory opinion of the ICJ on *Certain Expenses of the United Nations*:

> Without finance, the Organization could not perform its duties. Therefore, even in the absence of Article 17, paragraph 2, a general obligation for Member States collectively to finance the Organization would have to be read into the Charter, on the basis of the same principle as the Court applied in the *Injuries to United Nations Servants* case, namely "by necessary implication as being essential to the performance of its [i.e. the Organization's] duties" (*I.C.J. Reports 1949*, p. 182).[474]

(7)   The majority of the Commission maintained that no duty arose for members of an international organization under general international law to take all appropriate measures in order to provide the responsible organization with the means for fulfilling its obligation to make reparation. However, some members were of the contrary opinion, while still other members expressed the view that such an obligation should be stated as a rule of progressive development. This obligation would supplement any obligation existing under the rules of the organization.

CHAPTER III

SERIOUS BREACHES OF OBLIGATIONS UNDER PEREMPTORY NORMS OF GENERAL INTERNATIONAL LAW

Article 44 [43].   Application of this chapter

1.   This chapter applies to the international responsibility which is entailed by a serious breach by an international organization of an obligation arising under a peremptory norm of general international law.

2.   A breach of such an obligation is serious if it involves a gross or systematic failure by the responsible international organization to fulfil the obligation.

Commentary

(1)   The scope of Chapter III corresponds to the scope defined in article 40 of the draft articles on responsibility of States for internationally wrongful acts.[475] The breach of an obligation under a peremptory norm of general international law may be less likely on the part of international organizations than on the part of States. However, the risk that such a breach takes place cannot be entirely ruled out. If a serious breach does occur, it calls for the same consequences that are applicable to States.

(2)   The two paragraphs of the present article are identical to those of article 40 on the responsibility of States for internationally wrongful acts, but for the replacement of the term "State" with "international organization".

Article 45 [44].   Particular consequences of a serious breach of an obligation under this chapter

1.   States and international organizations shall cooperate to bring to an end through lawful means any serious breach within the meaning of article 44 [43].

2.   No State or international organization shall recognize as lawful a situation created by a serious breach within the meaning of article 44 [43], nor render aid or assistance in maintaining that situation.

3.   This article is without prejudice to the other consequences referred to in this Part and to such further consequences that a breach to which this chapter applies may entail under international law.

Commentary

(1)   This article sets out that, should an international organization commit a serious breach of an obligation under a peremptory norm of general international law, States and international organizations have duties corresponding to those applying to States according to article 41 of the draft articles on responsibility of States for internationally wrongful acts.[476] Therefore, the same wording is used here as in that article, with only the additions of the words "and international organizations" in paragraph 1 and "or international organization" in paragraph 2.

(2)   In response to a question raised by the Commission in its 2006 report to the General Assembly,[477] several States expressed the view that the legal situation of an international organization should be the same as that of a State having committed a similar breach.[478] Moreover,

---

[473] See the statements by the delegations of Denmark, on behalf of the Nordic countries (Denmark, Finland, Iceland, Norway and Sweden) (*Official Records of the General Assembly, Sixty-first Session, Sixth Committee*, 13th meeting, A/C.6/61/SR.13, para. 32); Belgium (*ibid.*, 14th meeting, A/C.6/61/SR.14, para. 42); Spain (*ibid.*, para. 53); France (*ibid.*, para. 63); and Switzerland (*ibid.*, 15th meeting, A/C.6/61/SR.15, para. 5). Also the Institute of International Law held that an obligation to put a responsible organization in funds only existed "pursuant to its Rules" (Institute of International Law, *Yearbook*, vol. 66 (1996), Session of Lisbon (1995), Part II, p. 451).

[474] *Certain Expenses of the United Nations (Article 17, paragraph 2, of the Charter), Advisory Opinion of 20 July 1962, I.C.J. Reports 1962*, p. 151, at p. 208.

[475] *Yearbook ... 2001*, vol. II (Part Two) and corrigendum, pp. 112–113.

[476] *Ibid.*, pp. 113–116.

[477] *Yearbook ... 2006*, vol. II (Part Two), p. 21, para. 28 (see footnote 386 above).

[478] See the interventions by Denmark, on behalf of the Nordic countries (Denmark, Finland, Iceland, Norway and Sweden) (*Official Records of the General Assembly, Sixty-first Session, Sixth Committee*, 13th meeting, A/C.6/61/SR.13, para. 33); Argentina (*ibid.*, para. 50); the

several States maintained that international organizations would also be under an obligation to cooperate to bring the breach to an end.[479]

(3) The Organization for the Prohibition of Chemical Weapons made the following observation:

States should definitely be under an obligation to cooperate to bring such a breach to an end because in the case when an international organization acts in breach of a peremptory norm of general international law, its position is not much different from that of a State.[480]

With regard to the obligation to cooperate on the part of international organizations, the same Organization noted that an international organization "must always act within its mandate and in accordance with its rules".[481]

(4) It is clear that the present article is not designed to vest international organizations with functions that are alien to their respective mandates. On the other hand, some international organizations may be entrusted with functions that go beyond what is required in the present article. This article is without prejudice to any function that an organization may have with regard to certain breaches of obligations under peremptory norms of general international law, as, for example, the United Nations in respect of aggression.

(5) While practice does not offer examples of cases in which the obligations stated in the present article were asserted in respect of a serious breach committed by an international organization, it is not insignificant that these obligations were considered to apply to international organizations when a breach was allegedly committed by a State.

(6) In this context it may be useful to recall that in the operative part of its advisory opinion on the *Legal Consequences of the Construction of a Wall in the Occupied Palestinian Territory* the ICJ first stated the obligation incumbent upon Israel to cease the works of construction of the wall and, "[g]iven the character and the importance of the rights and obligations involved", the obligation for all States "not to recognize the illegal situation resulting from the construction of the wall ... [and] not to render aid or assistance in maintaining the situation created by such construction".[482] The Court then added:

The United Nations, and especially the General Assembly and the Security Council, should consider what further action is required to bring to an end the illegal situation resulting from the construction of the wall and the associated régime, taking due account of the present Advisory Opinion.[483]

(7) Some instances of practice relating to serious breaches committed by States concern the duty of international organizations not to recognize as lawful a situation created by one of those breaches. For example, with regard to the annexation of Kuwait by Iraq, paragraph 2 of Security Council resolution 662 (1990) of 9 August 1990 called upon "all States, international organizations and specialized agencies not to recognize that annexation, and to refrain from any action or dealing that might be interpreted as an indirect recognition of the annexation". Another example is provided by the Declaration that member States of the European Community made in 1991 on the "Guidelines on the recognition of new States in Eastern Europe and in the Soviet Union".[484] This text included the following sentence: "The Community and its member States will not recognize entities which are the result of aggression."[485]

(8) The present article concerns the obligations set out for States and international organizations in case of a serious breach of an obligation under a peremptory norm of general international law by an international organization. It is not intended to exclude that similar obligations also exist for other persons or entities.

Netherlands (*ibid.*, 14th meeting, A/C.6/61/SR.14, para. 25); Belgium (*ibid.*, paras. 43–46); Spain (*ibid.*, para. 54); France (*ibid.*, para. 64); Belarus (*ibid.*, para. 101); Switzerland (*ibid.*, 15th meeting, A/C.6/61/SR.15, para. 8); Jordan (*ibid.*, 16th meeting, A/C.6/61/SR.16, para. 5); the Russian Federation (*ibid.*, 18th meeting, A/C.6/61/SR.18, para. 68); and Romania (*ibid.*, 19th meeting, A/C.6/61/SR.19, para. 60).

[479] Thus the interventions by Denmark, on behalf of the Nordic countries (Denmark, Finland, Iceland, Norway and Sweden) (*ibid., 13th meeting*, A/C.6/61/SR.13, para. 33); Argentina (*ibid.*, para. 50); the Netherlands (*ibid.*, 14th meeting, A/C.6/61/SR.14, para. 25); Belgium (*ibid.*, para. 45); Spain (*ibid.*, para. 54); France (*ibid.*, para. 64); Belarus (*ibid.*, para. 101); Switzerland (*ibid.*, 15th meeting, A/C.6/61/SR.15, para. 8); and the Russian Federation (*ibid.*, 18th meeting, A/C.6/61/SR.18, para. 68).

[480] A/CN.4/582 (see footnote 472 above), sect. II, U.2.

[481] *Ibid.* The International Monetary Fund went one step further in saying that "any obligation of international organizations to cooperate would be subject to, and limited by, provisions of their respective charters" (*ibid.*).

[482] *Legal Consequences of the Construction of a Wall in the Occupied Palestinian Territory* (see footnote 99 above), p. 200, para. 159. See also subparagraph (3) B and D of the operative paragraph, *ibid.*, pp. 201–202, para. 163.

[483] *Ibid.*, p. 202, para. 163, subparagraph (3) E of the operative paragraph. The same language appears in paragraph 160 of the advisory opinion, *ibid.*, p. 200.

[484] *Bulletin of the European Communities*, vol. 24, no. 12 (1991), pp. 119–120.

[485] European Community, Declaration on Yugoslavia and on the Guidelines on the Recognition of New States, 16 December 1991, reproduced in ILM, vol. 31 (1992), p. 1485, at p. 1487.

Chapter IX

THE OBLIGATION TO EXTRADITE OR PROSECUTE (*AUT DEDERE AUT JUDICARE*)

A. Introduction

345. The Commission, at its fifty-sixth session (2004), decided to include the topic "The obligation to extradite or prosecute (*aut dedere aut judicare*)" in its long-term programme of work.[486] During its fifty-seventh session (2005), the Commission, at its 2865th meeting, on 4 August 2005, decided to include the topic in its current programme of work and appointed Mr. Zdzisław Galicki as Special Rapporteur for the topic.[487] The General Assembly, in paragraph 5 of its resolution 60/22 of 23 November 2005, endorsed the decision of the Commission to include the topic in its programme of work.

346. At its fifty-eighth session (2006), the Commission received and considered the preliminary report of the Special Rapporteur.[488]

B. Consideration of the topic at the present session

347. At the present session, the Commission had before it the second report of the Special Rapporteur (A/CN.4/585 and Corr.1), as well as comments and information received from Governments (A/CN.4/579 and Add.1–4). The Commission considered the report at its 2945th to 2947th meetings, from 31 July to 3 August 2007.

1. INTRODUCTION BY THE SPECIAL RAPPORTEUR OF HIS SECOND REPORT

348. The Special Rapporteur observed that his second report summarized the main ideas and concepts presented in the preliminary report, in order to seek the views of the new Commission on the most controversial issues regarding this topic. He confirmed that the preliminary plan of action, contained in his preliminary report,[489] remained the main road map for his further work on the topic.

349. Among the main questions raised during the debate at the previous session, and on which the Special Rapporteur would welcome the views of the Commission, were the following: whether the source of the obligation *aut dedere aut judicare* was purely conventional or was also to be found in customary international law, at least for some categories of crimes (such as war crimes,

piracy, genocide and crimes against humanity); whether a clear distinction should be made between the obligation to extradite or prosecute and universal jurisdiction, and whether the latter should be considered in the context of this topic (and, if so, to what extent); whether the two alternative elements of the obligation to extradite or prosecute should be given equal footing, or whether one of them should have priority; whether the Commission should consider the so-called "triple alternative", consisting of the surrender of the alleged offender to a competent international criminal tribunal; and what should be the form of the final product of the Commission's work on the topic. The Special Rapporteur noted that a great variety of opinions had been expressed on these issues last year at the Commission and at the Sixth Committee.

350. The Special Rapporteur was however in a position, already at this stage, to present one draft article regarding the scope of application of the future draft articles on the obligation to extradite or prosecute.[490] The proposed provision contained three elements that would need to be dealt with by the Commission. With regard to the time element referred to in this provision, the draft articles would have to take into account the different periods in which the obligation was established, operated and produced its effects; the question of the source of the obligation was connected to the first period. With regard to the substantive element, the Commission would have to establish the existence and scope of the obligation to extradite or prosecute, thus determining *inter alia* whether one part of the alternative should have priority over the other, to what extent the custodial State has a margin of discretion in refusing a request for extradition, and whether the obligation includes the possibility of surrender to an international criminal tribunal. Finally, with regard to the personal element, the provision referred to alleged offenders under the jurisdiction of the States concerned, which raised the issue, also to be considered by the Commission, of the relationship of the obligation with the concept of universal jurisdiction. Together with the personal element, the Commission would also have to identify the crimes and offences covered by this obligation.

351. The Special Rapporteur also proposed a plan for further development and shared his ideas on articles to be drafted in the future. He indicated, in particular, that one draft article should contain a definition of the terms used, and that a further draft article (or set of draft articles) should be devoted to a description of the obligation

---

[486] *Yearbook ... 2004*, vol. II (Part Two), p. 120, paras. 362–363. A brief syllabus describing the possible overall structure and approach to the topic was annexed to that year's report of the Commission. The General Assembly, in resolution 59/41 of 2 December 2004, took note of the Commission's report concerning its long-term programme of work.

[487] *Yearbook ... 2005*, vol. II (Part Two), p. 92, para. 500.

[488] *Yearbook ... 2006*, vol. II (Part One), A/CN.4/571.

[489] *Ibid.*, p. 259, para. 61.

[490] Draft article 1 reads as follows:

"*Scope of application*

"The present draft articles shall apply to the establishment, content, operation and effects of the alternative obligation of States to extradite or prosecute persons under their jurisdiction."

to extradite or prosecute and its constitutive elements. The Special Rapporteur also envisaged a draft article that would provide that: "Each State is obliged to extradite or to prosecute an alleged offender if such an obligation is provided for by a treaty to which such State is a party." Other draft articles should take inspiration from the draft code of crimes against the peace and security of mankind adopted by the Commission at its forty-eighth session, in 1996.[491]

352.   The Special Rapporteur finally indicated the need to reiterate, at the present session, the request made for Governments to provide information on their legislation and practice with regard to the obligation to extradite or prosecute.

2.   SUMMARY OF THE DEBATE

(a)   *General comments*

353.   In their general comments, members of the Commission dealt, in particular, with the source of the obligation to extradite or prosecute, its relationship with universal jurisdiction, the scope of the obligation and its two constitutive elements, and the question of surrender of an alleged offender to an international criminal tribunal (the so-called "triple alternative" suggested by the Special Rapporteur).

354.   The view was expressed that the question of the source of the obligation to extradite or prosecute was central to the present topic and should be the object of rigorous analysis by the Commission, particularly given the position taken by some Governments in their comments. While acknowledging that the obligation to extradite or prosecute was often treaty-based, some members were of the view that it also had customary status, at least as far as crimes under international law were concerned. The question remained, however, whether this obligation was to apply only to certain crimes under customary international law or would also extend to other crimes provided for under international treaties, and whether it would also apply to ordinary crimes. According to some members, the Commission should focus on the identification of the crimes that are subject to the obligation to extradite or prosecute. Some other members considered that the Commission should not attempt to establish a list of such crimes (which would have the effect of hampering the progressive development of international law in this field), but should rather identify criteria allowing to determine those categories of crimes in relation to which States are *ipso jure* bound by that obligation. In this regard, it was suggested that the Commission should refer to the concept of "crimes against the peace and security of mankind" elaborated in its 1996 draft code. Some members noted that the Commission should also consider the question whether the obligation to extradite or prosecute could derive from a peremptory norm of general international law (*jus cogens*).

355.   It was further pointed out by some members that, in any event, the future draft should aim at regulating both those cases in which States were bound by the obligation

to extradite or prosecute under customary international law, and the problems that arose in the context of one or more treaties imposing such an obligation. Some other members, however, cautioned against limiting the recommendations of the Commission to treaty law.

356.   Some members stressed that, although the obligation to extradite or prosecute and universal jurisdiction shared the same objective (namely, to combat impunity by depriving the persons accused of certain crimes of "safe havens"), they should be distinguished from one another. Universal jurisdiction, which the Commission had decided not to include as a topic in its agenda, should therefore be considered only insofar as it related directly to the present topic. It was noted, in this regard, that the obligation to extradite or prosecute would only arise after the State concerned had established its jurisdiction and, in any event, if the person was present on the territory, or was under the control, of that State. Some other members pointed out that the custodial State often acquired jurisdiction only as a consequence of not extraditing the alleged offender. According to one view, the obligation *aut dedere aut judicare* was incumbent upon States for those crimes subject to universal jurisdiction. The proposal was made that the relationship between the obligation to extradite or prosecute and universal jurisdiction be addressed in a specific provision.

357.   With respect to the scope of the obligation, different views were expressed as to the two elements "to extradite" and "to prosecute", and their mutual relationship. According to some members, the custodial State had the power to decide, notably on the basis of its domestic legislation, which part of the obligation it would execute. Some other members noted that the obligation to extradite or prosecute may arise in different scenarios, which the Commission should take into account since they could be relevant for the determination of the scope of the obligation. Some members thought that to present the obligation as an alternative would tend to obscure its nature.

358.   With regard to the first part of the obligation, it was observed that, while the Commission would need to examine limitations on extradition (such as those concerning political offences, the nationals of the custodial State, or the case where specific safeguards for the protection of the rights of the individual would not be guaranteed by the State requesting extradition), it should be cautious not to embark into an analysis of the technical aspects of extradition law. The Commission would also need to determine the precise meaning of the part of the obligation referred to as "*judicare*".

359.   As regards the so-called "triple alternative", some members indicated that the surrender to an international criminal tribunal should not be dealt with in the present context, since it was submitted to different conditions, and posed different problems, from those arising from extradition. Some other members, however, observed that the Commission should address certain issues that were connected to the present topic; it was noted, for instance, that the duty for a State to surrender an individual to an international tribunal could paralyse the obligation to extradite or prosecute and that it should therefore be examined in the draft articles. Some members noted

that the constituent instruments of some international tribunals deal with the question of concurrent requests for
extradition and for surrender to the international tribunal.

(b) *Comments on draft article 1 proposed by the Special Rapporteur*

360. While some members found draft article 1 proposed by the Special Rapporteur to be acceptable in principle, other members pointed out that it was difficult for
the Commission to take a position on the scope of the draft
articles without knowing the views of the Special Rapporteur on subsequent issues, including that of the source
of the obligation to extradite or prosecute. Some members supported the reference to the different time periods
relating to this obligation, but criticized the terminology
used in the provision ("establishment, content, operation
and effects" of the obligation). Some other members suggested the deletion of this reference, favouring a simplified formulation of the provision. It was also considered
that the adjective "alternative" should be deleted since the
alternative character of the obligation was a matter that
the Commission would examine at a later stage. Some
members shared the Special Rapporteur's view that the
obligation to extradite or prosecute only existed in connection with natural persons; according to one view, the
situation of legal persons involved in the commission of
crimes should nonetheless be further explored. Divergent
opinions remained as to whether the Commission should
refer to *aut dedere aut judicare* as an "obligation" or a
"principle". A view was expressed that the word "jurisdiction" at the end of draft article 1 be replaced by "present
in their territories or under their control". This is to clarify
that the custodial State may not have criminal jurisdiction
over the alleged offender.

(c) *Comments on the future work of the Commission on the topic*

361. The plan for further development delineated in the
second report was favourably received by some members. In particular, the Special Rapporteur's intention to
follow the preliminary plan of action was supported, but
it was also indicated that the said plan should be further
elaborated to present a clear structure of the work ahead.
Some members agreed with the suggestions made by the
Special Rapporteur as to possible articles to be drafted in
the future, especially concerning the scope of the obligation to extradite or prosecute. The view was expressed,
however, that the wording of the provision that referred
to those cases in which the obligation is provided for by a
treaty could be seen as a restatement of the principle *pacta
sunt servanda* and should be carefully reviewed.

362. Support was also expressed for the proposal that
the Special Rapporteur present a systematic survey of the
relevant international treaties in the field. Some members observed, however, that consideration of the present
topic by the Commission required, in addition to a study
of treaties and customary international law, a comparative analysis of national legislation and judicial decisions
(including, as appropriate, the relevant opinions expressed
by individual judges at the ICJ). Although several States
had replied to the request for information made by the
Commission at the previous session, the debates in the

Sixth Committee and the comments received from Governments had not provided a sufficient basis to proceed.
Some members suggested that the request be repeated at
the current session. The view was expressed that the Special Rapporteur and the Commission should nonetheless
approach the topic on an independent basis, taking into
account comments made by States. According to some
members, the Commission should not hesitate, if it saw it
fit, to make proposals for the progressive development of
international law in the field.

363. On the question of the final form, some members
manifested their support to the formulation of a set of
draft articles.

3. SPECIAL RAPPORTEUR'S CONCLUDING REMARKS

364. The Special Rapporteur initially observed that the
debate in the Commission had confirmed his view that the
reference to an "obligation" to extradite or prosecute and
to the Latin maxim "*aut dedere aut judicare*" in the title
of the present topic should be retained.

365. He further noted that the debate had focused on
three main issues, namely: (*a*) the question of the source
of the obligation to extradite or prosecute; (*b*) the problem of the relationship between this obligation and the
concept of universal jurisdiction, and how it should be
reflected in the draft; and (*c*) the issue of the scope of the
said obligation. In his opinion, the different interventions
had clarified the views of the Commission on the topic.

366. As regards the first issue mentioned above, the
view that treaties constituted a source of the obligation
to extradite or prosecute had gathered general consensus,
but it had also been suggested that the Commission should
explore the possible customary status of the obligation, at
least with respect to some categories of crimes (such as
crimes under international law). The Special Rapporteur
noted that several members had expressed their opinion
on this possibility, and he agreed that any position taken
by the Commission would need to be based on a thorough analysis of treaties, national legislation and judicial
decisions. For this purpose, it was appropriate that the
Commission continue to request the assistance of Governments in collecting the relevant information.

367. With regard to the second issue, the Special Rapporteur observed that some members had suggested that
the concept of universal jurisdiction be examined by the
Commission to determine its relationship with the obligation to extradite or prosecute. He agreed with this suggestion, as well as with the view that the work of the
Commission should in any event remain focused on the
obligation *aut dedere aut judicare*.

368. As regards the third issue, the Special Rapporteur
concurred with the opinion of those members who had
pointed out that the obligation to extradite or prosecute
should not be described as an alternative one; he also
agreed that the mutual relationship and interdependence
between the two elements of this obligation (*dedere* and
judicare) should be carefully considered by the Commission. The Special Rapporteur reiterated his convic-
tion that the establishment, operation and effects of the

obligation to extradite or prosecute should be the object of separate analysis. He further indicated that, in light of the comments made, he would refrain from examining further the so-called "triple alternative", instead concentrating on those hypotheses in which the surrender of an individual to an international criminal tribunal could have an impact on the obligation to extradite or prosecute. As to draft article 1 proposed in his second report, the Special Rapporteur suggested that it be referred to the Drafting Committee at the next session, together with other draft provisions he would be presenting in due course.

Chapter X

OTHER DECISIONS AND CONCLUSIONS OF THE COMMISSION

A. Programme, procedures and working methods of the Commission and its documentation

369.   At its 2918th meeting, on 11 May 2007, the Commission established a Planning Group for the current session.

370.   The Planning Group held six meetings. It had before it Section G of the topical summary of the discussion held in the Sixth Committee of the General Assembly during its sixty-first session, prepared by the Secretariat and entitled "Other decisions and conclusions of the Commission" (A/CN.4/577), and General Assembly resolution 61/34 of 4 December 2006 on the report of the International Law Commission on the work of its fifty-eighth session, in particular paragraphs 7, 8, 9, 14, 15 and 19.

1. Relations between the Commission and the Sixth Committee

371.   The Commission considered it useful to discuss, on a regular basis, ways in which the dialogue between the Commission and the Sixth Committee could be further enhanced in the light of calls contained in annual resolutions of the General Assembly, and, in this regard, its Planning Group held discussions on the relationship between the Commission and the Sixth Committee of the General Assembly. These discussions will be continued at the Commission's session next year. Meanwhile, the Commission wishes to recall that the plenary meetings of the Commission are open to interested delegations and that its draft reports, issued in the A/CN.4/... series as documents for limited distribution (L-documents) and usually adopted during the last week of the Commission's session, are available for advance perusal, subject to changes that may be made during the adoption stage. The draft reports are available on the Official Documents System of the United Nations (ODS).[492] The Commission also welcomes the continued practice of informal consultations in the form of discussions between the members of the Sixth Committee and the members of the Commission attending sessions of the General Assembly as a useful means to enhance dialogue on the various topics on the Commission's agenda and would appreciate that, as far as possible, the number of such meetings be increased and some topics selected to guide the debate.

372.   The Planning Group is considering ways of improving Chapters II and III of the Commission's report to make them more user-friendly.

---

[492] http://documents.un.org.

2. Cost-saving measures

373.   The Commission, having considered paragraph 8 of General Assembly resolution 61/34 and the requirements of the programme of work of the Commission for the current session resulting from unforeseeable circumstances, decided that it should conclude the first part of the fifty-ninth session on 5 June 2007, thereby reducing the duration of the session by three days.

3. Working Group on Long-Term programme of work

374.   At its first meeting, held on 14 May 2007, the Planning Group decided to establish a Working Group on the Long-term programme of work for the present quinquennium, chaired by Mr. Enrique Candioti. The Working Group will submit its final report at the end of the quinquennium. The Chairperson of the Working Group submitted an oral progress report to the Planning Group on 25 July 2007, noting, *inter alia*, that the Working Group had held four meetings during which it considered some possible topics, including a topic concerning "Subsequent agreement and practice with respect to treaties", on the basis of a working paper prepared by Mr. Georg Nolte.

4. Inclusion of new topics on the programme of work of the Commission and establishment of working groups to consider feasibility of certain topics

375.   At its 2929th meeting, on 1 June 2007, the Commission decided to include on its programme of work the topic "Protection of persons in the event of disasters" and appointed Mr. Eduardo Valencia-Ospina as Special Rapporteur.

376.   At its 2940th meeting, on 20 July 2007, the Commission decided to include on its programme of work the topic "Immunity of State officials from foreign criminal jurisdiction" and appointed Mr. Roman Kolodkin as Special Rapporteur.

377.   At its 2929th meeting, on 1 June 2007, the Commission also established an open-ended Working Group on the most-favoured-Nation clause under the chairpersonship of Mr. Donald McRae to examine the possibility of including the topic "Most-favoured-nation clause" in its long-term programme of work. The Working Group held two meetings on 16 and 17 July 2007 and it had before it a working paper prepared by Mr. Donald McRae and Mr. A. Rohan Perera. It concluded that the Commission could play a useful role in providing clarification on the meaning and effect of the most-favoured-nation clause in the field of investment agreements and was favourable to the inclusion of the topic. Such work was seen as building on the past work

of the Commission on the most-favoured-nation clause.[493] At its 2944th meeting, on 27 July 2007, the Commission considered the report of the Working Group and decided to refer it to the Planning Group.

5. Work programme of the Commission for the remainder of the quinquennium

378. The Commission recalled that it was customary at the beginning of each quinquennium to prepare the Commission's work programme for the remainder of the quinquennium, setting out in general terms the anticipated goals in respect of each topic on the basis of indications by the Special Rapporteurs. It is the understanding of the Commission that the work programme has a tentative character since the nature and the complexities of the work preclude certainty in making predictions in advance.

Work programme (2008–2011)

(a) Reservations to treaties

2008

The Special Rapporteur will submit his thirteenth report on validity of reservations.

2009

The Special Rapporteur should submit his fourteenth report on effects of reservations and of objections to reservations, and probably on succession of States and international organizations with regard to reservations, which would permit the conclusion of the first reading of the draft guidelines.

2010–2011

The Special Rapporteur should submit his fifteenth and sixteenth reports in the light of observations from States, with a view to achieving the second reading of the draft guidelines in 2011.

(b) Expulsion of aliens

2008

The Special Rapporteur will submit an addendum to his third report on expulsion of aliens, dealing with the

---

[493] The Commission included the topic "The most-favoured-nation clause" in its programme of work at its twentieth session, in 1967 (*Yearbook ... 1967*, vol. II, document A/6709/Rev.1, p. 369, para. 48) and appointed Mr. Endre Ustor (*ibid.*) and Mr. Nikolaï Ushakov (*Yearbook ... 1977*, vol. II (Part Two), p. 124, para. 77) as the successive Special Rapporteurs. The Commission completed the second reading of the topic at its thirtieth session, in 1978 (*Yearbook ... 1978*, vol. II (Part Two), pp. 16–73, para. 74). At its thirty-fifth, thirty-sixth, thirty-eighth, fortieth and forty-third sessions (1980, 1981, 1983, 1985 and 1988), the General Assembly invited comments from Governments and intergovernmental organizations on the draft articles proposed by the Commission. At its forty-sixth session (1991) the General Assembly, in its decision 46/416 of 9 December 1991, took note with appreciation of the work of the Commission as well as views and comments by Governments and intergovernmental organizations and decided to bring the draft articles to the attention of Member States and intergovernmental organizations for their consideration in such cases and to the extent as they deemed appropriate. At its fifty-eighth session (2006), the Commission requested views of Governments on the topic (*Yearbook ... 2006*, vol. II (Part Two), p. 186, para. 259).

question of expulsion in case of dual or multiple nationals, and the question of expulsion following deprivation of nationality. He will also submit his fourth report on expulsion of aliens, dealing with the limits to the right of expulsion which relate to the fundamental rights of the human person.

2009

The Special Rapporteur will submit his fifth report on expulsion of aliens, dealing with the limits relating to the procedure to be followed in case of expulsion.

2010

The Special Rapporteur will submit his sixth report on expulsion of aliens, dealing with the grounds for expulsion.

2011

The Special Rapporteur will submit his seventh report on expulsion of aliens, dealing with the duration of stay as well as the property rights of the expelled person.

(c) Effects of armed conflicts on treaties

2008

The Drafting Committee would begin the consideration of the draft articles submitted by the Special Rapporteur, followed by the adoption of the draft articles.

2009

Work on the topic to be deferred so as to allow time for Governments to submit comments on draft articles adopted on first reading.

2010–2011

Further reports will be submitted by the Special Rapporteur containing proposals for the second reading of the draft articles, taking into account the comments and observations of Governments.

(d) Shared natural resources

2008

The Special Rapporteur will submit his fifth report containing the whole set of revised draft articles on transboundary aquifers. It is hoped that the Commission would complete the second reading of the draft articles in 2008.

2009

The Special Rapporteur does not plan to submit any report on transboundary aquifers. If the Commission cannot complete the second reading of the draft articles in 2008, it is hoped that it will complete such a reading in the first part of the session in 2009.

2010–2011

The Special Rapporteur would prepare studies in the light of any decision by the Commission on how to proceed with natural resources other than transboundary aquifers.

(e) Responsibility of international organizations

2008

The Special Rapporteur will submit his sixth report on the implementation of the responsibility of an international organization.

2009

The Commission would complete the first reading of the draft articles on responsibility of international organizations.

2010–2011

The Commission would proceed to the second reading of the draft articles following receipt of comments by Governments and international organizations.

(f) The obligation to extradite or prosecute (*aut dedere aut judicare*)

2008

The Special Rapporteur will submit his third report on the obligation to extradite or prosecute (*aut dedere aut judicare*).

2009

The Special Rapporteur will submit his fourth report on the obligation to extradite or prosecute (*aut dedere aut judicare*).

2010–2011

The Special Rapporteur will submit his fifth report, if necessary, and the Commission would complete the first reading of the draft articles on the obligation to extradite or prosecute (*aut dedere aut judicare*).

(g) Immunity of State officials from foreign criminal jurisdiction

2008

The Special Rapporteur will submit his preliminary report.

2009

The Special Rapporteur would submit his second report.

2010–2011

The Special Rapporteur would submit his subsequent reports in the light of developments in the Commission.

(h) Protection of persons in the event of disasters

2008

The Special Rapporteur will submit a preliminary report.

2009

The Special Rapporteur would submit the second report.

2010–2011

The Special Rapporteur would submit his subsequent reports in the light of developments in the Commission.

6. HONORARIA

379. The Commission reiterated once more its views concerning the question of honoraria, resulting from the adoption by the General Assembly of its resolution 56/272 of 27 March 2002, which were expressed in its previous reports.[494] The Commission emphasized again that the above resolution especially affects the Special Rapporteurs, in particular those from developing countries, as it compromises support for their research work. The Commission urges the General Assembly to reconsider this matter, with a view to restoring, at this stage, the honoraria for Special Rapporteurs.

7. DOCUMENTATION AND PUBLICATIONS

(a) External publication of International Law Commission documents

380. The Planning Group established a Working Group on the question of external publication of International Law Commission documents, under the chairpersonship of Mr. Giorgio Gaja. The Chairperson of the Working Group submitted an oral report to the Planning Group on 25 July 2007.

381. The Commission endorsed the following Guidelines on the Publication of Commission Documents prepared by the Working Group:

"Guidelines on the Publication of Commission Documents

"In order to ensure the proper attribution of the work of the International Law Commission, the following policy guidelines apply when present or former members of the Commission seek to publish documents relating to the work of the Commission:

"1. Documents of the Commission should be appropriately attributed, with a clear indication whether the author is the Commission as a whole, a body established by the Commission, a Special Rapporteur or any other member of the Commission;

"2. When the publication reproduces in whole or in part a document of the Commission this should be appropriately acknowledged;

---

[494] *Yearbook ... 2002*, vol. II (Part Two), pp. 102–103, paras. 525–531; *Yearbook ... 2003*, vol. II (Part Two), p. 101, para. 447; *Yearbook ... 2004*, vol. II (Part Two), pp. 120–121, para. 369; *Yearbook ... 2005*, vol. II (Part Two), p. 92, para. 501; and *Yearbook ... 2006*, vol. II (Part Two), p. 187, para. 269.

"3.   If the document to be published relates to a subject on which the Commission has come to some collective conclusion, even if provisional, reference should be made in the publication to that conclusion;

"4.   Documents of the Commission which are intended for publication by the United Nations should not be published, on the initiative of individual members, before the documents have been officially released, including through the website on the work of the Commission;

"5.   A copy of the publication should be provided to the Commission."

(b)   *Processing and issuance of reports of Special Rapporteurs*

382.   The Commission considered the question of the timely submission of reports by Special Rapporteurs. Bearing in mind the rules and regulations relating to the submission of documents in the United Nations as well as the heavy workload of the relevant services of the Organization, the Commission emphasizes once more the importance that it attaches to the timely submission of reports by Special Rapporteurs in view of both their processing and distribution sufficiently in advance to allow members to study the reports. In this connection, the Commission was reminded that the processing of documentation by the Secretariat was subject to very strict timetables on the basis of a slotting system within the Secretariat for the processing of documentation, established at the request of Member States.

383.   The Commission recalls operative paragraph 8 of General Assembly resolution 47/202 B of 22 December 1992, in which the General Assembly urged the substantive departments of the Secretariat to comply with the rule which requires them to submit pre-session documents to the relevant Secretariat Unit responsible for document processing at least 10 weeks before the beginning of sessions, in order to permit processing in time in all official languages. The Commission is aware of the special circumstances surrounding the timely submission of reports of Special Rapporteurs and took into consideration the recommendation made by the Department for General Assembly and Conference Management, and it formally endorses a time frame shorter than 10 weeks for the submission of such documents. Bearing in mind the principles governing the submission and issuance of documents in order to permit timely processing, the Commission requested that its documentation be exempted from the 10-week rule for submission of pre-session documents, on the understanding that the time for processing documents within the established word-limit is four weeks.

384.   The Commission reiterates the importance of providing and making available all evidence of State practice and other sources of international law relevant to the performance of the Commission's function of progressive development and codification of international law. While the Commission is aware of the advantages of being as concise as possible, it strongly believes that an *a priori* limitation cannot be placed on the length of its documentation and research projects and reports of Special Rapporteurs.

(c)   *Backlog relating to the Yearbook of the International Law Commission*

385.   The Commission expressed concern about the backlog relating to the *Yearbook of the International Law Commission*,[495] noting that the late publication of the *Yearbook* in the official languages of the United Nations had a negative impact on the work of the Commission, as well as in the teaching, training, research, dissemination and wider appreciation of the codification efforts of international law undertaken by the Commission. The Commission was cognizant of the need for concerted efforts to reduce the backlog. It stresses the importance of ensuring that the necessary budgetary resources are allocated for addressing the backlog under the relevant programme in the regular budget. It also proposed the establishment of a trust fund to address the backlog. In accordance with the relevant financial regulations and rules, voluntary contributions would be made by members, non-governmental organizations and private entities to such a worthy cause which was critical to the understanding of the Commission's work in the progressive development and codification of international law, as well as in the strengthening of the rule of law in international relations.

(d)   *Other publications and the assistance of the Codification Division*

386.   The Commission expressed its appreciation for the valuable assistance of the Codification Division of the Secretariat in its substantive servicing of the Commission and in preparation of research projects, by providing legal materials and their analysis. At its 2954th meeting, on 9 August 2007, the Commission requested the Secretariat to prepare a background study, initially limited to natural disasters, on the topic "Protection of persons in the event of disasters", as well as a background study on the topic "Immunity of State officials from foreign criminal jurisdiction".

387.   The Commission recognized the particular relevance and significant value to its work of the legal publications prepared by the Secretariat, namely: *The Work of the International Law Commission*; *The United Nations Juridical Yearbook*; the *Reports of International Arbitral Awards*; the *Analytical Guide to the Work of the International Law Commission*; the *United Nations Legislative Series*; and the *Repertory of Practice of United Nations Organs*; and reiterated its request that the Secretariat continue to provide the Commission with these publications.

---

[495] As at 30 June 2007, the backlog for the period 1994–2001 was as follows: *Yearbook ... 1994*, vol. I and vol. II (Parts One and Two): Chinese; *Yearbook ... 1995*, vol. I and vol. II (Parts One and Two): Chinese; *Yearbook ... 1996*, vol. II (Part One): Arabic, English, French, Russian and Spanish; and vol. I and vol. II (Parts One and Two): Chinese; *Yearbook ... 1997*, vol. II (Part One): Arabic, English, French, Russian and Spanish; and vol. I and vol. II (Parts One and Two): Chinese; *Yearbook ... 1998*, vol. II (Part One): Arabic, English, French, Russian and Spanish; and vol. I and vol. II (Parts One and Two): Chinese; *Yearbook ... 1999*, vol. II (Part One): Arabic, English, French, Russian and Spanish; and vol. I and vol. II (Parts One and Two): Chinese; *Yearbook... 2000*, vol. II (Part 1): Arabic, English, French, Russian and Spanish; and vol. I and vol. II (Parts One and Two): Chinese; *Yearbook ... 2001*, vol. II (Parts One and Two): Arabic, English, French and Spanish; and vol. I and vol. II (Parts One and Two): Russian and Chinese. From 2002 to the present, no volume has been issued in all the six official languages.

388.   Taking into account the importance of disseminating information about the Commission, the Commission welcomed the publication by the Codification Division of the seventh edition of *The Work of the International Law Commission*, a publication which provides a comprehensive, authoritative and up-to-date review of the Commission's contribution to the progressive development and codification of international law. It noted with appreciation that, as a result of its expanding desktop publishing initiative, the Codification Division issued this publication (in English only) for the first time at the beginning of the quinquennium and included the work of the Commission through the end of its previous quinquennium, a practice which the Codification Division should be encouraged to continue at future quinquennia. In addition, the Secretariat was requested to make every effort to issue this publication in the other five official languages prior to the beginning of the sixtieth session of the Commission.

389.   Noting the relevance to the Commission's consideration of present and future topics concerning international organizations, the Commission recognized the significant value of *The United Nations Juridical Yearbook* prepared by the Secretariat, which provides the most comprehensive and authoritative information on major legal developments and activities within the United Nations system as well as State practice with regard to international organizations. It noted that, as a result of its expanding desktop publishing initiative, the Codification Division was able to publish the *Juridical Yearbook* for 2003 and 2004 in less than a year as compared to five years for the most recently issued volume. The Secretariat was encouraged to continue this initiative with a view to expediting the preparation of future editions of this publication.

390.   In view of the importance of State practice in the work of the Commission, the Commission noted the usefulness of the publication entitled *Reports of International Arbitral Awards* prepared by the Codification Division, which contains international decisions involving substantive issues of public international law which have an enduring legal or historical significance. The Commission requested the Secretariat to continue its preparation of this publication.

391.   Bearing in mind the value of the publication the *Analytical Guide to the Work of the International Law Commission* as an indispensable research guide and the fact that the first edition was published in 2004, the Commission requested the Codification Division to begin the preparation of the second edition of the publication in commemoration of the sixtieth anniversary of the Commission in 2008.

392.   Mindful of the significance and utility of the Codification Division's publication the *United Nations Legislative Series*" for the Commission's work on several topics, by means of studying relevant national legislation, decisions of national tribunals, diplomatic and other official correspondence as well as treaty provisions, which has enabled the Commission to meaningfully carry out its responsibility of codification and progressive development of international law in several areas, the Commission requested the Secretariat to continue the publication of the *Legislative Series*.

393.   Recognizing the importance and usefulness of the Secretariat publication *Repertory of Practice of United Nations Organs* as the principal source of records for the analytical studies of the application and interpretation of the provisions of the Charter, the Commission took note of the progress made in the preparation of studies of the *Repertory* and their posting on the Internet in three languages.

394.   Recalling that the ICJ as the principal judicial organ of the United Nations has played an important role in adjudicating disputes among States in accordance with international law, the Commission requested the Secretariat to make every effort to continue the publication *Summaries of Judgements, Advisory Opinions and Orders of the International Court of Justice*, in all the official languages of the United Nations.

395.   The Commission also expressed its appreciation for the results of activity of the Secretariat in its continuous updating and management of its website on the International Law Commission.[496] It acknowledged in particular the establishment of a new website on the United Nations, *Reports of International Arbitral Awards*, including a full-text research option on all published volumes of the collection (25 volumes to date), which will then be updated to include any new volume. The Commission reiterated that the websites constitute an invaluable resource for the Commission in undertaking its work and for researchers of work of the Commission in the wider community, thereby contributing to the overall strengthening of the teaching, study, dissemination and wider appreciation of international law. The Commission would welcome the further development of the website on the work of the Commission with the inclusion of information on the current status of the topics on the agenda of the Commission.

8.   COMMEMORATION OF THE SIXTIETH ANNIVERSARY OF THE COMMISSION

396.   The Commission discussed various possibilities of commemorating the Commission's sixtieth anniversary session in 2008, and agreed upon the following recommendations:

(*a*)   that there should be a solemn meeting of the Commission to which dignitaries, including the Secretary-General, the President of the General Assembly, the President of the International Court of Justice, the United Nations High Commissioner for Human Rights, and representatives of the host Government, should be invited;

(*b*)   that there should be a one and a half day meeting with legal advisers dedicated to the work of the Commission;

(*c*)   that Member States, in association with existing regional organizations, professional associations, academic institutions and members of the Commission concerned, should be encouraged to convene national or regional meetings, which would be dedicated to the work of the Commission.

---

[496] Located at www.un.org/law/ilc/.

397.   The Commission recommended that the Secretariat, in consultation with a group of members of the Commission,[497] assist in making arrangements for the implementation of (*a*) and (*b*).

9.   MEETING WITH UNITED NATIONS AND OTHER HUMAN RIGHTS EXPERTS

398.   In accordance with article 25 (1) of its Statute,[498] the Commission held a meeting on 15 and 16 May 2007, with United Nations and other experts in the field of human rights, including representatives from human rights treaty bodies. Experts from regional human rights bodies were also invited. During the meeting, members of the Commission and the human rights experts[499] held a useful exchange of views on issues relating to reservations to human rights treaties, in particular on the causes of invalidity of reservations to human rights treaties and the appreciation of validity of reservations to human rights treaties.[500]

B.   Date and place of the sixtieth session of the Commission

399.   The Commission decided that the sixtieth session of the Commission be held in Geneva from 5 May to 6 June and 7 July to 8 August 2008.

C.   Cooperation with other bodies

400.   The Commission was represented at the forty-sixth session of the Asian–African Legal Consultative Organization, held in Cape Town, South Africa, from 2 to 6 July 2007, by Mr. Narinder Singh. The Commission also decided that it will be represented at the thirty-fourth meeting of the Committee of Legal Advisers on Public International Law to be held in Strasbourg on 10 and 11 September 2007, by Mr. Alain Pellet.

401.   At its 2933rd meeting, on 10 July 2007, Judge Rosalyn Higgins, President of the International Court of Justice, addressed the Commission and informed it of the Court's recent activities and of the cases currently before it.[501] An exchange of views followed.

402.   The Inter-American Juridical Committee was represented at the present session of the Commission by Mr. Mauricio Herdocia Sacasa, who addressed the Commission at its 2943rd meeting, on 26 July 2007.[502] An exchange of views followed.

403.   The Asian–African Legal Consultative Organization was represented at the present session of the Commission by its Secretary-General, Mr. Wafik Z. Kamil, who addressed the Commission at its 2944th meeting, on 27 July 2007.[503] An exchange of views followed.

404.   The European Committee on Legal Cooperation and the Committee of Legal Advisers on Public International Law of the Council of Europe were represented at the present session of the Commission by the Director of Legal Advice and Public International Law, Mr. Manuel Lezertua, who addressed the Commission at its 2952nd meeting, on 8 August 2007.[504] An exchange of views followed.

405.   On 11 July 2006 an informal exchange of views was held between members of the Commission and the International Committee of the Red Cross on topics of mutual interest.

D.   Representation at the sixty-second session of the General Assembly

406.   The Commission decided that it should be represented at the sixty-second session of the General Assembly by its Chairperson, Mr. Ian Brownlie.

407.   At its 2954th meeting, on 9 August 2007, the Commission requested Mr. Maurice Kamto, Special Rapporteur on the topic of "Expulsion of aliens", to attend the sixty-second session of the General Assembly under the terms of paragraph 5 of General Assembly resolution 44/35 of 4 December 1989.[505]

E.   International Law Seminar

408.   Pursuant to General Assembly resolution 61/34, the forty-third session of the International Law Seminar was held at the Palais des Nations from 9 to 27 July 2007, during the present session of the Commission. The Seminar is intended for advanced students specializing in international law and for young professors or government officials pursuing an academic or diplomatic career or in posts in the civil service in their country.

---

[497] The members of the Group are as follows: Mr. Enrique Candioti, Mr. Pedro Comissário Afonso, Mr. Zdzilsaw Galicki, Mr. Alain Pellet and Mr. Chusei Yamada. The Chairperson of the Commission and the Chairperson of the Planning Group would serve as *ex officio*.

[498] Article 25 (1) of the Statute of the International Law Commission provides: "The Commission may consult, if it considers it necessary, with any of the organs of the United Nations on any subject which is within the competence of that organ." See also General Assembly resolution 61/34.

[499] The participants were: Mr. Philippe Texier, Committee on Economic, Social and Cultural Rights; Mr. Nigel Rodley, Human Rights Committee; Mr. Guibril Camara, Committee against Torture; Mr. Jean Zermatten, Committee on the Rights of the Child; Mr. Alexandre Sicilianos, Committee on the Elimination of Racial Discrimination; Mr. Cees Flintermann, Committee on the Elimination of Discrimination against Women; Mr. Ahmed El Borai, Committee on the Protection of the Rights of All Migrant Workers and Members of Their Families; Ms. Liesbeth Lijnzaad, Council of Europe; Mr. Vincent Berger, European Court of Human Rights; Ms. Françoise Hampson, member of former Sub-Commission on the Promotion and Protection of Human Rights.

[500] The Special Rapporteur of the topic "Reservations to treaties" prepared a brief summary of his understanding (not attributable to the Commission) of what transpired in the discussion, which is on the website on the work of the Commission, located at www.un.org/law/ilc/.

[501] This statement is recorded in the summary record of that meeting and is also on the website on the work of the Commission.

[502] This statement is recorded in the summary record of that meeting.

[503] *Ibid.*

[504] *Ibid.*

[505] "The General Assembly, ... Invites the International Law Commission, when circumstances so warrant, to request a special rapporteur to attend the session of the General Assembly during the discussion of the topic for which that special rapporteur is responsible and requests the Secretary-General to make the necessary arrangements within existing resources."

409.   Twenty-five participants of different nationalities, mostly from developing countries, were able to take part in the session.[506] The participants in the Seminar observed plenary meetings of the Commission, attended specially arranged lectures, and participated in working groups on specific topics.

410.   The Seminar was opened by Mr. Ian Brownlie, Chairperson of the Commission. Mr. Ulrich von Blumenthal, Senior Legal Adviser of the United Nations Office at Geneva, was responsible for the administration, organization and conduct of the Seminar, assisted by Mr. Vittorio Mainetti, Legal Consultant at the United Nations Office at Geneva.

411.   Lectures were given by members of the Commission as follows: Mr. Giorgio Gaja: "Responsibility of International Organizations"; Ms. Paula Escarameia: "The ICC Statute: a Step Forward in International Law"; Mr. Alain Pellet: "The ILC—a View from Inside"; Mr. Chusei Yamada: "Codification of the Law of Shared Natural Resources"; Mr. Georg Nolte: "Assistance by States for Internationally Wrongful Acts by Other States—Issues of Responsibility and Development of the Law"; Mr. A. Rohan Perera: "Towards a Comprehensive Convention on Terrorism"; Mr. Zdzisław Galicki: "The Obligation to Extradite and Prosecute (*aut dedere aut judicare*)"; and Mr. Maurice Kamto: "Expulsion of Aliens".

412.   Lectures were also given by Mr. Vittorio Mainetti: "Introduction to the Work of the International Law Commission"; Mr. Daniel Müller, Assistant to Special Rapporteur Mr. Alain Pellet: "Reservations to Treaties", Ms. Jelena Pejic, Legal Adviser International Committee of the Red Cross: "Current Challenges to International Humanitarian Law"; and Mr. Markus Schmidt (OHCHR): "The Human Rights Council after its First Year: Trojan Horse or Real Progress?".

413.   A round table was also organized on the regional systems of protection of human rights. Two members of the Commission, Mr. Lucius Caflisch (former Judge at the European Court of Human Rights) and Mr. Edmundo Vargas-Carreño (former Executive Secretary of the Inter-American Commission of Human Rights) spoke respectively on the European and Inter-American systems, while Mr. Mutoy Mubiala, an official of the OHCHR, spoke on the African system. The discussion focused on

the comparative analysis and the reciprocal influence of the three regional systems.

414.   The seminar participants were invited to visit the WTO, where they attended briefing sessions by Ms. Gabrielle Marceau, Counsellor of the Director General, and Mr. Werner Zdouc, Director of the WTO Appellate Body Secretariat. The discussion focused on the current legal issues at the WTO and on the WTO Dispute Settlement System.

415.   Each Seminar participant was assigned to one of three working groups on "The ICC Statute: new and unsolved questions", "The obligation to extradite or prosecute", and "Reservations to treaties". Two members of the Commission, Ms. Paula Escarameia and Mr. Zdzisław Galicki, as well as Mr. Daniel Müller, provided guidance for the working groups. Each group wrote a report and presented their findings to the Seminar in a special session organized for this purpose. A collection of the reports was compiled and distributed to all participants.

416.   The Republic and Canton of Geneva offered its traditional hospitality to the participants with a guided visit of the Alabama Room at the City Hall, followed by a reception.

417.   Mr. Brownlie, Mr. von Blumenthal, and Ms. Yassin Alieu M'Boge, on behalf of the participants, addressed the Commission and the participants at the close of the Seminar. Each participant was presented with a certificate attesting to his or her participation in the forty-third session of the Seminar.

418.   The Commission noted with particular appreciation that the Governments of Cyprus, Finland, Germany, New Zealand, Switzerland and United Kingdom had made or pledged voluntary contributions to the United Nations Trust Fund for the International Law Seminar. The financial situation of the Fund enabled the awarding of a sufficient number of fellowships to deserving candidates from developing countries so that adequate geographical distribution of participants was achieved. This year, full fellowships (travel and subsistence allowance) were awarded to 14 candidates and partial fellowships (subsistence only) were awarded to two candidates.

419.   Since 1965, 979 participants, representing 160 nationalities, have taken part in the Seminar. Of them, 598 have received a fellowship.

420.   The Commission stresses the importance it attaches to the Seminar, which enables young lawyers, especially from developing countries, to familiarize themselves with the work of the Commission and the activities of the many international organizations which have their headquarters in Geneva. The Commission recommends that the General Assembly should again appeal to States to make voluntary contributions in order to secure the holding of the Seminar in 2008 with as broad participation as possible.

421.   The Commission noted with satisfaction that in 2007 comprehensive interpretation services were made available to the Seminar. It expresses the hope that the same services would be provided at the next session, within existing resources.

---

[506] The following persons participated in the forty-third session of the International Law Seminar: Ms. Tânia da Fonseca Alexandre (Portugal), Ms. María Eugenia Brunini (Uruguay), Mr. Víctor Cairo Palomo (Cuba), Mr. Alonso Chaverri Suárez (Costa Rica), Mr. Issaka Garba Abdou (Niger), Mr. Gabriel Herrera (Argentina), Ms. Bibian Isoto (Uganda), Mr. Ammar Jaber (Iraq), Ms. Melanie Khanna (United States of America), Ms. Man Anting (China), Ms. Yassin Alieu M'Boge (Gambia), Ms. Nuala Ní Mhuircheartaigh (Ireland), Mr. Yasuyuki Okazaki (Japan), Mr. Ahmed Haroune Ould (Mauritania), Ms. Priya Pillai (India), Mr. Sergio Puig de la Parra (Mexico), Mr. Aistis Radavicius (Lithuania), Ms. Velotiana Raobelina Rakotoasony (Madagascar), Ms. Ana Cristina Rodríguez Pineda (Guatemala), Ms. Vasilka Sancin (Slovenia), Ms. Marieme Sidibe (Mali), Ms. Simona Spinaru (Romania), Mr. Ton Van den Brandt (Netherlands), Ms. Anusha Wickramasinghe (Sri Lanka) and Ms. Aishath Zahir (Maldives). The Selection Committee, chaired by Mr. Jean-Marie Dufour (President of the Geneva International Academic Network), met on 25 April 2007, and selected 26 candidates out of 130 applications for participation in the Seminar. At the last minute, the 26th candidate selected failed to attend.

CHECKLIST OF DOCUMENTS OF THE FIFTY-NINTH SESSION

Document	Title	Observations and references
A/CN.4/576	Provisional agenda	Mimeographed. For agenda as adopted, see page 10 above.
A/CN.4/577 and Add.1–2	Topical summary of the discussion held in the Sixth Committee of the General Assembly during its sixty-first session, prepared by the Secretariat	Mimeographed.
A/CN.4/578 [and Corr.1]	Third report on the effects of armed conflicts on treaties, by Mr. Ian Brownlie, Special Rapporteur	Reproduced in *Yearbook ... 2007*, vol. II (Part One).
A/CN.4/579 and Add.1–4	The obligation to extradite or prosecute (*aut dedere aut judicare*): comments and information received from Governments	*Idem.*
A/CN.4/580	Fourth report on shared natural resources: transboundary groundwaters, by Mr. Chusei Yamada, Special Rapporteur	*Idem.*
A/CN.4/581	Third report on the expulsion of aliens, by Mr. Maurice Kamto, Special Rapporteur	*Idem.*
A/CN.4/582	Responsibility of international organizations: comments and observations received from international organizations	*Idem.*
A/CN.4/583	Fifth report on responsibility of international organizations, by Mr. Giorgio Gaja, Special Rapporteur	*Idem.*
A/CN.4/584 [and Corr.1]	Twelfth report on reservations to treaties, by Mr. Alain Pellet, Special Rapporteur	*Idem.*
A/CN.4/585 [and Corr.1]	Second report on the obligation to extradite or prosecute (*aut dedere aut judicare*), by Mr. Zdzislaw Galicki, Special Rapporteur	*Idem.*
A/CN.4/586	Reservations to treaties: note by the Special Rapporteur on draft guideline 2.1.9 (Statement of reasons for reservations)	*Idem.*
A/CN.4/L.705	Reservations to treaties	Mimeographed.
A/CN.4/L.706 and Add.1–3	Draft report of the Commission on the work of its fifty-ninth session: chapter IV (Reservations to treaties)	Mimeographed. For the adopted text, see *Official Records of the General Assembly, Sixty-second Session, Supplement No. 10* (A/62/10). The final text appears in the present volume, at page 15 above.
A/CN.4/L.707/Rev.1	*Idem*: chapter VI (Expulsion of aliens)	*Idem*, p. 61 above.
A/CN.4/L.708 [and Corr.1] and Add.1	*Idem*: chapter VII (Effects of armed conflicts on treaties)	*Idem*, p. 70 above.
A/CN.4/L.709 and Add.1	*Idem*: chapter V (Shared natural resources)	*Idem*, p. 56 above.
A/CN.4/L.710	*Idem*: chapter I (Organization of the session)	*Idem*, p. 9 above.
A/CN.4/L.711	*Idem*: chapter II (Summary of the work of the Commission at its fifty-ninth session)	*Idem*, p. 11 above.
A/CN.4/L.712	*Idem*: chapter III (Specific issues on which comments would be of particular interest to the Commission)	*Idem*, p. 13 above.
A/CN.4/L.713 and Add.1–3	*Idem*: chapter VIII (Responsibility of international organizations)	*Idem*, p. 79 above.
A/CN.4/L.714 and Add.1	*Idem*: chapter IX (The obligation to extradite or prosecute)	*Idem*, p. 94 above.
A/CN.4/L.715 and Add.1	*Idem*: chapter X (Other decisions and conclusions of the Commission)	*Idem*, p. 98 above.
A/CN.4/L.716	Programme, procedures and working methods of the Commission, and its documentation: report of the Planning Group	Mimeographed.
A/CN.4/L.717	Shared natural resources: report of the Working Group	*Idem.*
A/CN.4/L.718	Effects of armed conflicts on treaties: report of the Working Group	*Idem.*
A/CN.4/L.719	Most-favoured-nation clause: report of the Working Group	*Idem.*
A/CN.4/L.720	Responsibility of international organizations: titles and texts of draft articles 31 to 45 [44] adopted by the Drafting Committee on 18, 19, 20 and 25 July 2007	*Idem.*
ILC(LIX)/RT/CRP.1	Meeting with human rights bodies (15 and 16 May 2007): report by Mr. Alain Pellet, Special Rapporteur	*Idem.*
A/CN.4/SR.2914–A/CN.4/SR.2955	Provisional summary records of the 2914th to 2955th meetings	*Idem.* The final text appears in *Yearbook ... 2007*, vol. I.